Coming Alive  Five

MAYFIELD PUBLISHING COMPANY

Second Edition

Coming Alive from Nine to Five

THE CAREER SEARCH HANDBOOK

Betty Neville Michelozzi
MISSION COLLEGE

Library of Congress Catalog Card Number: 83-062827
International Standard Book Number: 0-87484-594-7

Manufactured in the United States of America
Mayfield Publishing Company
1240 Villa Street
Mountain View, California 94041

10   9   8   7

Sponsoring editor: Franklin C. Graham
Manuscript editor: Carol King
Managing editor: Pat Herbst
Art director: Nancy Sears
Cover designer: Deborah Hopping
Illustrator: Tom Durfee
Production manager: Cathy Willkie
Compositor: Publisher's Typography
Printer and binder: George Banta Company

Contents

Preface

Coming Alive from Nine to Five is a unique handbook that develops, demystifies, and integrates between two covers all the various facets of career search and choice. It is meant to be a comprehensive handbook: a handy reference book drawing together into one practical, easily usable and re-usable source the essentials of the career search process. It is flexible enough to be used in whole or in part, in individual counseling sessions, in workshops, or in semester-long courses. It is used in colleges and high schools, in industry and business, by people concerned about their own career development or that of others.

The handbook is intended for anyone who is making a life change. While it focuses specifically on careers, this topic can be translated into "meaningful life activity." The book contains valuable material for all phases of career choice even into retirement. The first edition has been used by a broad population ranging from high school students to persons approaching retirement, from managers of households to managers of corporations, from job trainees to career-changing professionals in transition. This updated and expanded edition focuses on career preparation not only for the 1980s and 1990s but for the next century as well. Using the same personal approach as the earlier text, the second edition expands awareness of the quality of work places and work styles as they relate to the whole of one's life. The dilemma of unemployment is addressed as well as trends that will shape the future.

Writing a second edition has provided a great opportunity to develop new, more effective material, to integrate text and exercises more fully, and to organize it all more smoothly. Feedback from those who used the first edition has been most helpful and supportive in the revision process. Exercises in value and skill assessment and in decision-making have been given greater focus. The material on trends and on work places and work styles was revised and expanded extensively. More group exercises have been added, yet kept separate from exercises that are immediately relevant to the individual career searcher. New material added to the leader/instructor's manual includes contributions from a variety of career educators.

Use of this handbook is most fruitful when the searcher approaches it in a relaxed, lighthearted manner. But a serious career search calls for commitment and motivation—and so does the handbook. The text is most helpful to those who become thoroughly involved in it. They will experience greater clarity about their lives and new confidence in themselves. Their goals will be easier to recognize and to reach. The career search will become a journey of personal growth on the path toward self-actualization.

B.N.M.

Acknowledgments

Private: Please do not read this.

Acknowledgments are a very personal thing. They point up the fact that it is impossible to accomplish anything of importance all alone. Thanks to:

Peter, my husband, for his caring support. He helped me keep perspective on life's deeper meanings when a sea of paper and words threatened to engulf me.

All the caring, careful typists who contributed from 'way back, most especially my neighbor Ruby Garcia, who has gone beyond neighborliness to heroism.

Supportive colleagues at Mission and West Valley Colleges who read, reviewed, and gave helpful feedback: Bill Allman, Veronese Anderson, Chloe Atkins, Don Cordero, Ken Gogstad, Carolyn Hennings, Jo Hernandez, Michael Herauf, Sharon Laurenza, Joyce McClellan, Gladys Penner, Richard Przybylski, Pat Space, Peter Thelin, Pat Weber, and Jan Winton, and the Mission library staff, who helped check references.

Aptos and Santa Cruz library staff, who at the drop of a phone call searched out many details and even called back—in minutes!

Academic reviewers who read an early draft of the manuscript and made valuable suggestions and comments: David J. Berilla of Western State College of Colorado, Naomi Lee of Washington State University, Robert A. Mantovani of Long Beach Community College, Steven Muck of El Camino College, and Cheryl A. Seyfang of the University of Toledo.

West Valley and Mission college students who taught me to teach Careers and Lifestyles and shared the beauty of their lives and their journeys, with special thanks to Carol Shawhan.

Career people who share their stories and give support and resources to career searchers; company people who share their workplaces with those who seek information.

Colleagues and resource people in many places who have been supportive, have given assistance and information: Judy Shernock for her work on the Personality Mosaic, Cora Alameda, Judy Appelt, Sally Brew, Dorothy Coffey, John French, H. B. Gelatt, Ritchie Lowry, John Maginley, Lillian Mattimore, Stephen Moody, Kay Ringel, Ed Watkins.

Instructors who shared class time to test materials, especially the Personality Mosaic: special thanks to Sue Coleman, Heather Hasseljian, Linda Lawson, and Barbara Lea.

People (past and present) at Mayfield who have been so great to work with: Liz Currie, Bob Erhart, Laraine Etchemendy-Bennett, Frank Graham, Pat Herbst, Yaeko Kashima, Pam Trainer.

Manuscript editor Carol King, who has contributed above and beyond the call of duty.

My family and friends who gave me "living love."

You have all enriched me.

Betty

Coming Alive from Nine to Five

Introduction

areer search can be a special, very precious time to orient and organize your life. It can be a time when you look deeply at yourself and what you have been doing. It can lead you to question how you intend to spend your life for a time, or your time for the rest of your life: to keep or not to keep certain goals, to change or not to change certain behaviors, to aspire or not to aspire to certain positions—all with a view toward greater life enrichment.

Career search involves more than simply figuring out what job might suit you best. That is the short-range view. The perspective expands when you ask yourself what you want that job to do for you. Very quickly you may find yourself face to face with some of your deepest values. Do you want money, power, status? Peace, harmony, love? Are some values incompatible with others? Can you have it all?

Can you work 60 hours a week moving up the corporate ladder, nurture loving relationships with family and friends, grow your own vegetables, recycle your cans on Saturday, jog daily, be a Scout leader, meditate, and do yoga? How fully can all of your interests and values be actualized in the real world? What is the purpose of work? What is the purpose of life?

Career search, then, can be a profound journey of personal growth—not just a superficial job hunt. A career can be a vital means of self-expression—not just a job. Besides providing a living, a career can satisfy some of your deepest longings.

Because it is important, some people approach a career decision with fear and trembling, lest they make a mistake. Others avoid the process altogether, certain that it will nail them down to a lifelong commitment they can never change. And still others feel that any job will do just to get them started on something! And then there are those who feel that even if they did a thorough career search, it would turn up absolutely nothing. In reality, a careful career search process can help everyone. It can help *you* to see many possibilities, and in turn give you flexibility and a great deal of confidence. The result can be greater career/life satisfaction.

3

What process does one use in making a career decision? Many people choose their first career using the "bumble-around method." They consider subjects they've liked in school: If it's math, then they'll be mathematicians; if its history, they'll be historians. They consider the careers of people they know and ask the advice of friends. Uncle Jim, the firefighter, is a family hero, and a new crop of firefighters is launched. If they fry hamburgers at McDonald's for a time, they're tempted to judge the whole world of business through the sizzle of French fries. If models and airline pilots capture their attention, they long for a glamorous life. An opportunity crops up; they grab it, and years later they ask, "Is this all there is?"

Many people spend their whole lives bumbling around, like Hobart Foote, who describes it this way:

I'm from Alabama, my wife and kids are Hoosiers. I was gonna work a few years and buy me a new car and head back south. Well, I met the wife now and that kinda changed my plans.

I might've been working in some small factory down south or I might have gone to Detroit where I worked before or I might have gone to Kalamazoo where I worked before. Or else I mighta stuck on a farm somewheres, just grubbing off a farm somewhere. You never know what you woulda did. You can't plan too far in advance, 'cause there's always a stumblin' block.[1]

Other folks make very early decisions: "I knew when I was two that I wanted to be a chimney sweep." Career choice can sometimes seem trivial. Adults ask six-year-olds what they want to be when they grow up. Are they going to sell shoes at Kinney's or invade the corporate complex of IBM? Will plumbing be their outlet or travel tours their bag? Yet many adults aren't always sure what their next job will be.

At least occasionally, however, the image of life's wholeness flashes before us and we see a large, work-filled part of it stretching into the future. We catch a glimpse of the time and energy that we will invest in work. We see that work will affect our lives in many ways. Unless we keep a tight lid on it, the ultimate question will eventually present itself: "What's it all about, Alfie?" If we deal in depth with career choice, we are bound to slip into a philosophic consideration of life's meaning. To do otherwise is to trivialize a profound experience.

Since you are reading this book, you're indicating you'd like to quit "bumbling around" and get on with it. Begin by looking at the stages and steps in the career search process. The search has four stages along a career choice continuum. For many people, the journey begins at ground zero with not an idea in sight. But as you gather career information, you reach a midpoint where you seem to be engulfed in too many ideas. In other words, things seem to get worse before they get better. Eventually you must begin to lighten the burden by choosing. You simply can't follow every career in one lifetime. The calmer you stay, the more easily you will arrive at your decision point. Where are you on the career choice continuum? Mark your position.

The steps to be taken must be part of a system that is clear and demystified,

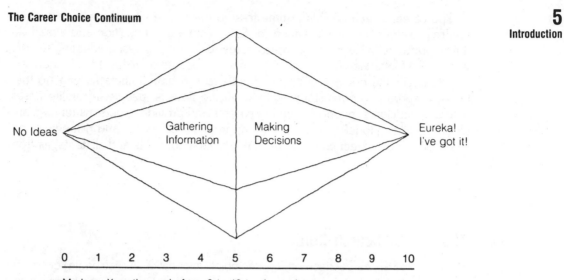

No Ideas

Gathering
Information

Making
Decisions

Eureka!
I've got it!

| 0 | 1 | 2 | 3 | 4 | 5 | 6 | 7 | 8 | 9 | 10 |

Mark an *X* on the scale from 0 to 10 to show where you are *now* on the
Career Choice Continuum.

that can be used many times in a lifetime: First, a system that helps people articulate who they are and what they do well. Second, a system that describes the work world as simply as possible. Third, a system that assists searchers to see where their personal characteristics fit into that world of work. Fourth, a system that "empowers" them to secure the job they have chosen by increasing their job hunting skills. Fifth, a system that raises their consciousness about work as only one part of their personal journey, one aspect of their total lifestyle. And finally, a system that addresses issues of global concern, showing how work is part of the world picture.

In *Coming Alive from Nine to Five* you will find such a system. It is based on finding clear values that lead to good decisions. At first glance this book may look like a conventional careers manual. Read the book, fill in the blanks, and (even if you're already over 40) you'll know what you want to be when you grow up.

You *will* find blanks to fill in as part of the step-by-step process of getting to know yourself and the job world. You will explore your needs, wants, and values. You will discover your personality orientation. You will examine your past and select the activities you've enjoyed, as well as skills you've developed over the years. A job group chart will help you to put *you* and *work* together in a meaningful way. And a final inventory will collect all this "you data" and help you to see it as a unified whole.

This book also touches on some of the heavier issues of life. How can you fulfill your potential? Be happy? Be content? It deals with such things lightly—sometimes whimsically—because life is joyful. But after a good chuckle we get serious and *think* again because our lives are also important and sometimes sad.

The career search is really a time to *stop out* to see who you are and where you're *growing*. This text is written for those who are in transition and would like the opportunity to learn a thought-full career decision process: graduating seniors, women no longer needed at home, the newly divorced or widowed, job changers, the disabled, the unemployed, grandmothers and grandfathers kicking up their heels, corporate tycoons stopping to smell the flowers, people in midlife crises, veterans, ex-clerics, people becoming parents and providers, persons retiring, and all others willing to let go of no longer appropriate behaviors and risk new ones.

A book about career choice is inevitably a book about life and all its stages from 19 to 99.

 ## The Career Search Guide

Most people base career decisions on incomplete information. As you begin your career search, it may help to focus on some important questions. Check (√) the items you feel are already answered satisfactorily for you.

1. Self-Assessment: A Guide
   a. Needs, wants, and shoulds
      What do you *need* to survive? What do you *want* to enrich your life? Do your *shoulds* help you or hold you back?
   b. Interests and values
      The choices you've made over your life have developed into a strong pattern of interests. These reflect what you value most in life. Are your values clear?
   c. Roles
      What *roles* do you play now? What expectations do you and others have about these roles? Do you wish to change or adapt these roles?
   d. Skills
      Analyze your most enjoyable activities. Through repeated choices in your areas of interest, you have developed many skills. Of all the skills you have, which do you enjoy using the most?

2. Job Market Exploration: Where to Start
   a. Research the job market
      Interest and skill inventories lead you to an overview of the entire job market. What jobs fit your self-image?
   b. Trends/workplaces
      Check the job market outlook and relate it to *trends* in society. Will there be a need for people to do the job you'd like? What workplace will you choose? Do you have alternatives?

FENWICK
Courtesy of Mal Hancock

c. Information interview
Talk to people in careers that interest you. Survey and evaluate possible work-places. Does the survey show that you need to re-evaluate your choices?

d. Tools for the job hunt
Learn how to portray yourself effectively through résumés, applications, interviews, letters. Can you talk fluently about yourself?

3. The Final Analysis: Wrap-Up
a. Decisions: Finalize your decision.
b. Goals: Set realistic goals with time lines.
c. Strategy: Develop a strategy for action.
d. Values/philosophy: Review the whole picture to make sure it fits your value system, your philosophy of life and work.

One

Needs, Wants, and Values:

Spotlighting YOU

o start the career process at its roots, ask yourself what you *really need*. A genuine need is something you must have to survive, something you cannot live without. After these basic needs are identified, begin to look at your *wants*. Wants enrich life beyond the level of needs. Then look at *shoulds* because sometimes they create confusion about what we really want. What we want reflects our *values* and gives meaning to our lives. Looking at needs, wants, shoulds and values, at the roots of a career search, can open a new phase of personal growth.

Four need levels are adapted here from the famous hierarchy of psychologist Abraham Maslow: physical, emotional, intellectual, and altruistic. Minimal survival needs on each of these levels are the basis for becoming a fulfilled and self-actualized person. All human beings have basically the same needs, with variations appropriate to innate capacity and stages of life.

Physical needs are the most basic. Without food, for example, we wouldn't survive many days. Gandhi said, "Even God cannot talk to a hungry man except in terms of bread." Air, water, food, clothing, shelter, health care, exercise, and the transportation required for these necessities are the elements of our physical need system. Accompanying our physical needs is the need to feel reasonably safe. It would be hard to concentrate on reading a great book in a burning building. But our physical safety can be threatened in many remote ways, too. We can let ourselves worry about future possibilities like illness from air pollution and chemical additives, our care in old age, meeting new and unfamiliar situations, and job security. Such continued worry can shrivel our physical well-being.

Yet we've heard stories about infants whose physical/safety needs were met, but nevertheless they died mysteriously. We've heard of old people "dying of loneliness" or of a person dying in a concentration camp after hearing of the death

9

of a loved one.[1] Human beings seem to need love, some kind of faith and assurance that they are lovable, someone who cares, someone with whom they can exchange affection, someone to give them courage. People's self-esteem can be badly damaged by real or imagined love deprivation. Their life energy seems to be diminished. Some level of emotional nurturing, then, is real and necessary for survival and growth.

Our minds also have the basic need to know and to grow in the knowledge necessary for survival. People learn in different ways: Those who relate best to the physical world seem to "learn through their hands." Some learn best from the emotion-filled words of people they love. Some learn best through their eyes, some through their ears. And media lovers learn easily from books, pictures, diagrams, and other symbols. But however we learn, the intellect lights our way.

On the altruistic level, human beings at times put their own desires aside to care for others. The survival of an infant depends upon this sort of self-sacrifice. The very survival of our planet may demand the same of all of us. Human survival would be endangered if we totally disregarded the needs of others. Imagine your daily commute: The freeway would become a free-for-all!

If you have survived modern life thus far and are reading and understanding this book, a good share of your basic needs have been fulfilled. Many people have contributed to your well-being on all levels along the way. Now, however, you may be facing a situation in which your basic physical needs are threatened. If you are next in line for a layoff, you may have seen friends losing their jobs and the unemployed losing their benefits. Unpaid bills, a baby on the way, and ailing parents can bring Joe Mechanic in Michigan or Martha Millhouse in North Carolina close to panic. At this point concerns about emotional, intellectual, and altruistic needs can fly out the window! But perhaps this is the time to gather some emotional support from family and friends, to come together with others to share all available support, resources, and ideas, to use every bit of intelligence and knowledge to carve out a survival path. It may seem silly to do career planning during a crisis, when any job will do. But the insights gathered may be just what is needed to boost confidence and morale and open up unsuspected possibilities. In any case, to lead a balanced and satisfying life, we need to develop our potential as far as possible in all areas.

Needs Relate to Wants

Very soon in life we begin to go beyond mere survival to a place of enriched choice where we actualize our wants. According to psychologists Nena and George O'Neill, who wrote a book called *Shifting Gears,* it's important to differentiate between needs and wants.[2] Risks such as changing jobs are less frightening when we know we can survive on very little. Once needs are satisfied, we can work more calmly toward achieving our own set of wants. But sometimes our wants can lead us far from our goals. We can choose things, relationships, and activities that are either nurturing or harmful. It has been said that "everything you own owns you." So we must plan our journey carefully. We don't want to find ourselves "halfway down the block without realizing we've turned the corner."

Needs and Wants Relate to Feelings and Shoulds

How did our own individual sets of wants come to be? Basically, they come from two divergent areas: what feels good to us and the reasoned and not-so-reasoned judgment of others.

Running free feels good to a child, but the reasoned judgment of an adult says that a busy street is not a good place to exercise this freedom. The child learns to curb good feelings by using reasoned judgment. But if not-so-reasoned judgment and excess caution inspire anxiety about every venture, the child will lose the joy of trying new things. He or she will become a slave to shoulds, according to college counselor Carolyn Hennings. When you say "I should," you are implying that you neither need nor want to do this thing, but something or someone outside of you is saying you must. Shoulds are energy drains because they create a feeling of resistance and apathy. They cause us to shift responsibility for our choices somewhere else. When making life changes it's important to know if your shoulds are value-inspired. A should thus explored will either evaporate as unimportant or, if value-related, will become a want.

As adults, then, we need to look at the things we want and value—things that are important to us. On the one hand, we need to see if we are acting on feelings and sabotaging our real needs by not using reasoned judgment. On the other hand, the opposite may be true: By absorbing the not-too-reasoned judgments of others, we may have lost touch with some things that would give us joy. We are afraid of our feelings, or we have exchanged true feelings for unreal fear or frustration.

When we try to ignore authentic feelings, they may come out in inappropriate ways. We explode over a minor irritation because we've been "saving up" our anger. We can experience bodily tension by denying feelings—sometimes to such an extent that we become ill. It is difficult to exercise good judgment and make life decisions when feelings are troublesome. Learning to deal with feelings in a straightforward way is an important growth step.

Carl Rogers, the psychologist who first used the term "unconditional positive regard," believes that a person grows best and most positively when he or she can explore feelings freely in a caring, nonjudgmental atmosphere. If we agree that feelings are a physiological phenomenon, we cannot judge others' feelings, but must accept them as useful indicators. Anger and fear are physical reactions to our environment. By focusing directly on these feelings, experiencing them, and sharing and exploring them with others, we can learn to channel our emotional energy and use it in a more effective way.

All personal growth activities are aimed at understanding oneself better in relationship to others and the environment. When I begin to understand myself, I can learn to take responsibility for what I feel. Instead of blaming others for my feelings, I may realize that my troublesome reactions are largely based on past experiences instead of present realities. I may catch myself misinterpreting another's words or actions and thinking the worst, without checking the facts.

Self-deception results when one feeling masks another. Suppose I feel angry at a meeting when someone speaks well, expressing an idea I couldn't put into words. My anger may mask hurt pride. My hurt pride may mask feelings of inferiority and insecurity, which in turn mask a profound feeling of being unesteemed by others. If I learned to recognize the truth, I might say, "I feel profoundly unesteemed when others articulate ideas well." This statement puts me in touch with an absurdity and helps me to become aware of my esteem needs. I may then find ways to meet my needs. And incidentally, I may become aware that I seldom, if ever, compliment or give esteem to others.

If I care about my relationships with others, I will share my feelings with them when appropriate in an honest and caring way, taking responsibility for the feelings, and experiencing them without denial or delay so that I can deal with them clearly. I will be neither timid nor aggressive but assertive. Both the timid and the aggressive person create dissonance wherever they go: one by "nitpicking around the bush," the other by bulldozing the bush out of existence. And who wants to spend a lifetime "picking nits or dozing bulls?" (Some of us alternate between the two extremes: first being polite and suppressing feelings, and then exploding.) The assertive person, then, is a growing, balanced person who is centered within self, feels comfortable with life, has little need to fear or control people, is more able to love and value self and others. Such a person will be loved and valued.

We can create our own happiness and solve our "feeling problems" by changing what can be changed and then changing our attitude about the unchangeable. Negative emotions can be rechanneled if we catch them at the first inkling. They are all related. We begin by wanting something that we think we need. If it doesn't come easily, we begin to fear we won't get it. This anxiety can turn to frustration and anger and even hate for others who seem to block our path. If we choose to let those emotions overwhelm us, judgment gets fogged up. But used well, strong feelings can be a source of good power. It takes practice. But since feelings so often get in the way of effective action, it can be worth the effort. We have a choice. We can choose our feelings! Some people find it helpful to talk to a counselor when they are experiencing strong emotions. It's difficult to make decisions about careers when you feel overwhelmed by other problems.

As we become more clear about what we feel and balance those feelings with good judgment, we are becoming aware of what we cherish most in life. Decisionmaking and action are easier when we know what we value and when we recognize the order of our priorities. We are then able to seek, search, and risk. In the words of Ken Keyes, Jr., a humanist who developed a system for handling strong feelings, we thus create our own world, and "a loving person lives in a loving world."[3]

Needs, Wants, and Feelings Relate to Values

What I *need* is an absolute survival minimum on the physical, emotional, intellectual, and altruistic levels. What I *want* goes beyond survival to a place of enriched choices. Changing shoulds to wants and getting in touch with what I *feel* clarifies my needs and wants and helps me to consider what I really *value*.

Becoming aware of what we really value and cherish is a lifetime process. To find out whether an action of yours truly reflects a value, ask yourself

- Did I have a choice?
- Did I weigh my choices carefully?
- Did I choose freely?
- Am I happy with my choice?
- Has my choice become a part of my life pattern?

Values are what we *do*, not what we *say*. Our struggles, disappointments, worries, hopes, and dreams are all indicators of value areas. And also, a true set of values is indicated when we feel confident, enthusiastic, and clear about ourselves and others.

On the other hand, murky values can result in many conflicts. We see these conflicts in people who are apparently turned off, confused, changeable, complaining, alienated, or "lazy." The person who over-conforms or over-rebels probably has problems clarifying values.

If we are clear about our values, we won't let our wants disguise our needs. When people substitute possessions for love needs, for example, they acquire all sorts of status symbols. They are hoping for attention and love, but may alienate those they are trying to impress. A person with clear values goes right to the heart of the matter and works on improving relationships by good communications and caring.

The values each person cherishes are an individual expression of self. For King Midas, gold was everything. Most people are astounded when someone leaves a million dollars to a pet cat. All aspects of life are value-laden: family, love and friendship, religion and virtue, work and leisure.[4]

Values Influence Your Lifestyle

The values you esteem will lead you to make decisions about the whole of your life, not just your career. All the elements of your life, including family, friends,

The Flowering of Personal Growth

The flowering of our growth brings aliveness, effortlessness, individuality, playfulness, completion, richness.

SELF-ACTUALIZATION

BEAUTY JUSTICE PERFECTION

GOODNESS ORDER

TRUTH MEANING

WHAT

DO

YOU

NEED?

WANT?

VALUE?

CREATE CREATE

FULFILL FULFILL

RELATE RELATE

SURVIVE SURVIVE

Begin here to nurture the growth of self-actualization.

SELF-ACTUALIZATION

4. ALTRUISTIC NEEDS: We all must interact with others to survive, but to live life fully is to have that generous, loving spirit that promotes truth, goodness, beauty, justice, perfection, order, meaning, and all that is noble and good in the world.

3. INTELLECTUAL NEEDS: A degree of knowledge and understanding are necessary for survival, but a truly developed mind is one in which wisdom and creativity flourish.

2. EMOTIONAL NEEDS: Basic caring from others is necessary for our growth. Rich relationships bring us joy and the courage that comes from emotional support love, and respect.

1. PHYSICAL NEEDS: We all have needs for food, clothing, shelter, safety—the things that keep us alive. Our carefully chosen wants enrich us and enable us to simplify our lives and feel self-sufficient.

home and work environments, religious preference, education, and recreation make up the components of your unique lifestyle.

It may seem difficult or impossible at times to align all these elements with your values. Life is seldom that obliging. The Great American Novel may be on your dream agenda, yet you find yourself typing engineering specs. The reality is that at present you value feeding yourself and your family over feeding your love for art. Being clear about your values and the order of preference can eliminate a great deal of conflict. And if you know that something is very important to you, you will set aside other things to make room for it. When you have a goal and see it as realistic, you will have a far greater possibility of actualizing your dream than you will have if you see it as impossible.

There is no doubt that your career will influence your entire life in many subtle and not so subtle ways.

Work and its consequent lifestyle are bound up tightly with self-image, ego, and status. Sometimes we put much undue emphasis on "what a person does" that we overlook the person. In fact, some people find it hard to relate to new acquaintances without knowing what they do for a living. The point is that your career choice will change you. You will learn new skills, change some behaviors to fit your new role, make new friends, and learn a new vocabulary. Your work can lead to new involvements, new values, and even new ways of seeing yourself.[5] Its implications reach far beyond the workplace. In short, your lifestyle will reflect your most cherished values.

In this book you will be clarifying many values as you learn about yourself and your characteristics in reference to the work world. You will be making decisions based on those values. This process is bound to enhance your personal growth.

Personal Growth

Getting re-acquainted with ourselves—our feelings, needs, wants, and most cherished values, while transforming our shoulds—is a continuous process. But at certain stages of life the quest for self becomes imperative. We find that we have grown out of familiar roles: nurturer, business dynamo, provider, supermom. Life has a way of forcing us to make changes. When children start school, and especially when they leave home, a person can no longer be a parent in the same old sense. When a young person graduates from college, takes a job, marries and has children, he or she can no longer be a full-time, carefree young adult. When a person achieves success in a job and reaches the top, or realizes she or he is not going to reach the top, what then?

Growing as a person means changing, adjusting to both inner and outer reality. The need for growth on all levels is a powerful force within us. It means expansion into new and exciting areas of life. Never before in the history of humankind have people had such opportunity for growth at later stages of life—simply because people have never lived this long. Very old people were rare.

We are slowly beginning to perceive a new dimension to our lives. We see people going back to school at 70 and 80, getting degrees, starting businesses, publishing their first books, painting, initiating nationwide political action groups, teaching swimming! We are confused: Whatever happened to that obsolete object, the rocking chair? People are discovering that their powers are about as strong as their attitudes: physical (including sexual) ability, the ability to learn, to grow and develop new ideas. Limits seem to be vanishing like desert mirages. My mother went to work at a publishing company at age 70 with not much training or work experience. Her success at correcting material and supervising other workers was a source of amazement and delight to her.

The alternative to growth is: a diminished life that closes out *self* by put-downs, lack of confidence, many shoulds; closes out *others* by bitter, angry thoughts, blaming/projecting, many shoulds; closes out *life* by tension, anxiety, and finding fault on all sides.

Personal growth means: not getting stuck, but moving on; not clinging to an obsolete role, but trying on new ones until one fits; not denying, but accepting reality.

Times of transition are fearful periods when life seems so empty that we'd give anything not to face reality. But when we do face it, we are amazed at how much more there is of all good and joyful things, especially love for ourselves and others. We gradually begin to see life differently. Self-awareness leads to self-acceptance, which leads to self-confidence. We are on the way to self-actualization.

A self-actualized person might be described as follows:

- Authentic, open, doesn't hide behind roles or masks
- Is not ruled by either ego or emotion
- Simple, natural, with little need for status symbols
- Autonomous, centered, not pulled along with every fad
- Able to make decisions, take responsibility
- Takes life seriously with a generous touch of whimsy
- Can see through the "put-ons" of others with a benign view and maybe even a chuckle
- Emotionally balanced, enjoying peak experiences, delighting in people, art, and nature, yet able to "get the job done"
- Not burdened with the anxiety, guilt, or shame that go with shoulds
- Spontaneous, passionate, creative, enjoyer of life, and yet moral, ethical, concerned
- Sees all useful work as dignified and treats all workers with respect
- Takes time for self-renewal and relaxation
- Can be alone or in a group with equal ease
- Values privacy, yet feels one with humankind
- Tends to form deep personal relationships based on love and caring with other self-actualized people

- Has a basic set of beliefs, a philosophy of life
- Acts not out of greed, fear, or anger but out of love and caring for the whole world

The process by which we grow is not always easy. Author Bill Cane asks, "Is it possible to accurately plot out a lifetime without budgeting in the possibility of change, darkness, and personal pain?" Yet some people even seem to go beyond self-actualization. Heroic deeds based on minimal needs make up the fabric of their joyful lives. So when minimal needs are fulfilled on every level, when our wants are becoming reality, when our shoulds have dissolved or turned to wants, when our feelings are helping, not hindering the process, it seems that endless vistas of growth open up for us. As Maslow said, "We may still often (if not always) expect that a new discontent and restlessness will soon develop, unless the individual is doing what he's fitted for. A musician must make music, an artist must paint, a poet must write, if he is to be ultimately at peace. What a person can be, he must be. This need we call self-actualization."[6]

A self-actualized person, then, has solved most of life's problems. The human person is born to grow, to be open in spirit, to become self-actualized. Like trees, we can't grow backward. No matter where we are or what our past has been, we can reach a better place.

THE UNEXAMINED
life is not worth living.
SOCRATES

A Global/Philosophic View of Work

The work we choose will fulfill many of our needs and wants, directly reflect our values, and affect not only our own lives but the nation and the world. It's value-laden! Work can be rewarding, exciting, fulfilling, exasperating, exhausting, and dreadful—sometimes all at once. Work is often hard work!

What is work? There are many definitions, including some that overlap or contradict. Without getting too technical and precise, let's say that work is activity that provides goods and services to others while providing some reward for the worker.

We humans don't do anything without motivation. And our motivators are our needs and wants. Most people work for money to fulfill their various needs in the hierarchy as seen by Maslow. Those with enough resources to fulfill their basic needs then work for other reasons. A housewife works to care for husband and children. Her rewards may vary from love and mutual support to avoidance of disapproval.

Some people work because the work is intrinsically satisfying to their personalities. Others go to work to be with people, get noticed, be approved, and for a whole host of unique and individual enticements. But along the way, work must also be useful to others. "Work is the way that we tend the world, the way people connect. It is the most vigorous, vivid sign of life—in individuals and civilization."[7]

W I T H O U T   W O R K
all life goes rotten.
But when work is soulless,
life stifles and dies.
ALBERT CAMUS

Day and night the world hums with the activities of people and machines making goods for one another. Mines and forests, oceans and fields yield raw substances to make a myriad of *things*. Wood and metal, coal and cotton, and thousands of other materials are baled and baked, pounded and pummeled, mixed and milled, cut and checked, piled and packed for delivery to the world. Trucks and trains, ships and planes move endlessly huffing and hauling it all to other factories and farms, stores, and homes.

Things! They are bought, sold, used, recycled, worn out, and finally discarded to become endless piles of debris. Some of it returns to the earth, some of it remains to pollute and plague us. These things are made more easily than ever before because technology saves us from many back-breaking tasks. But our view of this change is limited because Americans are accustomed to having many things—more than any other country on earth. We take them for granted.

Along with the production of goods, work involves those often intangible "services rendered." From answering phones and directing traffic to designing systems and supervising workers, more and more people are involved in transactions, interactions, communications, "deals." We seem to be struggling into a new era that emphasizes information, ideas, and people over things.

Many affluent people clustered in suburbs believe they are "average Americans," while average Americans look mighty prosperous to much of the world. The information society, in which information jobs predominate over production jobs, accounts for only a small percentage of the world population. Some human beings do not survive because they lack even food, clothing, and shelter. As population expands, societies that were once self-sustaining are no longer able to supply their own necessities. Trade and travel arose very early in human history in response to the need for imported goods. But even today, transportation of basic goods is a necessity sadly lacking in many parts of the world. While great numbers of the world's people barely subsist, the affluent countries produce luxuries unheard of even by the most powerful emperors of old. Many ordinary children own television sets, stereos, video games, calculators, ten-speed bikes, and other magical gadgets.

As a nation we have entered an era of affluence and high living standards never before seen in all of history. In two centuries we have changed from an agrarian society, involved with simple necessities, to a technically oriented one involved with complex necessities and many luxuries. We are the richest nation on earth; we use the most energy and resources per capita of any country. And our powerful influence causes others to rush to imitate us.

But the provision of goods and services (called *work*), to those willing to pay for them, is costly in more than dollars and souls. It is costing us dearly in terms of irreplaceable energy and resources and in irreversible damage to the environment. The United States seems to be leading the world on a collision course with nature.

Decisions are needed, but we don't see clearly what to decide. Every possible choice causes some group somewhere to protest. Environmentalists vie with labor, and labor struggles with government, as government conflicts with business over their special interests. And the resulting tension and fear of the future affect us all as we try to see our own personal direction. Work affects our souls!

We are at an exciting crossroads where careful choices could create a better world. But there are no simple answers. So far, individuals' suggested alternatives have resounded like voices crying in the wilderness. Buckminster Fuller shows us complex geometric dwellings; Paolo Soleri builds a strange city in the desert; E. F. Schumacher says "intermediate technology" might be more humane and waste less energy.

Little by little, however, the message is becoming clear: decisions are in order. But before decisions can be made, values must be clarified. First we must know what we need and want and we must realize what our wants will cost in larger terms. To line up our values, we might agree that work should be a self-fulfilling, leisurely, meaningful activity that produces worthwhile products and services through peaceful, nonpolluting, resource-conserving methods. We are surprised that not everyone agrees what these products and services shall be. Such issues have social, political, and economic ramifications. For example, *peaceful* means "peace-keeping" to many people And thus the national defense budget consumes about 56 percent of the personal income tax collected yearly. We may agree to provide services to our weaker members: the disabled, the elderly, the needy minorities, the unwanted young, the uneducated, the poor, the imprisoned. But then our tax bill comes and we rebel. The United Nations Center for Disarmament puts it into perspective by telling us, "The money required to provide adequate food, water, education, health and housing for everyone in the world has been estimated at about $18.5 billion a year. It is a huge sum of money . . . about as much as the world spends on arms every two weeks."[8]

Perhaps corporations could cut down on profits. But this "remedy" strikes at the heart of the free enterprise system, and many companies are on a slim profit margin as it is.

Any move we make to cut back will change or short-change the money flow in some way. In the extreme view, we are caught in a bind of building/producing/ doing more and more of what we could perhaps use less and less of. We exhaust ourselves and the environment to keep the economy going.

When we get to the ultimate point (the one just before "no return"), will we have to start paying to dismantle it all? Garrett DeBell fantasizes this happening in "A Future That Makes Ecological Sense." Maybe it has already started. A parking lot in Yosemite National Park has been turned into a meadow![9]

At any rate, a national and global clarification of values continues. Your individual soul-searching will add to the pool of collective consciousness. Again, how much of what things do you want and need? How do your choices fit the global view? How do these choices affect your soul?

The Work Ethic: A Personal Philosophic View

An integral part of our value system is our attitude toward work, our work ethic. Is work really necessary? Is it valuable? Vocational educator, Terrence E. Carroll responds by saying, "Work is necessary, of course, and sometimes enjoyable. However, there is no intrinsic virtue in work in and of itself. Virtue is attached to it by individual attitudes that have been learned, and the fact that a great many individuals in our society share that attitude does not mean either that all people should share it or that it is even a healthy attitude for all who do. The human personality is capable of enjoyment and was meant to enjoy, not merely to consume; to create, not merely to produce."[10] Edward Kennedy tells that during his first campaign for the U.S. Senate, his opponent said scornfully in a debate, "This man has never worked a day in his life!" Kennedy says that the next morning as he was shaking hands at a factory gate one worker leaned toward him and confided, "You ain't missed a goddammed thing."[11]

Not everyone shares Carroll's attitude toward work, of course. (Thar's them 'ats fer it, 'n them 'ats agin it.) A strong work ethic stems from early colonial days, when "Idleness is the Devil's workshop" was a truth not to be questioned, like Ben Franklin's dictum that "Time is money." Americans value those who have "made it," and look down upon poor achievers with feelings ranging from compassion to moral outrage. People should do their work as a God-given duty, and only then can they expect a just reward: happiness and a home in the suburbs. So goes the common principle. Thus by and large we are work addicts—striving, struggling, even being ruthless and immoral to succeed. (*Work* sometimes becomes the Devil's workshop!)

The backlash from our national policies and attitudes was described in *Work in*

America, a 1972 Special Task Force report to the Secretary of Health, Education, and Welfare:

> Because work is central to the lives of most Americans, either the absence of work or employment in meaningless work is creating an increasingly intolerable situation. The human costs of this state of affairs are manifested in worker alienation, alcoholism, drug addiction, and other symptoms of poor mental health. Moreover, much of our tax money is expended in an effort to compensate for problems with at least a part of their genesis in the world of work. A great part of the staggering national bill in the areas of crime and delinquency, mental, physical health, manpower and welfare are generated in our national policies and attitudes toward work. Likewise, industry is paying for its continued attachment to Tayloristic practices through low worker productivity and high rates of sabotage, absenteeism, and turnover. Unions are paying through the faltering loyalty of a young membership that is increasingly concerned about the apparent disinterest of its leadership in problems of job satisfaction. Most important, there are the high costs of lost opportunities to encourage citizen participation: the discontent of women, minorities, bluecollar workers, youth, and older adults would be considerably less were these Americans to have had an active voice in the decisions in the workplace that most directly affect their lives.[12]

Mainly, however, we seem to be in a period of rising expectations about ourselves and about work even in a shrinking job market. Well, why not? Why not expand our vision? "The true person is as yet a dream of the future." Why keep that idea forever in the future? Why not make it present reality? The premise of this manual is that work, and maybe even life, can be joy! For the first time in history we can allow ourselves the luxury of considering work as fulfilling. And each person will find that fulfillment in a unique and special way.

If we can find a place where we feel some measure of success, some value, we shall find new energy to put into our work. Dr. Hans Selye talks about the relationship between aging, work, and stress: "Work wears you out mainly through the frustrations of failure. Most of the eminent among hard workers in almost any field lived a long life. Since work is a basic need of man, the question is not whether to work but what kind of work is play."[13] And Yehudi Menuhin expresses it best when he says, "All my life I have reveled in the sound of the violin."

We have many resources of mind and spirit. Can we move to a place of more joy in work and in life? Personal growth is essential. Each person can help by expanding his/her awareness of self and others. We seem to long for a less pressured, more serene life, with less frantic activity. Busy people are asserting their need for daily meditation, yoga, or other forms of relaxation to help them get in touch with deeper values.

We have merely touched the surface of a few of the concerns, global and personal, that relate to work. But each individual must garner the courage to fashion a meaningful existence, to find the balance between personal needs and the needs of others. We are responsible to ourselves for the quality of our own lives. We can be friends or enemies to ourselves by the choices we make, which in turn make up the lives we live. Real caring about ourselves is the first step in caring for others and in solving global concerns.

May your career choice contribute to your dream of the future.

 ## Self-Assessment Exercises

The following exercises are designed to help you with your inward search. *Use only the ones that seem useful to you. You may not need to do them all.* They will help you explore your feelings, needs, wants, and values. A self-portrait will assist you to look at your "free-spirit years," school experiences, and various other periods in your life. Ideas for an autobiography can be used to help with life planning. From this you can see how you've been having fun all your life and what has been most satisfying.

Chapter 9, "Work Affects the Soul: The Final Analysis," has been set aside for summaries of some of the Self-Assessment Exercises. You may note the results of your surveys there as you go along. Or you may wait until you reach the end of the book and then go back and collect them all. It's up to you.

1. Tapping into Feelings

How do you habitually respond to life situations? Do feelings get in your way and block your effectiveness? Growth can result from looking at your habits and choosing which ones you'd like to change.

On the list below, circle the words that describe your feelings and attitudes most of the time. Then mark with a plus sign (+) any that you'd like to develop more. Use a minus sign (−) to show those you'd like to deal with more effectively or eliminate as responses to life situations. Use a zero (0) for words that seldom or never describe you.

_____ Agitated	_____ Disgusted	_____ Optimistic
_____ Angry	_____ Encouraged	_____ Pessimistic
_____ Apathetic	_____ Enthusiastic	_____ Resentful
_____ Bored	_____ Fearful	_____ Satisfied
_____ Calm	_____ Frustrated	_____ Serious
_____ Compassionate	_____ Happy	_____ Skeptical
_____ Confident	_____ Hostile	_____ Stimulated
_____ Confused	_____ Hurt	_____ Violent
_____ Cynical	_____ Involved	_____ Weary
_____ Depressed	_____ Loving	_____ Withdrawn
_____ Discouraged	_____ Not sure	_____ Worried

Well, what have we here?

THE PICK OF PUNCH

2. Life Problems Checklist

a. Identify the factors that are holding you back. Rate the items listed on the next page by checking the appropriate columns. The column heads signify the following:

A: No problem—happy here
B: Slight problem
Y: Moderate problem
Z: A great problem
Year +: A great problem for more than a year
Chronic: A problem throughout your life

	A	B	Y	Z	Year +	Chronic
1. Parents/brothers/sisters						
2. Spouse/children						
3. Family closeness						
4. Friends/relationships/love						
5. Privacy/freedom						
6. Dwelling						
7. Work						
8. Finances						
9. Personal achievement/success						
10. Confidence						
11. Health						
12. Diet/drugs/drinking/smoking						
13. Exercise						
14. Your appearance						
15. Physical well-being						
16. Hectic lifestyle						
17. Recreation/hobbies						
18. Spiritual/religious well-being						
19. Emotional/mental well-being						
20. Status						
21. Intellectual ability						
22. Artistic ability						
23. Education						
24. Social concern						
25. Political concern						

b. Circle the numbers of the items you would like to change. Perhaps see a counselor
to discuss your feelings. It's easier to make a good career decision if anxieties
are not getting in the way.

3. Needs and Wants and Shoulds

What do you value? Write your answers in the space provided.

a. Survival Needs Plus

What lifestyle is important to you? Dream—let your imagination soar—describe your ideal.

Your home _____

Your clothing _____

Your food _____

Your family _____

Your friends _____

Your associates _____

Your transportation _____

Your pets/plants _____

Your gadgets and playthings _____

Your activities _____

Other _____

b. People Needs

What do you expect from each group around you? What would you like to change?

_____

_____

_____

_____

_____

c. Fulfillment Needs

Dream again! If you could instantly have your career choice and be already trained and skilled, what would you do:

1. To amaze your family and friends and delight yourself?

_____

_____

_____

2. To improve the world?

_____

_____

_____

d. List and examine the shoulds that hold you back. Are they related to your values? Can you drop them or change them to wants?

_____

_____

_____

e. Take charge! Today, what immediate steps, little or big, can you take to improve your life?

_____

_____

_____

_____

f. Today, what immediate steps, little or big, can you take to make your world a better place?

_____

_____

_____

g. Check the balance in your life. List things you do, over and above absolute need, to contribute to your well-being on each of the four levels.

Physical _____

Emotional _____

Intellectual _____

Altruistic _____

4. Rating Values

Here are five incomplete sentences that encourage you to think about values. In the lists that follow each one, check *every* word that finishes the statement correctly *for you*. Feel free to add, delete, or change words on each list.

After you have marked each list, rank order the values you've checked—that is, number them in the order of importance to you within each category.

a. Career value: In my career, I would like to _____

_____ Be secure

_____ Have fun

_____ Have status

_____ Design systems

_____ Help people

_____ Be physically active

_____ Make things

_____ Create ideas

_____ Be independent

_____ Take risks

_____ Create beauty

_____ Explore ideas

_____ Follow directions

_____ Take responsibility

_____ Experience variety

_____ Make money

_____ Improve society

_____ Organize things

b. Result values: I'd like to have _____

_____ Adventure   _____ Money

_____ Beautiful surroundings   _____ Pleasure

_____ Comfort   _____ Power

_____ Fun   _____ Possessions

_____ Happiness   _____ Prestige

_____ Independence   _____ Security

_____ Leisure time   _____ Structure

c. Personal qualities: I want to be _____

_____ Accepting   _____ Honest

_____ Achieving   _____ Intelligent

_____ Affectionate   _____ Intense

_____ Brave   _____ Joyful

_____ Bright   _____ Kind

_____ Caring   _____ Loyal

_____ Clean   _____ Mature

_____ Clear thinking   _____ Neat

_____ Competitive   _____ Needed

_____ Confident   _____ Peaceful

_____ Conscientious   _____ Powerful

_____ Creative   _____ Self-accepting

_____ Decisive   _____ Sensitive

_____ Disciplined   _____ Tough

_____ Efficient   _____ Trusting

_____ Free   _____ Understanding

_____ Genuine   _____ Verbal

_____ Good looking   _____ Warm

_____ Healthy   _____ Wise

d. People satisfiers: I'd like close relationships with _____

_____ Spouse/lover   _____ Children

_____ Relatives   _____ Friends

_____ Parents   _____ Neighbors

_____ Siblings   _____ Colleagues

_____ In-laws   _____ Supervisors

e. Personal growth satisfiers: The areas in which I'd like to develop are _____

_____ Physical   _____ Intellectual

_____ Emotional   _____ Altruistic/spiritual

f. Global values: I would like to work toward _____

_____ Arms control   _____ Industrial development

_____ Brotherhood   _____ Peace

_____ Economic development   _____ Prosperity

_____ Environmental preservation   _____ Technological development

_____ Harmony   _____ World food supply

_____ Human rights   _____ World order

5. Drawing a Self-Portrait

Many people find it helpful, when making a life change, to review their past experiences. An important clue to your skills and interests is to become aware of what you've been doing all your life. Pay attention to what gave you satisfaction. Your disappointments are important too, since they wouldn't be disappointing if they meant nothing to you. Some people find great motivation striving for success in a so-called area of failure. The following exercises are designed to help you recall some important happenings in your life.

a. Your Free-Spirit Years

One important time was your pre-teen years when you were a "free spirit." At about age five or six you began to be independent enough to cross the street alone and make some choices. During that time you may have chosen friends and activities without too much parental guidance. You weren't too worried about what people thought. What did you enjoy most during those years?

Make a list of activities you were involved with when you were 5 to 10 years old. Remember various seasons, indoors, outdoors; remember friends you played with. Check (√) the things you enjoyed most.

_____   _____

_____   _____

_____   _____

_____   _____

_____   _____

b. Your Life Line

Beginning with the "young childhood" period, draw a "life line" representing the ups and downs of your experience at various times of your life. Draw your first impressions without concern about detail. After you have plotted your life line, answer the questions that follow.

	Young Childhood Teddy Bears/Goblins 3–5 years	Elementary School Free-Spirit Years 6–13 years	High School Teen-age Traumas Teen-age Triumphs 14–17 years	New Beginnings College/Work 18–22 years	Developing an Adult Lifestyle 23–28 years	Family Career Involvement Commitment 29–39 years	Midlife Crisis Is There Life After 40? 40–45	Settling In Facing Up 45–55 years	Putting It All Together Once More Preretirement 56–70 years	Reflecting/Integrating A Time for Wisdom 70+
High Points										
Low Points										

1. Mark the high points on your life line with a star (*). List them:

_____

_____

_____

2. Double-star your important successes (**). List them:

_____

_____

_____

3. Mark the low points on your life line with the letter *Z*. List them:

_____

_____

_____

4. Mark your deepest disappointments with the letter *X*. List them:

_____

_____

_____

5. Circle points of important decisions. List them:

_____

_____

_____

_____

6. On the life line, list the people who influenced you most at each stage (teachers, writers, etc.). How important is their influence now? Rate them by:

1 = Very important
2 = Important
3 = So so
4 = No longer important

7. Your past can get better! How can this be so? Write your answer here:

_____

_____

_____

6. Candid Camera—3-D

Your life in 3-D will help you *discover* who you are, *decide* your goals, and *design* your strategies.

a. Loves: Make a list of things you love to do—not like or "should" but *love!*

_____

_____

_____

_____

b. Jobs: List every job you've held for pay at each stage of your life—way back to your babysitting/lawn-mowing days.

_____

_____

_____

_____

c. Other: List every school extracurricular activity, household task, and community volunteer job you've done at each stage of your life. Include arts and crafts, sports, hobbies, and recreation.

_____

_____

_____

_____

Now comes the very important part. Take a separate sheet of paper for each activity listed above and write the name of the activity at the top of the page. Then write all the things you had to do to accomplish that activity. Imagine that a photographer was taking pictures of you minute by minute. Tell exactly what you were doing.

People often underestimate all the things they've done. To do something like going skiing requires many steps: Buying equipment; deciding where to go, how to get there, and with whom; and budgeting funds are only a few of the decisions to be made and carried out.

One student developed the following lists:

Human Relations	Materials/Maintenance
Worked well with customers/employers/co-workers (good teamwork)	Inventoried, ordered, stored, prepared materials
Oriented, trained, evaluated employees	Noticed and took care of details
Organized, scheduled work	Did maintenance/repair
Settled customer/employee arguments	Opened and closed business
	Handled cash/cash register

Can you guess her job? She worked in a fast-food restaurant. At first, she had said, "But all I did was make hamburgers!" But when talking informally about her job, this is what she said she did:

"I notice when things are running low and order supplies and put them away."

"When the owners are away, I am in charge."

"I show new clerks what to do."

"Sometimes I fix the kitchen equipment."

"I make all the sauces."

"I settle arguments between kids and clerks about orders."

"I can always tell when a new clerk isn't going to work out."

This student had actually been in a supervisory position for four years and had often acted as manager. In developing a résumé for a management trainee position in a small restaurant, she might say:

Supervisor/Clerk

Inventory, order, prepare, and stock food supplies. Settle employee and customer problems and complaints. Orient/train new employees; informally evaluate employee performance. Do minor repairs/maintenance. As occasional acting manager, open and close shop, handle cash/cash register.

Spend at least an hour working intensely on this activity. Then save the lists and keep working on them, refining them, adding to them. You need to do them only once in your life. Later, they'll need only updating.

Some people have found it helpful to organize all the information about each job and important activity on separate file cards. Include company, address, supervisor, salary, dates worked, and each job title. This will be a good start on a "You Data" file. They will provide data you can use for a résumé and interviews when you job hunt.

Here are some examples of file cards turned in by one student. They nicely summarize activities she had done in several jobs, some of them volunteer. Notice that activities like fund raising and costume making could be expanded with many details.

Photo—Tree   Date: 1980 to present
870 Saratoga Ave.
San Jose, Ca.

Job title: Photo-processer

Supervisor: Dorena Penner

Salary: By the job @ $5.00 per hr.

Responsibilities:
  - choose and order the prints
  - arrange the albums
  - put together orders
  - re-order if necessary

Church   Date: 1975-79
Santa Clara, Ca.

Job: Leader in Women's Organization
          (Homemaking leader)
Salary: Volunteer
Responsibilities:
  - taught adults
  - organized lessons
  - shopped for materials
  - put on displays
  - set up lectures
  - dealt with people

Church   Date: 1973-75
Santa Clara, Ca.

Job: Counselor in children's organization
Salary: Volunteer
Responsibilities:
  - organized fund-raiser for children's hospital
    - talks
    - P.R.
  - organized programs, holiday activities
  - taught
  - made decisions
  - made costumes

Courtesy of Kathy Kidder

7. Creating an Autobiography

Many people find that creating an autobiography is a valuable way to rediscover themselves. To start your autobiography, use one of these suggestions:

a. Write the story of your life.

b. Write a summary of Exercise 5b, "Your Life Line."

c. Using Exercise 5b, "Your Life Line," write about the people who influenced you. What were their messages?

d. Make a poster or collage out of magazine pictures that illustrate you and your life line.

e. Make up your own idea for telling your life story.

f. Use the three circles below as a basis for examining yourself. Discuss each item in the past, present, and future circles as it applies to your life.

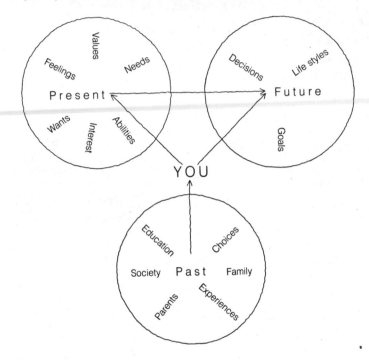

 Group Discussion Questions

1. Name the last five items you've purchased. What basic needs did they fulfill? What wants? Could you get along without them for a year?

2. What products do you consider useless? Harmful? What would happen if people stopped buying them?

3. List all the devices in your home that use electricity. On a scale of 1 to 10, rate how necessary each appliance is to you. If you could use only five, which ones would you choose? Is electricity a basic human need?

4. Fantasize about the changes you would make if you had to keep all your discards and throw nothing away. How would your life style change? Do we ever *really* throw anything away completely?

5. What limits and demands do your personal wants place on your career choice?

6. In prehistoric times, how were these seven basic workplace functions carried out:

business, industry, education, entertainment/communication, health, government, and military?

7. What are the major differences in the way work was carried out in prehistoric times and now?

8. Do the basic human needs change over time?

9. What is the connection between our needs and wants and the work that we and others do?

10. Give as many answers as you can to this question: Why do we work?

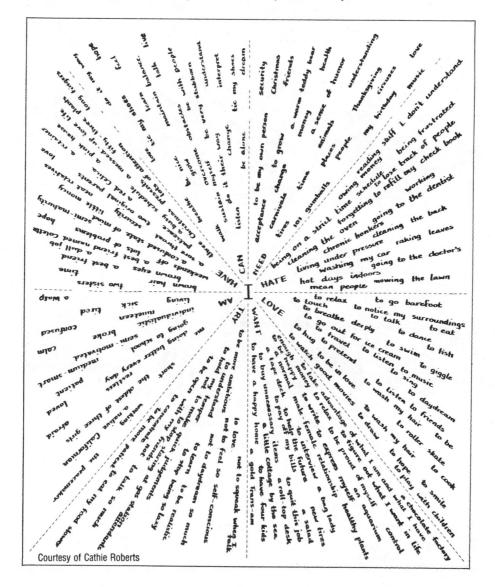

Courtesy of Cathie Roberts

Two

Roles and Realities: Sinking the Stereotypes

I t's easy to overlook some important factors in making a career decision. One of these, deeply imbedded in your being, motivated by your needs and wants and closely related to your values, has to do with the roles you play. Everyone functions in a variety of roles: male, female, mother, father, spouse, child, student, senior citizen, disabled, minority, immigrant/refugee—plus career roles from accountant to zookeeper. People play these roles for many reasons: Some roles they're born into, others they feel pressured to assume, and still others they choose freely. Sometimes stereotypes about how these roles "should" be played can influence your career and lifestyle decisions.

People seldom feel that they make decisions based on stereotypes, but everybody does it. A stereotype is a way of understanding and organizing information. It saves time but also imposes limitations on your thinking. Some obvious and useful stereotypes: A doctor can fix your sagging back, a carpenter can fix your sagging door. But some are based on faulty assumptions: for example, women can't handle engineering because they can't do math and are "too emotional"; men should always know how to fix things and should never, never cry! Years and years and layers and layers of conditioning about roles can subtly color your perceptions when you think about careers and your lifestyle, unless you stay open to new ideas about yourself.

To start, it may help you to explore the American Dream. This stereotype involved roles in a lifestyle thought to be achievable for most Americans following World War II. The dream has been and continues to be a motivator for the life choices of many men and women.

The American Dream included a cozy house in the suburbs with two cars in the garage and two healthy, bright children: an older boy and a younger girl. Father

39

commuted to work in a proper suit and tie and worked hard supporting his family as a successful manager. His loving wife "did not work" but stayed at home, dusting up a bit, attending to child problems, preparing each day for her husband's return to their little nest. If she ever worked, it was at a "feminine" position and only temporarily, until she could entrust herself to the care of a man. Marriage meant "living happily ever after."

Until the mid-1960s, many couples had an opportunity to make the dream come true. (Of course, their chances were better if they were white, Anglo-Saxon, and Protestant.) But today, only about 7 percent of the population resembles the idealized family described above. A large number of Americans live in cities. A great many are struggling to survive on very small incomes. Many have more than two children, some have none. Many are unmarried, separated, divorced, widowed, remarried with various sets of children, his and hers.

FAMILY PORTRAITS: U.S.A.

- In 1980, 23 percent of children were living in single-parent families. In 1970, the comparable figure was 15 percent.
- Overall, 10.3 percent of families were living in poverty in 1980.
- From 1970 to 1980, family households increased 13.5 percent, and nonfamily households increased 73 percent.

SOURCE: *Statistical Abstract of the United States* (Washington, D.C.: Bureau of the Census, 1981), p. 49. *U.S. Statistics in Brief* (Washington, D.C.: Bureau of the Census, 1981).

In a society beset with problems of permissiveness, casual sex, drugs, crime, violence, and a shaky economy, parenting is not pure bliss. It seems at times a thankless job to those who have made sacrifices for their children. Men and women are questioning their basic roles and struggling to sort out their values. Women run away from home. Men become househusbands and rear children. Many people—especially the elderly, the disabled, minorities, immigrants, and refugees—are poor and isolated from the mainstream of society. Today only 7 percent of American families fit the pattern of the suburban family of four.

Thus, the American Dream, which we had assumed was the "average American" way of life, turns out to be the 7 percent stereotype and therefore a myth for most people. But many still see this lifestyle as ideal and still believe that a great many Americans live this way. The media, especially television commercials, support this view despite real-life evidence to the contrary.

Old Images, New Imperatives

Females, males, minorities, refugees and immigrants, the disabled, teenagers, and the aging all have hopes and dreams that can be actualized through their career and life choices. As you read on, you can analyze each role as it relates to you and those around you. You can gain an understanding of the struggles that people experience in achieving their goals. You may be able to pinpoint ways to avoid some of these problems for yourself. You might also decide to what extent the American Dream motivates your thinking.

Male/Female Roles

At every age and every stage of life, male/female roles are most basic. Daniel J. Levinson writes, in *The Seasons of a Man's Life*, "During the last several hundred years, there has been a slow reduction in the ancient gender distinctions. There is greater recognition that women are not categorically different from men, that they have much the same desires as men and can develop much the same skills."[1] No one has ever been able to prove how much of our male/female attitudes and behavior are due to societal expectations and how much due to our physical make-up. But almost everyone has strong opinions about this issue. Consider the battle to pass the Equal Rights Amendment. It has touched on the deepest issues about the ways in which men and women view themselves. It has raised questions that we will be trying to answer for years to come.

Our experience tells us that both male and female behavior can be found all along a spectrum. This spectrum ranges from the Victorian, mythical, fragile, fainting female to the tough "Annie, Get Your Gun" figure; from the "Little Lord Fauntleroy" sissy male, getting sand kicked in his face on the beach, to the gun-toting, mighty, macho male. In the case of both males and females the range is from timid to tough.

You play your role according to a variety of images you've absorbed over time. Where are you on the Timid/Tough Spectrum? As people become more educated, they tend to move somewhat toward the middle. Most people realize that they need to balance these extreme qualities to survive modern life. Yet many very tough men and women feel they need to fight the world to protect themselves, and many timid men and women run away for protection. But it can be just as dangerous to safety to be armed to the teeth for battle as it is to be cowardly.

No matter how wide a range of behavior both men and women display, the truth is that in today's job market men are wa-a-a-ay ahead of women in earnings and job status. Early expectations have encouraged men to aim for success and prestige and women to downplay their role as achievers. Women typically say things like, "I could never do math!" or "I'm so helpless around machinery!" and finally, "I'm just a housewife!" But frustration over past inequities is beside the

The Timid/Tough Spectrum

Here are some words to describe people along the Timid/Tough Spectrum.

The Fragile, Fainting Female The "Little Lord Fauntleroy," Sissy Male	The Humorous, Humane Human	The Mighty, Macho Male The "Annie, Get Your Gun" Female
Timid	**Assertive/Balanced**	**Tough**
soft	strong	powerful
cowardly	confident	tough
dependent	equal	superior
gives up	persistent effort	keeps going beyond reason
aloof	cooperative	competitive
overwhelmed by harsh feelings	accepts all feelings	denies tender feelings
motivated by approval	self-motivated	motivated by power/money/fear
acts emotionally	blends intuition and logic	acts rationally
sacrifices all	asks for what is needed	demands all
manipulates	cooperates	dominates
withdraws	negotiates	attacks
inept, insecure	learning, open, growing	knows all, can do all
rigid	spontaneous	reckless

The Timid Person *is*	The Assertive Person *is*	The Tough, Aggressive Person *is*
indirect, inhibited, self-conscious, unsure	direct, clear, open, centered, accepting	direct, overbearing, domineering, controlling, insensitive
and feels	*and feels*	*and feels*
tearful, shaky, angry, hurt	strong, buoyant, self-respecting, confident	angry, explosive, superior, demanding, pseudo-confident
and experiences	*and experiences*	*and experiences*
uncertainty, domination, disregard, disrespect, annoyance from others.	acceptance, clarity, respect, cooperation from others.	lack of cooperation, isolation, confusion, anger, hurt, guilt from others.

Where are you on the Timid/Tough Spectrum?
Where would you like to be?

TIMID   BALANCED   TOUGH

point. Let's look at some facts about the status of women in relationship to men today—facts that don't fit the stereotype in the American Dream. The discussion will of necessity focus on the dilemma of being female in the workplace.

Eighty percent of women still tend to cluster in low paying, low status, stereotypical jobs. They still receive different education, training, and counseling. They work less overtime because of such factors as family care. They get started later on their careers for the same reason. Many women are lacking in confidence and experience fear and ambivalence. Men's salaries increase dramatically with a B.A. or B.S. degree, women's only modestly. With advanced degrees, however, the gap narrows.

Fifteen Facts: Women in the Workplace

1. Fifty-one percent of the population is female; 49 percent is male.
2. More than 90 percent of all women work sometime in their lives, two-thirds out of economic necessity because they are divorced, widowed, or married to men earning less than $10,000 per year. In 1980 the average woman could expect to spend 34 years of her life in the work force, compared to 38.3 years for men. By the year 2000 the average is expected to be 40 years for women.
3. Women accounted for nearly 60 percent of the increase in the civilian labor force between 1970 and 1980—about 13 million women compared with more than 9 million men. The highest percentages of working women are in the age ranges 18–24 and 35–54—that is, women not likely involved with full-time child rearing. The life expectancy of a female born in 1979 is 77.8 years. In 1920, it was 55 years. The life expectancy of a male born in 1979 is 70 years. In 1920, it was 54 years.
4. The average woman worker is as well educated as the average man worker; both have completed a median of 12.6 years of schooling.
5. Many women tend to cluster in low paying, dead-end jobs: 60 percent of all working women are clerks, saleswomen, waitresses, and hairdressers. As a result, the average woman worker earns only about 60 percent of what a man earns, even when both work full-time year-round. A man, then, earns 166 percent of the salary of a woman. Fifteen percent of women workers are unionized. These women earn 33 percent higher salaries, have better benefits, and have recourse to grievance procedures. The median weekly salary in 1980:

White men	$329
Minority men	$242
White women	$206
Minority women	$183

6. The unemployment rate is lowest for adult white men (20 and over) and highest for young black women.

7. One percent of women and 12 percent of males earn more than $25,000 a year.

8. Only 7 percent of American families have a working father, a dependent mother, and two children.

9. Forty percent of mothers with children under the age of 6 are working.

10. Fifty-one percent of all working women are married; 49 percent are single, widowed, or divorced, many with dependent children.

11. Eighty-four percent of all children whose mothers must work can find no government-licensed day care.

12. Women who head families earn 50 percent less than men who head families. Half of all widows and single women exist on poverty-level incomes.

13. Seventy-four percent of all divorced fathers default in the first year of court-ordered child support.

14. A nurse with 14.2 years of education earns 5.8 percent less than a deliveryman. A secretary with 13.2 years of education earns less than a truck driver with 9 years of education.

15. According to the United Nations' Women's Conference (1980): Two out of every three illiterates in the world are women. Although women account for one-third of the labor force, they put in two-thirds of the work hours, earn one-tenth of the world's income, and own less than 1 percent of the property.

The reality then is that women work mainly because they must work to survive, and yet their financial condition has improved little if at all in the last two and a half decades, although their needs have increased.

Many inequities must be addressed before equality in the workplace is a reality. By 1990, 72.4 percent of women between the ages of 25 and 54 will be working, mostly at traditional jobs. They will comprise 45 percent of the workplace.[2]

In a unique way women are striving to come into their own in the 1980s. While the statistics seem discouraging, they represent a tremendous transition point. From the early days of the United States, women have seen themselves as achievers and movers in the larger society, struggling for their place. Abigail Adams, for example, wrote to her husband John, the country's second president (1797–1801), interceding for women's rights.

At age 72, Elizabeth Cady Stanton, speaking to the International Council of Women, said, "The younger women are starting with great advantages over us. They have the results of our experience; they have superior opportunities for education; they will find a more enlightened public sentiment for discussion; they will have more courage to take the rights which belong to them. . . . Thus far, women have been the mere echoes of men. Our laws and constitution, our creeds and codes, and the customs of social life are all of masculine origin. The true woman is as yet a dream of the future." Somehow that quotation sounds more recent than 1888! In the 1980s, the true woman is still a "dream of the future."[3]

The struggle for women's rights continued into the 1940s. But after World War II, the stereotypical, mythical woman in the American Dream evolved. She was first a wife, next a mother, rarely herself as a woman. Her life was defined by the roles of others, and she served their needs. Betty Friedan called this new role limitation, "this problem that has no name," the "feminine mystique."[4] It began to occur to many that this American Dream model was not the "true woman." Certainly it did not describe every woman. Historically, about 20 percent of American women do not marry, and many women, especially minorities and immigrants, have always worked in factories and service jobs. Cottage industries were a way of life before the industrial revolution, and even as late as the 1940s, farms where women worked beside men, claimed 25 percent of the population.

In the early 1980s, inflation accelerated the movement of women into the workplace. Many older women who had not been socialized or educated to see themselves in careers have headed for low paying, dead-end jobs. But younger women have had a different perspective. Planning for a career is higher on their agendas. Older women with experience are also moving up in the workplace. The general trend is toward improvement and opportunity for working women.

New Directions for Men

While women are trying to define new roles, men also face dilemmas because their role is too rigidly defined. Society says that their careers are primary and their families secondary, so men have to keep on working and moving up the ladder of success until they are forced to retire. But we are becoming aware that a man's whole future isn't determined when he chooses a career, and the white male executive doesn't always rise to the top in an easy, direct ascent.

Levinson writes in *The Seasons of a Man's Life* that male adult development takes place in three overlapping, age-linked eras marking early, middle, and late adulthood. Many men experience traumatic crises as they make the thirties, forties (midlife), and sixties transitions. During these transitions, many men reevaluate at least two and possibly three components of the life structure. One's career is most important in that it is a vehicle for contributing to society and fulfilling one's dream about oneself. Marriage and family are usually an integral support for the dream. Friendships/peer relationships, ethnicity/religion, and sometimes leisure—especially sports—come in for their share of scrutiny.

Decisions made at these times are value-dependent and highly interrelated. Salary, prestige, commuting time, overtime, pressure, travel, and colleagues all have an impact, either positive or negative, on family life. Approaching the final settling-down period of one's life with a very flawed life structure can prove intolerable for many men.[5]

Much energy goes into the daily competition for success in the marketplace.

Men who have "made it" have to work hard to "keep it." For men, making business contacts is as natural as breathing. Or is it? The stereotype is that the old boys' network begins at age 6 with the soccer team and works its way up to the college/military fraternity. The hearty handshake and exchange of business cards isn't the road to success for every male, however, and images like these put needless pressure on many men, especially minorities with little access to the power structure. Many feel hostile at now having to share a piece of the pie with women and in some cases to be passed by while a woman is promoted. Often men come to a dead end where no more promotions are possible, and they have to relinquish their life ambitions. The same old job has become too familiar; all the challenge is gone. Like many women, many men feel trapped in monotonous, demanding, or demeaning jobs. Many workers of both sexes seem dissatisfied with their jobs.

Unfortunately, career success does not prevent the crisis. Some men achieve their long-sought goals only to ask, "Was it worth it?" Perhaps they have moved up into administration and now find themselves in prestigious positions they do not enjoy. Sometimes these jobs involve long hours, trips away from home, and frequent moving. The result is alienation from the family—a loss of nurturing that can be critical, especially in times of crisis. Many marriages don't survive this stress.

Whether equal to the task or not, men have had full economic responsibility for their families. Often they are expected to spend weekends and vacations doing heavy work at home, with little time for rest and recreation. As children grow older and require less care, a husband may resent a wife who stays home enjoying her leisure and playing cards with her friends. For men who try to be "househusbands," re-entry to the job market is much more difficult and viewed with more disapproval than for women. Enculturated to deny many human feelings, men are allowed to get angry, but not to show fears or tears. The successful man, as well as the unsuccessful, may be leading a life of "quiet desperation."

Yet the alternatives may seem frightening. Changing careers may mean stepping down, with a resulting loss of income and possibly a feeling of defeat. Instead of retraining for a new line of work, the dissatisfied working man will probably decide to "stick it out" until retirement or to look for a new company with a fresh outlook. He seems to have fewer choices than his wife, who can change her life dramatically by going back to college or taking a job outside the home. For both husband and wife, in most instances, the immediate goal is not self-actualization, but paying off the mortgage, educating the children, and caring for their elderly parents.

Midlife is a crucial time, a time to realize that *dis*-illusionment means seeing more clearly. It is a time to re-order values, build confidence, face areas of deficiency, and develop neglected segments of one's life. Midlife can be a healing time, a time for growth, the time to befriend oneself by putting one's world into perspective—a time to ask, "What do I really want out of life?"

As they face the issues and *grow* through this crisis, some men develop a new, deeper, more mature outlook that restores their energy and vitality. Some are amazed to learn that they need better skills in human relations and communications, instead of a new job or a new kind of work. Some find the courage to make needed changes in work or home life, go back to school, break out of old patterns. The

"It seems like only yesterday I was on the verge of getting it all together."

need to let go of the past is a common human experience that can bring us closer to the real meaning of life. Learning this and not feeling that one should "have it all together" once and for all can be liberating. Both men and women need support when they are experiencing these critical periods in the normal course of human development.

DON'T LET LIFE
discourage you;
everyone who got where he is
had to begin where he was.
—RICHARD L. EVANS

Family, Career, or Both?

Every person has to resolve questions that involve family versus career. In the past men found themselves on a career path early in life, supporting a wife who reared the children. But the questioning sixties seemed to turn all the guideposts around as choices multiplied. The issues are many and complex. Their solutions will be found by the usual muddling that takes place in human existence. And for the majority, the results will continue to be unclear.

What are some of the issues that beset us as we try to fulfill basic needs and wants in the context of family versus career? Family life fulfills some of the deepest longings of men and women. It fulfills needs and wants on many levels for physical, emotional, intellectual, and altruistic support and growth. Families are people who, theoretically, see one through the ups and downs of life and are enduringly present in a special way.

Today we see people opting for all sorts of new family lifestyles: from traditional marriage to live-in roommates or divorce; from large families to delayed families or no children by choice; from single parents to remarried parents or communal parenting. But the questions asked by men and women are vastly different. Women wonder if and how they can combine a family with a career. Men, remaining career oriented, wonder if they need a family, especially one that might include a very liberated wife.

So while it is still quite acceptable for a man to be career oriented, the ambivalence remains for a woman. She may forgo marriage and children, opting for a full-time career. The struggle to "make it" is still greater for women than for men. Women are still competing, for the most part, in a male world. If a woman chooses to marry and have children, she will be largely responsible for their care. She may choose full-time wifing and mothering. She may then find herself out of a job or in need of a job before she can say (to wit), "women in transition!"

In the small nuclear family of today, full-time child rearing can be expected to take only seven to ten years of a 75-year existence. If a woman remains at home until age 35 or 40, she still has 25 to 30 years to fill with some kind of activity before she reaches retirement age. The nuclear family makes even grandmothering a part-time job—if babysitting is needed at all, since grandmother and grandchildren may be living in widely separated geographic areas. Where kids once played and coffee flowed freely among friends, an empty nest in daytime-desolate suburbia has become the lot of the middle-class woman.

When volunteering and playing bridge and golf wear thin, work involvement is felt as a compelling need. Women need work for the same reasons men do: money and fulfillment. No one seems to doubt that men need work. Even the Kennedys and the Rockefellers work. We sympathize with men who are out of work more than a few months and with those in forced retirement, but we rarely feel concern for women in the same position. Skills can get rusty and confidence eroded while women are staying at home. Just getting dressed and leaving the house in the morning can be invigorating for some, especially when child rearing is finished.

For others the empty nest is a delight of peace and quiet after years of mothering. Work offers opportunity for personal growth, but so does family and community involvement.

For the mother with children still at home, working can sometimes be a bowl of lemons. One working mother, after dropping off her children in the morning at different schools, taking one to the dentist during lunch hour, and making a trip to the shoe store after work, arrived home at 6:30 to find her husband late and the refrigerator empty. She asked herself, "Is this liberation?" Contrast this person, who was working at an unfulfilling job and besieged by demands both at work and at home, with a fulfilled wife and mother who finds homemaking a satisfying career. Running a home creatively with love and care, experimenting with voluntary (or involuntary) simplicity, practicing innovative nutrition, gardening, sewing, and entertaining can be interesting and stimulating for some women when economic needs aren't urgent. Being with children at those special and irreplaceable moments is a greater reward than career development for many mothers.

But women who are successful in their careers may well be happier wives and mothers than those who feel trapped at home. Many women who have chosen motherhood are exploring viable ways to do it well and still have successful careers. Some employers let women work part-time for a few years, share a job with another person, or act as consultants during the child-rearing period. Studies show increased productivity as a surprising result of this flexibility.

People are concerned that men will be pushed out of jobs if too many women come into the labor market and also that wages will fall. Barbara R. Bergman, speaking on the economics of the women's movement, estimates that if the 40-hour work week fell to 31, all potential workers could be accommodated and end up with more leisure. She also adds that working women use more goods and services, not fewer, thus further increasing productivity.[6] Many husbands welcome the increased economic security that a wife's income provides. One man remarked that he "loves being dependently wealthy!" Others feel threatened by the thought of a working wife. Long accustomed to seeing themselves as "sole provider," they see their main role in life eroding. But Bess Myerson, a nationally prominent woman of many careers, says, "When it comes to machismo versus mouths to feed, machismo is a luxury no family can afford."[7] Self-fulfillment also may be a necessity, not a luxury.

But even if a woman is not one of the 66 percent who must work because of economic necessity, there is some danger in turning over to another the complete responsibility for economic support. Women need career skills as insurance against a crisis, such as divorce or widowhood. If a woman has made a total, lifetime commitment to marriage and family, only a crisis propels her to seek a career. If she is divorced or widowed at 40 or 50, she hasn't been trained to cope in today's world.

And it is still true that some women, especially older women, come back to work for enrichment and a little extra money. They are ambivalent about "going for it." Sometimes their ambivalence translates—to the eye of the beholder—as lack of commitment. The woman chooses to go home and cook dinner instead of working overtime. She skips a weekend conference in order to be with family.

As Kevin Starr wrote in the *San Francsico Chronicle-Examiner,* "She finds herself traumatized by all those steely-eyed, perfectly groomed, 25-year-old MBA's in slit skirts about whom she reads in the newspapers when they receive promotions to vice presidencies. These women seem so positively untouched by the pieties and sentiments that dominated her at a comparable age."

In truth, these 25-year-old women are a minority in a sea of young women struggling with the newfound image of female success. Many of them are raising children alone without child support or alimony, going to school, and holding a job at or near the poverty level. Juggling career and family is a necessity. They may take two steps forward, but step back at those crucial times of decisions, such as seeking more education, or choosing lucrative career fields with more responsibility. Many women begin well, getting the "right degree" and a good job. But research shows that by midmanagement time, women start lagging and rarely make it to the top. Women still have a way to go!

In most cases working wives and mothers can expect to carry the burden of household chores and child care. Working women don't have wives at home. Alice Cook, Cornell professor and scholar in residence at Stanford University's Center for Research on Women, surveyed 19 nations and in 1976 published a report entitled "The Working Mother." She concluded, "The husband spends very little more time assisting the wife and mother with household tasks when she works outside the home than when she does not."[8] A February 1982 *Better Homes and Gardens* survey found most working women still caring for household tasks. Younger and better educated couples are an exception, but not yet numerous enough even today to affect the statistics significantly.

Eve Steadman, a wife who returned to school, wrote this fantasy about men and housework:

> Women have always worked. The term "working women" usually indicates that these women are working for pay and that they have some choice about the kind of work they will perform. Many years ago, when I felt trapped in a future of endless diapers, dishes, and debris, I used to speculate about what would happen if the work situation pushed upon women were also applied to men. First of all, men could have no choice; every man by virtue of his biology would have exactly the same work. Second, this work would be comparable with that of women, that is, featuring monotony, drudgery, and repetition. Suppose, I thought, every man regardless of talents and interests were forced to be a ditchdigger. The man would not only dig all day, but every night while he slept someone would come by and push all the dirt back into the ditch! When he faced the dirt next morning, he would be expected to look glamorous and cheerful. Under these conditions, the Men's Revolution would not have been long in coming!

But Caryl Rivers of Boston University is optimistic for the future of liberated marriage, which she defines as one in which there is rough parity of both "the dirt

I'm unhappy and I don't even know if it's me or my stereotype.

THE NOW SOCIETY by William Hamilton
Copyright 1979
by Universal Press Syndicate

work and the glory."[9] Each woman—each couple—who is going to change from the traditional lifestyle will have to make adjustments. Some men have been strongly socialized to see housework as very unmasculine. But many people value a reasonably clean house and occasional home-cooked meals. The business of living, of maintaining oneself and one's home, is necessary, is hard work, and is not often perceived as stimulating. These facts can become friction.

Add babies—add more of the above. Who's to take care of it all if a wife works? Some women overcompensate by emphasizing feminine appearance and behavior. If a woman tries to be the perfect housewife/mother, she may experience a physically and emotionally exhausting way of life.[10]

Child Care

Along with household management, working parents must be concerned with finding effective child care where there is supervised play, learning, and social life. Day care, which was widespread and federally and industrially funded during World

War II, is now available only in private centers. Very few companies provide child care, but some employers will agree to a part-time or flexible work schedule that enables a parent to be at home when the children come home from school. Sometimes a close friend or relative is willing to care for the children, or a live-in babysitter will exchange services in return for room and board. Some parents organize their own co-ops. Others arrange for child care through help-wanted ads in company, school, or church newsletters.

Before enrolling a child at a day-care facility, it is important to be sure that the place provides clean and safe surroundings, nutritious meals, growth promoting activities, and a loving/caring environment. Child care must be reliable, especially if a mother is competing with men at work. Panic over babysitters is no help to the serious pursuit of a career, nor is worry over a sick or distressed child. Parents' needs for leisure on weekends and holidays should be considered. Many men, long socialized to see responsibility for children as someone else's problem, do not "see" what needs to be done, but leave it entirely up to Mother.

It would seem wise, then, to look at male/female roles as they relate to family versus career. Should women feel free to choose either full-time work or full-time motherhood, or whatever combination meets their needs, without being pressured by the expectations of others? If so, then society should value their contributions as important on every level, and men should become more involved with life at home. Both partners in the relationship can benefit from a more balanced lifestyle. Some men whose wives enjoy working are cutting down on their own work hours, again moving toward a better balance. Children can benefit in many ways from the care and concern of two involved parents.

The Single Woman

Women who choose careers over family life have been viewed with a wide range of feelings, from disapproval to awe. For the unmarried working woman, ambivalence over career vs. family can last for years and undermine a serious commitment to a career. Since her career change is not viewed as problematic by society, the individual struggles alone to make the decision, while often working at a low paying and unsatisfying job. Society provides few support systems to assist her with career advancement or change.

Fortunately, these attitudes are changing. Society views the working woman of the '80s with less disapproval, more awe and great interest. But the path is not without obstacles, and the ambivalence between career and family still persists. The high divorce rate can make marriage and children seem like great risks. The single woman is under pressure as she struggles to succeed in what is still largely a man's world. A career change, or a return to college, can be a lonely and frightening decision. Many working women have begun to form support groups or "new girl networks" to help each other—a step in the right direction.

Teenagers and Young Adults

Teenagers who have done well in high school are usually confident and college-bound—but they are *not* the majority. Many of their peers have not yet learned necessary survival skills or experienced any feeling of achievement. They lack both the job skills and the sophistication that are needed to find work in a tight job market. Their sagging self-image is not improved when they are rejected by prospective employers who have neither the time nor the budget to train raw recruits.

Today business and industry are engaged in myriad mysterious machinations that challenge the understanding of even the brightest adult. No wonder young people, fresh out of senior government class, are lost! Some high schools acknowledge students' needs by offering work experience and career observation and exploration programs. Often the shyest, least successful students will not even apply. For many, approaching the first rung of the career ladder is the most difficult step in the entire lifetime career process. Statistics show that the unemployment rate for young adults is two to three times higher than the rate for the remainder of the population.

Walter Williams, who teaches at Temple University, favors a lower minimum age and wage for teenagers. He maintains such changes would increase employment for the young, especially minorities, allowing them to step up onto the first rung of the career ladder and gain badly needed work experience. Such services as movie usher and car hop might be reinstated without taking jobs away from older people. [11]

Nontraditional careers have little appeal. Many women are willing to accept the higher pay and status of "male" jobs, but most men are ashamed to accept the low pay and inferior status of traditionally "female" jobs. The young, inexperienced, untried job seeker is reluctant to strike out into these uncharted waters. Few do, especially among those who do not have a chance to mature and explore their potential in college. In truth, the young are rushing at a snail's pace in this direction.

When young adults have personal and financial responsibilities, very few will take time out to completely retool for a nontraditional career. But despite the obstacles in launching a satisfying career, taking that first step, however small, can be a rewarding experience at any age.

The Aging

Opportunities for rewarding work become fewer for both men and women as they grow older. After age 40, job hunting becomes even more difficult. Many workers stay at jobs they've outgrown rather than face possible rejection. Our youth-oriented, throw-away culture sees little value in older people. In playwright Lillian Hellman's words, they have "the wisdom that comes with age that we can't make use of." [12]

Unemployment and economic need for work is higher among older women, especially minorities, than among younger white women. A national council reports these findings: Though unemployed longer when seeking work, older women job hunt harder, hold a job longer with less absenteeism, perform as well or better, are more reliable, and are more willing to learn than men or younger women. Yet many older women earn poor pay and face a future of poverty in their retirement years.[13] When "sexism meets ageism, poverty is no longer on the doorstep—it moves in," according to Tish Sommers, coordinator of a task force on older women for the National Organization for Women.[14]

Yet a 1981 report on the White House Conference on Aging shows that as a group, older Americans are the "wealthiest, best fed, best housed, healthiest, most self-reliant older population in our history." This statement is small comfort to those living below the poverty line on meager fixed incomes, but it does explode some of the myths and fears that lurk in the aging psyche. Opportunities for moving in and up in a large company may shrink but many older people begin successful small businesses, volunteer in satisfying activities, and stay active for many years. They have few role models because in previous generations the life expectancy was much shorter and expectations of life were fewer. They are plowing new ground.

Employers are beginning to recognize that the mature person can bring a great deal of stability and responsibility to a position. One doesn't lose ability and experience on the eve of one's 65th or 70th birthday any more than one grows up instantly at age 21.

Minorities

Minorities, particularly blacks and Hispanics, also are caught in the stereotype bind. If they cluster in ghettoes, they struggle just to stay even. Their expectations are low because, among the poor, young people rarely get a chance to observe adult role models in successful positions. When minority people move up, many also move away from those they might have helped. The young are left to find themselves, often in a hostile environment, cut off from the mainstream. As they watch others making decisions that affect them and getting the lion's share of affluence, the future may seem hopeless. Minorities in decision-making roles are barely visible. Unemployment for minorities is dramatically higher, while wages are noticeably lower. Among minority youth in cities, the unemployment rate is over 50 percent. Many are unable to begin careers because opportunities are limited or withheld. While the number of black businesses has risen greatly, for example, they are still relatively few. Inflation, recession, and unemployment have jeopardized their positions.

Refugees/Immigrants

Never before in history have so many people migrated in fear and suffering during such a short period of time as this past decade. This migration has been due in part, according to former President Jimmy Carter, "to the failure on the part of the world to live by principles of peace and human rights."[15] If the career search is demanding for everyone, imagine the added stress of coping with a new language in a new culture—and worrying about the family and friends left behind. Many immigrants feel trapped in low-status jobs, a mismatched work ethic, an ambiguous dress-for-success code, and a U.S. brand of go-for-it assertiveness.

The immigrant's first and most important task is to learn the language of the host country. People who feel unable to communicate are tempted to withdraw, isolating themselves from the larger society. In the long run, this isolation is usually self-defeating. Americans meet newcomers with emotions ranging from compassion to resentment over possible competition for jobs. Americans tend to forget that our ancestors were either American Indians or "boat people."

Non-English-Speaking Immigrants to the United States, 1971–1979

Mexico	583,700
Philippines	312,700
Dominican Republic	310,800
Cuba	249,700
West Indies	237,400
South Korea	235,400
Vietnam	129,300
Other Asia	140,300

SOURCE: *Statistical Abstract of the United States* (Washington, D.C.: Bureau of the Census, 1981), p. 87.

Persons with Handicaps

Society has never been successful at dealing with people who are noticeably disabled. A silent minority, too, they were expected to stay in their place, which was one of low expectations. They have often struggled with a poor self-image and feelings of hopelessness about making even a living, much less a contribution to society.

In the present climate of focus on individual rights, people with limitations are asking for rightful recognition of the skills they possess. They are demanding more access to government, business, industry, education, and all phases of life. Society is forced to take note that here are people able to make a living and to make valuable contributions.

The Economic Perspective

Counselor Veronese Anderson sees society with mainly the white, affluent, successful male at the top and his family with him by association. At the lower levels are those of poor to modest incomes: Minorities exist at these levels in percentages far out of proportion to their numbers. In 1980, the median income for white families was $21,904; for black families, it was $13,843. As the levels rise, the numbers diminish. Figure 2-1 shows this disparity as a sort of socioeconomic tower.

In 1980 nearly 25 million (and by some definitions, 48 million) Americans were living in poverty. In the 1980s the shift may be toward less overall poverty but a frightening increase of impoverished women, children, and minorities. Growth in the private sector does not "trickle down" to them. If this shift continues, by the year 2000 the poverty population will consist almost solely of children and women, many alone and over 65. Recessions and job layoffs make the problem worse.

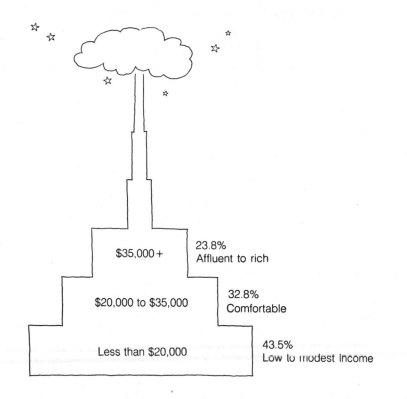

Figure 2-1 Income Distribution of All U.S. Families, 1981

Source: *Statistical Abstract of the United States, 1982–1983* (Washington, D.C.: Bureau of the Census, 1983), p. 432.

And the U.S. Census Bureau shows that weekly spendable earnings dropped between 1970 and 1980, with an even sharper drop to 1981.[16]

Some people see discrimination against women and other groups as part of capitalistic planning. As economist Marilyn Power Goldberg points out, we need a "marginal workforce to smooth over cycles in the economy and to perform vital but menial and poorly paid jobs. We need to keep reinforcing their image of inferiority."[17]

John Kenneth Galbraith also sees society using the concept of the "convenient social virtue" to keep women (and various minorities) in a position of free service. Galbraith says: "'The convenient social virtue' ascribes merit to any pattern of behavior, however uncomfortable or unnatural for the individual involved, that serves the comfort or well-being of the more powerful members of the community." The nurse, the teacher, the nun, the community volunteer, the "cheerful, dutiful draftee": All have accepted social approval instead of pay. The economy benefits from free service. Galbraith sees the cheerful housewife of the nuclear family, who takes pride in her virtue as provider of goods, as the "consumer par excellence," another advantage to the economy.[18] But the cheerful drudge and the dutiful draftee are both fading into the past.

New Themes, Changing Attitudes

Today, after more than two decades of consciousness raising, everyone wants access to an enriched life. Perhaps most Americans agree, in theory if not in practice, that no one should be denied self-fulfillment because of sex, creed, color, nationality, disability, or age. But sweeping innovations in traditional roles require a willingness to take risks and change attitudes—beginning with our own. Men and women who want others to change are often surprised to learn that they must change themselves first. The result may be alienation or—with much effort—a more rewarding closeness. The key is good communication.

Improving Communication

Most breakdowns in communication take place because of misunderstandings over needs poorly stated as demands or blame. To improve communication, avoid starting sentences with "you never" or "no matter what you say." The listener translates such messages to "I don't care what you say or think," which becomes "I don't care about YOU!" Hurt and anger result, and strong feelings block clear thinking. A minor or even major war erupts—hot or cold depending on whether fight or flight is used to solve the problem.

Here are some guidelines for improving relationships through good communication. They focus on solving problems instead of getting caught in an emotional vortex.

Use "I" statements instead of "you" statements. Describe your feelings, needs, and wants instead of attacking or blaming. "I would really enjoy taking an evening class this term if you could take care of the children" would probably work better than "You never take care of the children so that I can get out once in a while."

Take responsibility for your feelings. We *choose* our feelings, based on strong patterns of behavior that began in early childhood. We are the only ones who can change those patterns. Since others cannot *make* us have certain feelings, it makes no sense to say, "You make me angry." You take responsibility for your feelings when you say, "I become angry when . . ."

A NO-WIN GAME

In a restaurant, a woman is juggling a fussy baby on her shoulder while she tries to eat her meal. She tells her husband that child rearing is beginning to get her down.

Her husband replies, "I'd trade places with you anytime, honey. Just tell me when you're ready to go out and earn a living, and we'll switch."

According to writer Alice De Armand, "Who's got it worse?" is a no-win game. The wife tends to overestimate the "glamour" and "excitement" of going out into the world of work every day. The husband tends to overestimate the amount of "freedom" and "leisure time" that a woman has when she stays at home with the children.

A caring response would accomplish more than the futile game of "Who's got it worse?" Each spouse could learn to say, "I know how hard you work. I'm impressed with the way you handle your job, and I'd like to help you more than I do." Many thoughtful husbands would add, "Here, let me hold the baby for a while."

SOURCE: Santa Cruz *Weekly,* October 14, 1981.

Change yourself, not others. Trying to force others to change usually results in resistance and resentment. "If you don't pick up your clothes [threat . . . threat]" becomes, "I choose not to wash clothes that are left lying around the house!"

Communication that facilitates intimacy rather than destroys it is a skill that can be learned. Sometimes feelings *are* strong. Avoid fight or flight, focus on the problem, and look for compromises. Careful listening and understanding may be necessary until the other person calms down.

It may seem difficult to handle problems of this sort alone. During a time of decision, you may want to join a counseling support group or get some individual help. Sorting out feelings and learning to share them in a caring way is important for personal growth. It may take skill and effort and risk and courage, as you travel through tears and fears, but the results over time will be well worthwhile.

Changing Lifestyles

Changes are in the air everywhere as people try new styles of living and then evaluate and adjust. Women are more willing to accept power and responsibility in the workplace. Men are learning to provide nurturance for children. In *The Second Stage*, Betty Friedan admits that one failure of the women's movement was a blind spot about the family. She urges a revitalization and sharing of the traditional role of nurturer.[19]

Many writers, like Marilyn Ferguson, applaud the emergence of this "feminine principle" in society. Men are beginning to see that operating behind a shield of power is sometimes cowardly. Some men are refusing to relocate, take promotions, or travel if it means more time away from their families. Men need liberation, too. Author Mark Gerzon says that men need new heroes.[20] Some say that changes from dominance to nurturance will make possible our survival as a planet and a race.

Many women have achieved glamorous and rewarding positions, but they are now learning—as men have to learn—how to cope with job burnout. The frustration and weariness of sustaining success has taken its toll on some women, just as it has on some men. But women have often had to work much harder than men and overcome more obstacles on the road to success. Women, too, will have to learn to balance the need for career achievement with enrichment in other areas of life.

Aging people are returning to school not only for enrichment but to learn new skills. It's memorable to see a 72-year-old grandmother receive a degree, cheered on by a group of balloon-waving grandchildren. A 65-year-old who received her M.A. degree in psychonutrition now supports herself by giving seminars and workshops.

Minorities also are moving up, becoming more visible in every area of life. The disabled are wheeling and whizzing out of isolation and assertively speaking up about their needs. Like the elderly, they are beginning to feel a sense of energy and ability to change their lot in life.

Marilyn Ferguson speaks of a conspiracy of people beginning to "take charge of their lives," to make changes that deal with the transformation of the person and could ultimately change society. Some of the changes she predicts could be described as balancing the Timid/Tough Spectrum or becoming a self-actualized person.[21] Jean Houston's exciting brain/mind research asks, "What is the possible human?" and shows us on the verge of a giant step forward toward new forms of consciousness and fulfillment. She affirms that our human systems are vastly superior to anything that technology could invent; we have only begun to plumb the depths of our inner selves. We may be reaching a "golden age of body/mind control that challenges us to a new humanity."[22] It's a time for all of us to make "thought-full" decisions about what we wish to be and what roles we want to play.

Growing as a person means changing, adjusting to both inner and outer reality. It means expansion into new and exciting areas of life. Stereotypes about how we *should* be keep us from becoming what we *could* be.

It seems that in our society we have come to a time of decision about how we want to be. More aware of our fragile environment, our energy shortage, our waste of resources, we know that we can't "have it all." But a further look at our needs, wants, and values might show us that we can have more than enough. It can be a good time for us if we act wisely, giving all of us a chance to develop more balanced lives and to free ourselves from stereotypes. To paraphrase Elizabeth Cady Stanton, "the true person is as yet a dream of the future." Let's hope that future is not too distant.

 ## Self-Assessment Exercises

The following exercises are designed to start you thinking about roles and considering their effects on your life and work.

1. Thinking About Stereotypes

a. What are the various roles you play in life?

_____

_____

_____

b. What is expected of you in each of these roles?

_____

_____

_____

c. Do you live your roles as you choose or as others expect you to? Explain.

_____

_____

_____

We've locked the director in the broom closet—we're busting out of the joint tonight.

2. The Timid/Tough Spectrum

a. Check (√) where you stand on the Timid/Tough Spectrum:

_____ Timid _____ Balanced _____ Tough

b. Discuss how your gender limits or liberates you.

_____

_____

_____

_____

_____

3. Looking at Drawbacks

Do you permit stereotypes to hinder your career choice? ("I can't be a nurse because I'm a man.") Check (√) any items you consider drawbacks on the following list:

_____ Gender   _____ Nationality

_____ Race   _____ Socioeconomic background

_____ Age   _____ Health

4. Identifying Major Components of Your Life

a. Rank the components of your life structure in order of importance to you. Think of how you would list them if you were starting with none of them.

_____ Career   _____ Ethnic/national ties

_____ Marriage   _____ Religion/spiritual development

_____ Family   _____ Leisure

_____ Education   _____ What else?

b. Do the significant people in your life agree with your ranking?

Yes _____ No _____

c. What problems do you see in integrating each of these components into your life? Into the life structure of those around you?

_____

_____

_____

5. Affirming Who You Are

Fill in the blanks:

Because I am _____ , I can _____

_____

_____

_____

_____

6. Planning for the Future

What practical steps can you take to balance your role behavior and liberate yourself from stereotypes?

_____

_____

_____

_____

 ## Group Discussion Questions

1. Talking About Stereotypes

a. Can a woman who is a wife and a mother be liberated? Can a man who is a husband and a father be liberated?

b. Pair with someone of a different age, sex, or ethnic background (or all three). Finish the following statements:

Men/women are

Men/women should

Young/old people are

Young/old people should

Minorities are

Minorities should

2. Deciding Specific Cases

a. The Institute of Occupational Health and Safety states that women hold a disproportionate share of the ten most stressful jobs. Secretary is second on the list of most stressful jobs. Do you agree? Why or why not?

b. In Santa Clara County, California, 75 highly skilled secretaries employed by the state demonstrated because the state paid a car washer $300 more per month than a secretary made. Were the secretaries justified in demonstrating? Do you believe in equal pay for comparable worth?

3. Ordering Priorities

William Brodhead (D-Mich.) resigned from Congress "to spend more time with family" and because of ethical concerns about increasing pressure to take money in exchange for votes.

a. List in order of importance Representative Brodhead's life components as evident from that decision.

b. What values did he have to give up in resigning from Congress?

c. What values did he enhance?

4. Summing It Up

Discuss in class or write your answers on a separate sheet of paper:

a. What have you learned from this chapter?

b. What stereotypes and prejudices would you like to change in yourself and in society?

Three   Personality and Performance:

Pieces of the Puzzle

You are gathering information to match a special person—you and your needs, wants, and values—with satisfying positions in the world of work. When you finally enter the workplace, you may have to make some compromises, but the ideal is to minimize the compromises and maximize the match.

A major decision point is that of interest area. Where do you, with all the unique facets of your personality, feel most comfortable? The human personality can be likened to a stained-glass window—a mosaic of light and color. A stained-glass window is an enduring object of carefully chosen colors, yet it changes with the changing sun. In darkness, it seems to disappear, but in the light it comes alive with color.

> *It takes*
> *its life from light*
> *it sleeps at night*
> *and comes ablaze at dawn*
> *it holds the day*
> *'til shadows fade*
> *its brilliance strangely gone.*

Analogously, the human personality can be seen as a mosaic of six major themes.

Areas of Interest: The Personality Mosaic

Psychologist and vocational counselor John Holland says that one of six major personality types—or perhaps a combination of two or more types—plays a highly important role in an individual's career choice.

Most of us probably cannot deal with many areas of interest. We become preoccupied with a certain one early in life. It becomes our focal point, largely because of choices that stem from our needs, wants, and values.[1]

You can observe others as they focus on certain interests. When friends or relatives arrive for the weekend, they generally scatter in the directions of their wants and values: The refrigerator, the stereo, the football game on TV, the garden, the new drapes, the video game, the grandparents, the children, the new car, a good discussion, a crossword puzzle—each will be a magnet for someone's attention. Since each person notices and experiences things differently, you are unique in the combination of things that interest you. Generally, the interests that predominate and point to a particular personality mosaic are among the most important keys to career satisfaction.

Being aware of your "lesser lights" can also shed some illumination and enrichment. Personal growth leads to the discovery of new dimensions in ourselves. We are all born with innumerable possibilities. Some talents remain undeveloped for half a lifetime; then new lights surface in time to bring joy to our middle and senior years.

Perhaps, too, we can see as an ideal the "universal person" of the Renaissance: able to be all things with apparently equal ease, at home in all settings and with all people, truly self-actualized.

In this chapter, you can identify the predominant orientation of your personality in an inventory called the Personality Mosaic. It's important to take this inventory before reading the interpretation that follows. Then you can analyze the kinds of activities you've been enjoying all your life. Having reminded yourself of your interests, you will be ready to tie this data into the job market in Chapter 4.

Personality Mosaic

Circle the numbers of statements that clearly sound like something you might say or do or think—something that feels like *you*. Check (√) the numbers of items that you aren't sure of to see how they change your score. Put the letter *X* on the numbers of statements that are *not you* to get a negative total.

1. It's important for me to have a strong, agile body.
2. I need to understand things thoroughly.
3. Music, color, beauty of any kind can really affect my moods.
4. People enrich my life and give it meaning.
5. I have confidence in myself that I can make things happen.
6. I need clear directions so I know exactly what to do.
7. I can usually carry/build/fix things myself.
8. I can get absorbed for hours in thinking something out.
9. I appreciate beautiful surroundings; color and design mean a lot to me.

10. I'll spend time finding ways to help people through personal crises.
11. I enjoy competing.
12. I'll spend time getting carefully organized before I start a project.
13. I enjoy making things with my hands.
14. It's satisfying to explore new ideas.
15. I always seem to be looking for new ways to express my creativity.
16. I value being able to share personal concerns with people.
17. Being a key person in a group is very satisfying to me.
18. I take pride in being very careful about all the details of my work.
19. I don't mind getting my hands dirty.
20. I see education as a lifelong process of developing and sharpening my mind.
21. I love to dress in unusual ways, to try new colors and styles.
22. I can often sense when a person needs to talk to someone.
23. I enjoy getting people organized and on the move.
24. I'd rather be safe than adventurous in making decisions.
25. I like to buy sensible things I can make or work on myself.
26. Sometimes I can sit for long periods of time and work on puzzles or read or just think about life.
27. I have a great imagination.
28. I like to help people develop their talents and abilities.
29. I like to have people rely on me to get the job done.
30. I usually prepare carefully ahead of time if I have to handle a new situation
31. I'd rather be on my own doing practical, hands-on activities.
32. I'm eager to read about any subject that arouses my curiosity.
33. I love to try creative new ideas.
34. If I have a problem with someone, I'll keep trying to resolve it peacefully.
35. To be successful, it's important to aim high.
36. I don't like to have responsibility for big decisions.
37. I say what's on my mind and don't beat around the bush.
38. I need to analyze a problem pretty thoroughly before I act on it.
39. I like to rearrange my surroundings to make them unique and different.
40. I often solve my personal problems by talking them out with someone.
41. I get projects started and let others take care of details.
42. Being on time is very important to me.
43. It's invigorating to do things outdoors.
44. I keep asking "why?"
45. I like my work to be an expression of my moods and feelings.
46. I like to help people find ways to care more for each other.

47. It's exciting to take part in important decisions.
48. I usually have things around me in order.
49. I like my surroundings to be plain and practical.
50. I need to stay with a problem until I figure out an answer.
51. The beauty of nature touches something deep inside me.
52. Close personal relationships are important to me.
53. Promotion and advancement are important to me.
54. I feel more secure when my day is well planned.
55. A strong system of law and order is important to prevent chaos.
56. Thought-provoking books always broaden my perspective.
57. I look forward to seeing art shows, plays, and good films.
58. I can deal with and understand people who express strong feelings.
59. It's exciting to influence people.
60. When I say I'll do it, I follow through on every detail.
61. Good, hard physical work never hurt anyone.
62. I'd like to learn all there is to know about subjects that interest me.
63. I don't want to be like everyone else; I like to do things differently.
64. When people have a problem, I go out of my way to be flexible and caring.
65. I'm willing to take some risks to get ahead.
66. I feel more secure when I follow rules.
67. The first thing I look for in a car is a well-built engine.
68. I like a conversation to be intellectually stimulating.
69. When I'm creating, I tend to let everything else go.
70. I feel concerned that so many people in our society need help.
71. It's fun to get ideas across to people.
72. I'm very good about checking details.
73. I usually know how to take care of things in an emergency.
74. Just reading about those new discoveries is exciting.
75. I like to create happenings.
76. I often go out of my way to pay attention to people who seem lonely and friendless.
77. I love to bargain.
78. I like to be very careful about spending money.
79. Sports are important in building strong bodies.
80. I've always been curious about the way nature works.
81. It's fun to be in a mood to try or do something unusual.
82. I am a good listener when people talk about personal problems.

83. If I don't make it the first time, I usually bounce back with energy and enthusiasm.
84. I need to know exactly what people expect of me.
85. I like to take things apart to see if I can fix them.
86. Don't get excited. We can think it out and plan the right move logically.
87. It would be hard to imagine my life without beauty around me.
88. People often seem to tell me their problems.
89. I can usually connect with people who get me in touch with a network of resources.
90. It's very satisfying to do a task carefully and completely.

Scoring Your Answers

To score, circle the numbers that you circled on the Personality Mosaic.

R	I	A	S	E	C
1	2	3	4	5	6
7	8	9	10	11	12
13	14	15	16	17	18
19	20	21	22	23	24
25	26	27	28	29	30
31	32	33	34	35	36
37	38	39	40	41	42
43	44	45	46	47	48
49	50	51	52	53	54
55	56	57	58	59	60
61	62	63	64	65	66
67	68	69	70	71	72
73	74	75	76	77	78
79	80	81	82	83	84
85	86	87	88	89	90

Count the number of circles in each column and write the totals in the spaces below:

R _____ I _____ A _____ S _____ E _____ C _____

List the letters R, I, A, S, E, and C, according to your scores, from highest to lowest:

1st _____   4th _____

2nd _____   5th _____

3rd _____   6th _____

Does adding in the items you're unsure of (✓) change the order? _____

How? _____

In which areas do you have the most negatives (X)? _____

Do you have a tie score in two or more columns? If so, the remainder of this chapter will help you to decide which column represents the "real you."

To get more in touch with yourself, read aloud some of the statements for each orientation from the Personality Mosaic. Be that kind of person. Embellish and dramatize the statements to see how that kind of behavior feels. You may want to role-play this activity in a group.

Interpreting the Personality Mosaic

The inventory you have just taken is based on the six personality orientations identified by John Holland. As you can see from your score, you are not just one personality type—that is, you are not a person with fifteen circles in one area and no circles in any of the others. In most people, one or two characteristics are dominant, two or three are of medium intensity, and one or two may be of low intensity. A few people score high in each category because they have many interests. Others, who don't have many strong interests, score rather low in all areas.

Here is an overview of the six personality types, followed by a discussion of each orientation and its relationship to the others. Try to find yourself in the following descriptions:

- *Realistic Personality*

    Hands-on people who enjoy exploring things, fixing things, making things with their hands

    Express themselves and achieve primarily through their bodies rather than through words, thoughts, feelings

    Usually independent, practical-minded, strong, well coordinated, aggressive, conservative

    Like the challenge of physical risk, being outdoors, using tools and machinery

    Prefer concrete rather than abstract problems

    Solve problems by doing something physical

- *Investigative Personality*

    Persons who "live" very much in their minds

    Unconventional and independent thinkers, intellectually curious, very insightful, logical, and persistent

Express themselves and achieve primarily through their minds rather than through association with people or involvement with things

Like to explore ideas through reading, discussing

Enjoy complex and abstract mental challenges

Solve problems by thinking and analyzing

- ### Artistic Personality

  Persons who are creative, sensitive, aesthetic, introspective, intuitive, visionary

  See new possibilities and want to express them in creative ways

  Particularly attuned to perception of color, form, sound, feeling

  Prefer to work alone and independently rather than with others

  Enjoy beauty, variety, the unusual in sight, sound, word, texture, people

  Need fairly unstructured environment to provide opportunities for creative expression

  Solve problems by creating something new

- ### Social Personality

  People persons who "live" primarily in their feelings

  Sensitive to others, genuine, humanistic, supportive, responsible, tactful, perceptive

  Focus on people and their concerns rather than on things or deep intellectual activity

  Enjoy closeness with others, sharing feelings, being in groups, unstructured settings that allow for flexibility and humaneness

  Solve problems primarily by feeling and intuition, by helping

- ### Enterprising Personality

  Project persons who are thoroughly absorbed in their involvements

  Energetic, enthusiastic, confident, dominant, political, verbal, assertive, quick decision-makers

  Leaders who are talented at organizing, persuading, managing

  Achieve primarily by using these skills in dealing with people and projects

  Enjoy money, power, and status, being in charge

  Solve problems by risking

- ### Conventional Personality

  Persons who "live" primarily in their orderliness

  Quiet, careful, accurate, responsible, practical, persevering, well-organized, and task-oriented

  Have strong need to feel secure and certain, to get things finished, to attend to every detail

Prefer to identify with someone of power and status rather than be in such a position themselves

Solve problems by appealing to and following rules

FOR THE MOST PART
I do the thing which my
own nature drives
me to do.

—ALBERT EINSTEIN

Realistic Personality

Realistic individuals are capable and confident when using their bodies to relate to the physical world. They focus on *things*, learn through their hands, and have little need for conversation. Because of their facility with physical objects, they are often good in emergencies. Their ability to deal with the physical world often makes them very independent. Since these characteristics describe the stereotypical male, many women shrink from displaying any capability in this area, and often women are discouraged from doing so. Realistic people sometimes get so absorbed in putting *things* right that they can forget about everything else.

Investigative Personality

The investigative type deals with the "real world" of things, but at a distance. These individuals prefer to read, study, and use books, charts, and other data instead of getting their hands into *things*. When involved with people, they tend to focus on ideas. Wherever they are, they will collect information and analyze the situation before making a decision. If they enjoy the outdoors, it's because they are curious, not because they enjoy rugged, heavy, physical work. Their curiosity sometimes leads them to explore their ideas to the exclusion of all else.

Artistic Personality

The artistic type is creative, but not necessarily with paint and canvas. These individuals express creativity not only with material objects, but with data and systems as well. The weaver designs and makes fabric; the poet creates with words; the choreographer arranges dancers in flowing patterns. The industrialist creates new systems for the flow of goods; the program planner creates better delivery of services in a variety of settings. Creative people see possibilities beyond the usual.

They would rather create ideas than study them. They like variety and are not afraid to experiment, often disregarding rules. Their ideas don't always please others, but opposition doesn't discourage them for long.

Artistic types focus on whatever strikes their creative fancies. Sensitivity to sight, sound, and touch will draw some of them to the fine arts, such as drama, music, and literature. Others will be content just to enjoy aesthetic experiences, while still others will create new ways of doing things—new systems. If they like the outdoors, it is from an aesthetic standpoint. They love its beauty and its power to inspire their creativity—but not its ability to make them perspire with heavy work. Their irrepressible spirits and enthusiasm can often keep them focused on a creative project to the exclusion of all else. Not producing up to standard (their own) can plunge them to the depths.

Social Personality

The social personality focuses on people and their concerns. Sensitive to people's moods and feelings, these individuals enjoy company and make friends easily. Their level of caring may range from one person to the entire human race. Their relationships with people depend on their ability to communicate both verbally and nonverbally, listening as well as speaking. Their empathy and ability to intuit emotional cues help them to solve people problems before others are even aware of them. They can pull people together and generate positive energy for a good cause. Since the social orientation seems to describe the "typical female," many men shrink from expressing or dealing with deep feelings. The social personality types sometimes focus on people concerns to the exclusion of all else. They sometimes appear "impractical," especially to the realistic types.

Enterprising Personality

The enterprising person is a leader who initiates projects but often gets others to carry them out. Instead of doing research, they rely on intuition about what will work. They may strike an observer as restless and irresponsible since they often drop these projects after the job is underway. But many activities would never get off the ground without their energizing influence. They have a need to be part of the "in crowd." But since their relationships center around tasks, they may focus so dynamically on the project that people's concerns go unnoticed.

Conventional Personality

The conventional person also is task oriented, but prefers to carry out tasks initiated by others. Since they are careful of detail, these individuals keep the world's records and transmit its messages. They obey rules and they value order in the data world. Their sense of responsibility keeps the world going as they focus on the task at hand to the exclusion of all else.

Figure 3-1 Personality Types: Similarities and Differences

Source: Adapted from John Holland, *Making Vocational Choices: A Theory of Careers* (Engle-wood Cliffs, N.J.: Prentice-Hall, 1973), copyright © 1970, by special permission of John Holland and Prentice-Hall, Inc. See also John Holland, *Self-Directed Search* (Palo Alto:, Calif.: Consulting Psychologists Press), copyright © 1970.

The Personality Hexagon

The six personality orientations can be arranged in a hexagon. In Figure 3-1, the types next to one another are most similar. The words linking them indicate their shared traits or interests. For example, realistic and investigative people focus on things. The *R* person does something to the thing; the *I* person analyzes it. Investigative and artistic types are both idea people. The *I* explores ideas logically; the *A* invents them intuitively. Artistic and social people need to be in tune with their feelings. Social and enterprising people are people leaders; the *S* being concerned about people, the *E* wishing to get a task underway. The conventional person will carry out the details of the task to the last period. Both *C* and *R* types value order: The *C* values data/paper order; the *R* values physical order.

People find that they are most comfortable with others of similar personality. They seek out work activities that enable them to be with these types of people. Workplaces, too, tend to gather like types, and reflect the style of these workers.

The types opposite each other on the hexagon are most dissimilar. For example, the artistic personality is independent, doesn't mind disorder, and likes to try new things. The conventional person depends more on other people, likes order, and would prefer things to stay the same.

Two people who are strongly opposite in personality can improve their relationship by understanding the differences between them. A realistic person doesn't deal much with people's feelings, while a social person sees much of life through

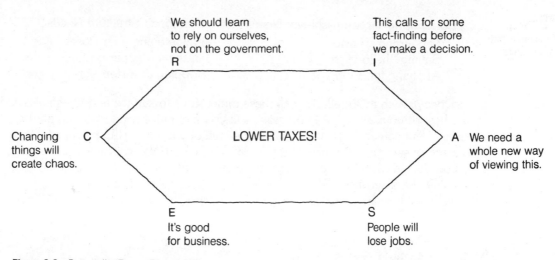

Figure 3-2 Personality Types: Typical Talk

feelings. That's just the way they are. The introspective *I* person is amazed at the outgoing *E* person's ability to act without doing much research. Since opposites complement each other, it can be advantageous to see a conflicting personality as a source of support. Wise employers will hire those whose personality orientation is needed for the work to be done.

Imagine six people sitting around the hexagon. Each person is a strong representative of a personality type. Give the group an issue to discuss (such as lower taxes, in Figure 3-2), and each person will look at it in a different way.

Sometimes we have personality conflicts within us. We'd like to be creative, to try something different, but our conventional nature tells us that's a "no-no." We'd like to take an enterprising risk, but our investigative side wants to gather all the facts before deciding. (Decisions are difficult for the *I* person who has little *E*.) Even folks who like to be alone dealing with physical objects (*R*) need some people interaction, too.

Understanding your personality can facilitate a good career decision. Understanding the personality of others can improve human relationships and ease acceptance of the choices others make. Every day we all act in these six modes to some extent:

Realistic: Physical Needs
> Running on the beach
> Eating meals
> Fixing the sink

Investigative: Mind Needs
> Discussing politics
> Reading *War and Peace*
> Planning a trip to Europe

Artistic: Aesthetic Needs
> Enjoying a sunset
> Wearing complementary colors
> Decorating a cake

Social: People Needs
> Laughing with a friend
> Hugging the baby
> Going to a party

77

Enterprising: Accomplishment Needs	Conventional: Structure Needs
Organizing a party	Straightening your closet
Saying "hello" first	Finishing a paper on time
Applying for a job	Stopping at a stop sign

Does growth mean allowing all these dimensions to surface and to actualize to the best of your ability? As you grow, will you feel more comfortable in all these areas? Your career decision may fall in the area of your dominant personality type, a blend of several, or in an area that is difficult for you. You will need extra energy if you veer away from your dominant orientations. Discuss your dominant personality characteristics and tell someone why they feel right to you.

Now we'll begin to analyze the interests and activities you've been involved with all your life.

Activity Analysis

In Exercise 6, "Candid Camera—3-D," in Chapter 1, you listed just about every activity you could think of that you've done in your life: jobs, community and extracurricular activities, education, and other projects. Then you listed all the things you had to do to accomplish each activity. This analysis produced your expanded activity list—data that will help you choose satisfying life activities.

If your lists are now as long as you can make them, code all the activities like this:

P = Interacting directly with people

T = Interacting directly with things

D = Using ideas and information without interacting with people or things

Then star (*) every activity you've enjoyed and wouldn't mind repeating. These favorite activities reflect your interests and values and will influence your future decisions

Skills

When you've *done* any activity, that means you *can* do it! You've shown you have the ability and that ability is a *skill!* Many people think they have no skills because they can't play the oboe or type 100 words per minute. But in reality they have been accomplishing things successfully for many years and have the capacity to accomplish much more. One huge factor is confidence. If you *think* you can, then you can. At least you can probably do something closely related to your dream job.

A teacher completed an interest inventory that suggested a career in the performing arts. Acting seemed intriguing but not likely to provide much income for

Courtesy of Mal Hancock

a beginner. It suddenly dawned on the teacher how much she loved "appearing" in a class or workshop, making people laugh and appreciate her. She loved to perform well for her students! She remembered that when she first became a teacher, she had had little confidence and either over- or underdisciplined her classes as a result. Confidence grew with the realization that she could teach and have fun doing it. Now she rarely misses a chance to talk with a group.

It's helpful to realize that only eight basic activities enable people to do everything. They are the basis of all our abilities or aptitudes—or, to use the more popular term, skills. Here are the basic eight:

1. *Intelligence:* You concentrate and use your MIND to figure things out.
2. *Verbal proficiency:* You use WORDS to read, talk, and listen to get and give information.
3. *Numerical proficiency:* You use NUMBERS to figure things out.
4. *Form-space awareness:* You VISUALIZE how things will look.
5. *Clerical perception:* You CHECK words and numbers for accuracy
6. *Color sense:* You use COLOR.
7. *Finger-hand agility:* You use your FINGERS/HANDS to do things.
8. *Body coordination:* You coordinate your WHOLE BODY to do things

Your interests are usually a good clue to your skills. Most people acquire skills in areas they enjoy and tend to neglect other areas. If you like something, you spend time doing it . . . get better at it and like it more . . . and spend more time . . . And it's comforting to note that most jobs, by definition, require only average skills.

We come into this world already well equipped for action. Unless there is a serious defect, our growth and potential growth are phenomenal. Look at a 6-month-old and be amazed at the complexity of skills compared to a newborn infant. Compare with a 6-year-old and be further astounded!

But somewhere along the line our confidence and energy may begin to lag. Jean Houston, brain researcher, says that by age 17 we are using only 17 percent of our body's potential for flexible movement compared to our use at age 3. And she says that as the body goes, so does the mind. Houston finds that even the very elderly, with correct exercise, can "remake" their bodies in six months. Their mental and emotional powers are greatly enhanced.[2] "The true person is as yet a dream of the future."

Only as a mental exercise can we divide the human person into mind, body and emotions. Philosophers have struggled through the centuries to understand these everyday terms. Since our educational system stresses mental activities, we sometimes infer that men and women who work with their hands are not "using their heads." In reality the two cannot be separated; they can only be examined separately as two different modes of living and learning.

 Identifying Favorite Activities

From your expanded activity list, write your favorite activities in the "Favorite Activities Chart" on the facing page. Be sure to state what you *did* as specifically as possible. Then check (√) the numbers of the basic eight skills you used to perform each favorite activity. For example, if you ordered supplies by phone, you would check 2, 3, and 5. If you arranged food attractively on a plate, you would check 4, 6, and 7.

The Skills Trio

There are three kinds of skills: transferable, work-specific, and personal responsibility skills.[3] The basic eight activities, or skills, are *transferable skills* because they can be used in many kinds of activities and transferred from one job to another. Speaking or visualizing, for example, can be used in hundreds of jobs. Perhaps 80 to 90 percent of the content of most jobs requires transferable skills—those you already have. The other 10 to 20 percent may require on-the-job training (OJT), further education, or both. A salesperson, for example, depends largely on transferable skills and can learn the needed *work-specific skills* quickly. Some jobs require quite a bit of special training, especially in science, technical fields, and the arts. This special training gives us work-specific skills such as those used by electronics

Favorite Activities Chart

Activity	Mind 1	Words 2	Num- bers 3	Visual- izing 4	Check- ing 5	Color 6	Fingers Hands 7	Whole Body 8

Which of the basic eight activities do you like to use the most? _____

technicians, business managers, doctors, and ballerinas. But all of these people need transferable skills, too. Managers include, for example, teachers and house-wives since both manage complex organizations. Even though they may have limited business experience, they have been using management skills. They have supervised *people;* organized data, people, and things; managed records and budgets; made decisions; and resolved conflicts. As Ray Killian says, "Much of this experience can be transfered . . . to supervisory skills."[4]

If you are enthusiastic, committed, careful, prompt, cheerful, and able to use common sense, you have *personal responsibility skills.* Such skills sometimes develop at an early age, often independent of education. They reflect how well you manage *yourself* in regard to data, people, and things. Do you manage yourself responsibly, creatively, and with initiative? Do you use common sense? Common sense, energy, dedication, responsibility, intuition, creativity—all are traits that can be learned, that develop with the help of both achievement and disappointment, no one knows how! You have survived modern life so far. Your physical, mental, emotional, social, and financial well-being have depended upon your abilities. You *must* possess a good measure of skills in all areas.

Dealing with Data, People, and Things

Skills give our minds and bodies the power to act on the world around us, to use the basic eight skills in a multitude of combinations. And that world has only three areas that we can relate to: ideas and information (that "mind stuff" called data), people, and things.

Data: A human mind can take in and give out great quantities of information, or data, in the form of words, numbers, and symbols. All day long the mind clicks away expressing complex thoughts and ideas, often creatively, and always in a way unique to the individual. When you notice you are out of milk and jot it down on the grocery list, you've just processed some data. Reading, writing, speaking, and listening all deal with data (ideas and information). Every activity deals with data from simple to complex. The cry of the newborn gives us data about how the baby feels. Some people think of data as complex numbers and computer printouts. But data includes all kinds of ideas and information: the words you speak, read, listen to; the music you enjoy; the smiles of your friends; the colors of the sunset. Anything that is not a person or a concrete object is called data.

People: Another kind of activity depends upon interaction with people, ranging from saying hello to helping someone solve a personal problem, from simple to serious. We use a great deal of data to deal with other humans. We involve all sorts of body/mind perceptions and linguistic skills. The emotions, which are physical responses to sensory information, permeate our mental processes and influence our behavior and relationships with others.

Who would think that the ability to use love and affection would make a manager more effective? Harold Leavitt, professor of organization behavior at the Stanford University Graduate School of Business, says, "Worker expectations and job values are changing, and being in management is going to require a lot more love and

You've got people skills. You fire him.

THE NOW SOCIETY by William Hamilton

© Chronicle Publishing Co., 1975

affection—more emphasis on vicarious and helpful behavior . . . less on control and competition. . . . Managing software programs is less disciplined, more artsy than managing hardware programs . . . harder to control except by building goodwill."[5] So the balanced manager can draw on many types of skills and behaviors along the Timid/Tough Spectrum.

Things: We relate to physical objects in any number of ways: building, repairing, carrying, making, running machines, tinkering with gadgets from food processors to power saws. The human body uses data from the physical world, and its skills depend on its degree of strength, agility, and coordination in relating to other physical objects. The way the body fixes and builds things often requires creative ability.

You learned to deal with data, people, and things at all levels early in life. Look again at your "Candid Camera" lists (p. 32). How many times have you planned events, organized people, or repaired objects in your lifetime? Your skills with data, people, and things work together in a blend of mental and physical abilities, emotionally expressed in creating music, art, literature, and in scientific and technical works. But stop and think: Every day, using your mind, body, and emotions, *you* create your life.

Instead of groaning at your "lack of talent," think of all the talents you've used effectively in dealing with a life filled with data, people, and things. And since the majority of workers have only average skills, most people can do most jobs. And that includes you! The question is, then, of all the skills you possess, which do you enjoy using? And more important, which would you like to use in a work setting? Do you prefer to work primarily with data, people, or things? And of all the jobs you *can* do, which would you *like* to do?

Observe yourself. What skills are you motivated to acquire and develop to get where you would like to be? In what ways would you like to focus your transferable skills to work-specific skills? If you have good finger dexterity, for example, would you prefer to become adept at the guitar, the typewriter, brain surgery, or all three? Are you willing to devote some time to further training and education to acquire work-specific skills? Which personal responsibility skills are your strengths? Which will you work to improve? These are important decision points.

**If you think you can't
You won't!
If you think you can,
You will!**

In this chapter, then, you've discovered your very own Personality Mosaic. You have identified skills that have motivated you to act successfully in the past and will carry you into the future. And you are putting together some extremely valuable pieces of the career decision puzzle. In short, you have been gathering important words to describe the one and only YOU!

Self-Assessment Exercises

1. Six Personality Types

Circle the personality types that describe you best: realistic, investigative, artistic, social, enterprising, conventional.

2. Basic Eight Skills

Circle the basic skills that you prefer to use: mind, words, numbers, visualizing, checking, color, fingers/hands, whole body.

Go away! I'm peopled out.

GUINDON

3. Proud Accomplishment Articulator

From your activity list, pick out an important accomplishment that you especially enjoyed and wouldn't mind repeating. Then on the following tables, check the action verbs and adjectives that describe what you did. If possible, tell one person or a small group what actions the activity required. For another perspective, ask which action verbs and adjectives the group thinks apply to you.

Action Verb Checklist

Check off the action verbs that apply to you. Double-check the actions you enjoy and wouldn't mind repeating.

In the past when using DATA I have:	Interacting with PEOPLE I have:	Dealing with THINGS I have:
_____ Administered	_____ Assigned	_____ Adjusted
_____ Analyzed	_____ Assisted	_____ Altered
_____ Budgeted	_____ Cared for	_____ Arranged

continued

Action Verb Checklist continued

Check off the action verbs that apply to you. Double-check the actions you enjoy and wouldn't mind repeating.

In the past when using DATA I have:	Interacting with PEOPLE I have:	Dealing with THINGS I have:
_____ Compared	_____ Communicated	_____ Assembled
_____ Computed	_____ Coordinated	_____ Balanced
_____ Compiled	_____ Consulted	_____ Built
_____ Coordinated	_____ Counseled	_____ Cleaned
_____ Decided	_____ Developed	_____ Cut
_____ Designed	_____ Directed	_____ Decorated
_____ Developed	_____ Encouraged	_____ Driven
_____ Evaluated	_____ Entertained	_____ Fabricated
_____ Illustrated	_____ Evaluated	_____ Fitted
_____ Implemented	_____ Hired	_____ Guarded
_____ Innovated	_____ Instructed	_____ Guided
_____ Interpreted	_____ Interviewed	_____ Handled
_____ Learned	_____ Led	_____ Improved
_____ Marketed	_____ Listened	_____ Inspected
_____ Organized	_____ Managed	_____ Installed
_____ Planned	_____ Motivated	_____ Lifted
_____ Promoted	_____ Negotiated	_____ Made
_____ Publicized	_____ Organized	_____ Measured
_____ Read	_____ Persuaded	_____ Mixed
_____ Recorded	_____ Protected	_____ Moved
_____ Reported	_____ Referred	_____ Operated
_____ Researched	_____ Represented	_____ Processed
_____ Scheduled	_____ Served	_____ Repaired
_____ Synthesized	_____ Shared	_____ Set up
_____ Theorized	_____ Sold	_____ Shaped
_____ Visualized	_____ Supervised	_____ Tended
_____ Written	_____ Trained	_____ Tested

Adjective Checklist

Check off the adjectives that apply to you personally and
describe your method of work.

I am:	My work is:
_____ Articulate	_____ Complete
_____ Conscientious	_____ Effective
_____ Committed	_____ Major
_____ Competent	_____ Positive
_____ Confident	_____ Profitable
_____ Consistent	_____ Proven
_____ Creative	_____ Results-oriented
_____ Decisive	_____ Significant
_____ Dependable	_____ Substantial
_____ Efficient	_____ Successful
_____ Energetic	_____ Sound
_____ Enthusiastic	_____ Thorough
_____ Experienced	_____ Vigorous
_____ Flexible	
_____ Knowledgeable	
_____ Loyal	
_____ Perceptive	
_____ Persistent	
_____ Persuasive	
_____ Positive	
_____ Productive	
_____ Qualified	
_____ Reliable	
_____ Resourceful	
_____ Responsible	
_____ Sensitive	
_____ Self-motivated	
_____ Stable	
_____ Successful	
_____ Thorough	
_____ Verbal	
_____ Well-organized	

4. Abstract Skills Articulator

Sometimes people with an abundance of the more abstract skills, especially mental and verbal, have difficulty recognizing and articulating their abilities. These skills tend to be more diffused, more generalized, not as easy to pin down and identify as the more visible concrete skills. If you are one of these people, use these exercises to increase your appreciation of the wealth of ability in mental and verbal skills. By finding key words to identify and by articulating them, you will build a background for an impressive résumé and an effective job interview. Circle the aspects of mental and verbal skills that describe yourself.

a. Logical Mental Skills

Logical, rational thinking exercised primarily to investigate, plan, and organize (called "left brain" activity by some researchers)

Investigate: Research, compile, analyze, synthesize, understand data

Plan: Establish goals and objectives; develop programs, products, systems; set policies and procedures; forecast; schedule, evaluate, revise programs

Organize: Set up systems to coordinate data, people, things, or all three, to produce events, programs, materials

b. Intuitive Mental Skills

Creative, intuitive thinking exercised primarily to imagine, design, innovate, perceive, intuit (called "right brain" activity by some researchers)

Imagine, design, innovate: See new possibilities, new combinations, new applications

Perceive, intuit: Sense qualities not easily measured, see things not immediately evident, apprehend holistically rather than analytically

c. Verbal Skills

Use of words to read, speak, write, listen, teach, sell, supervise

Read: Research, study, decipher, scan

Speak: Deliver speeches, lead/facilitate/chair small groups, resolve conflicts, counsel, question, advise, interview, summarize, perform

Write: Reports, technical manuals, curricula, instructions, handbooks, news, speeches, publicity, orders

Listen: Perceive clearly, attune oneself deeply, attend fully to words and feelings

Teach: Train, instruct, explain, encourage, motivate

Sell: Bargain, convince, persuade, influence, negotiate, motivate, promote

Supervise: Explain, direct, assign, motivate, delegate, evaluate, convey, discuss, hire, terminate

5. Personal Skills Checklist

Evaluate yourself and your ability to handle data, people, and things. Check (√) "Good" or "Could improve" after each statement.

	Good	Could improve
a. Evaluate YOURSELF.		
I usually:		
Dress appropriately for work	_____	_____
Manage needs and wants without interfering with the rights of others	_____	_____
Control and channel impulses and feelings in an effective way	_____	_____
Display common sense, enthusiasm, a sense of humor	_____	_____
b. How well do you interact with PEOPLE?		
I usually:		
Respond with tact and courtesy	_____	_____
Accept criticism without anger and learn from others	_____	_____
Respect and compliment the ideas and good work of others	_____	_____
Share with and assist others; enjoy teamwork; admit mistakes; know when to apologize; communicate assertively without attacking or blaming others	_____	_____

	Good	Could improve
c. How well do you deal with DATA/THINGS?		
I usually:		
Work independently without many questions or much outside help	_____	_____
Am flexible and willing to try new and unfamiliar things	_____	_____
Carry through on difficult or pressured work on time, without excuses	_____	_____
Take good care of property, equipment	_____	_____
Follow rules and help make them more effective, more reasonable	_____	_____

6. Work-Specific Skills

List your work-specific skills—those acquired by education or training to do a particular job:

_____   _____

_____   _____

_____   _____

_____   _____

_____   _____

7. Sharing Your Discoveries

In the space that follows, write an enthusiastic paragraph or letter about yourself and your abilities to a friend. Use as many of the skill words from this chapter as possible to describe yourself and show that you would be an effective worker.

Four

The Career Connection:

Finding Your Job Satisfiers

When you have surveyed your life activities and discovered your personality types, you are ready to rate yourself on three inventories that connect directly to all the jobs in the United States. About 20,000 different occupations have been identified and defined by the U.S. Department of Labor. The results of this investigation are contained in a monumental work called the *Dictionary of Occupational Titles (DOT)*.[1] The book is a gold mine of information—if you know how to dig for the gold. Because of alternate titles for the same job, the 20,000 occupations result in about 40,000 listings. Job titles are listed both alphabetically and by industry. The alphabetical listing gives the code number needed to find a short description of each job among descriptions grouped by occupational area. These clusters of similar jobs make the search easier.

The *DOT* supplement, *Guide for Occupational Exploration*,[2] provides additional help by classifying jobs into 66 groups. A job group is a cluster of occupations that call for similar worker characteristics. In this chapter you will rate yourself on some of these characteristics and your enjoyment in expressing them. Then you will be able to identify jobs that have these enjoyable characteristics and thus will prove satisfying for you. Sixty-six job groups with 20,000 jobs! There must be a job for you!

The first inventory is the Data, People, Things Indicator, in which you will decide at what level(s) you would like to be involved with data, people, and things on your job.

In the second inventory, you will look at ten qualities associated with work and decide which you must have on the job: repetition, precision, intuition, production, variety, business contact, influence, personal contact, prestige, and adventure. These are all qualities that any life activity might offer. For example, if you worked many similar addition problems in second grade, that activity involved repetition and precision. If you were ever in debate, discussion, or argument, you definitely tried to influence others. We do that at a very early age.

In the third inventory, you will rate yourself on the degree to which you wish to use the basic eight skills on your job.

Try to respond through feelings as well as thoughts. The results of these inventories depend on self-awareness. They are designed not so much to tell you about yourself, but to encourage you to think about the qualities you possess. Use pencil for all inventories so that you can go back and revise. Then record all your inventory results on the tally sheet that follows (p. 99).

Don't imagine that you will be ready for the ultimate career decision when these inventories are completed. Look at them instead as the first round of a serious investigation. The results will then need to be sharpened, refined, and pinpointed. This sort of information about self isn't absorbed instantly. Like good brew, it needs time to percolate. After you have taken the inventories, and recorded the results on the tally sheet, you will be ready to look at the whole job market.

Data, People, or Things?

In Chapter 3 you identified activities in which you have dealt with data, people, and things. You've learned that there are various levels of responsibility and complexity with each. Here you will indicate the degree of involvement you prefer with data, people, things, or all three. We will soon look at all the jobs that will give you satisfiers in these areas.

Data, People, Things Indicator

Working with Data

How deeply do you want to get involved with and use data on the job?

Decide which description fits you best; then check (√) the appropriate box.

I prefer doing work that is uncomplicated and easy to learn. I don't mind using information in a simple way if it doesn't require too much mental energy.	Low data

I like keeping track of and working with verbal or numerical information in an orderly way. I prefer having others take responsibility for directing this kind of work.	Medium data

> I would enjoy putting ideas and information together to understand operations, plan and organize work, and develop new ideas and new ways to do things.

High data

Involvement with People

To what extent do you want to be involved with people as a part of your work?

Decide which description fits you best; then check (√) the appropriate box.

> I prefer involvement with information or things, but minimal interaction with people.
>
> Being friendly and cooperative with people, giving them information, serving them in some way, is enough people involvement for me.

Low people

> I think I would like discussing procedures and business problems; organizing and motivating people to do a task.
>
> I enjoy entertaining people or being a key person in a group.

Medium people

> I believe I'd enjoy teaching people, exchanging ideas, negotiating, promoting others' personal growth and development.
>
> I would enjoy helping people deal with complicated personal problems.

High people

Handling Things

To what extent would you like to work with things as part of your job?

Decide which description fits you best; then check (√) the appropriate box.

> I prefer little involvement with things on my job.
>
> If I had to work with things, I'd prefer uncomplicated, easy-to-learn procedures.

Low things

> I would do a good job running equipment carefully and correctly but . . .
>
> I'd prefer not to have too much responsibility for directing this kind of work.

Medium things

> I would enjoy using my hands to work with intricate tools and machines.
>
> I'd like to be responsible for a complex piece of equipment.

☐ High things

Now you know a little about *you* and the big three—data, people, and things. Indicate your rating of *H, M,* or *L* (high, medium, or low) for each category in the spaces provided below.

Data _____

People _____

Things _____

Work Qualities and Characteristics

The work we do can have a number of different qualities or characteristics. It can be repetitive or varied; it can require precision or intuition. We can produce *things* or talk with people to negotiate a deal; we can persuade people to change or help them to grow. Some work is prestigious; some is physically dangerous. Our work may have only one or two of these qualities and thus be very simple, or it may have many and be more complex. Some jobs with a variety of duties may involve many characteristics that change from day to day. The Work Qualities Inventory is a list of ten basic qualities of work. If you can identify those that are important to you, you will be better able to zero in on satisfying job groups.

Work Qualities Inventory

Here are ten descriptions of various qualities of work. Examine each statement and decide whether you would like your work to have that quality. Circle the number if you feel your work *must have* that quality. Put an *X* on the number if you wish to avoid that quality. (If you have never held a job and find it hard to imagine what various jobs are like, think of these statements as descriptions of work you've done in school.)

1. Work in which you follow a set way of doing things—sometimes over and over again. (Repetition)
2. Work in which you have to be very exact, accurate, and/or make decisions based on set rules or measurements. (Precision)
3. Work in which you have to make decisions based on your best guesses, intuition, or common sense without rules or measurements to go by. (Intuition)
4. Work in which you make, repair, test, process, or otherwise deal with things by using tools, machines, and/or special techniques. (Production)
5. Work in which your duties change often and require you to use different knowledge and skills as they change. (Variety)

6. Work in which you have business contact with people in order to manage, supervise, negotiate with, teach, or serve them in some way. (Business contact)

7. Work in which you try to persuade/influence people to think or behave in a certain way by interpreting/communicating ideas, facts, or feelings—sometimes very creatively. (Influencing)

8. Work in which you need to get involved in people's personal problems. (Personal contact)

9. Work in which you are recognized as someone important or prestigious or in authority. (Prestige)

10. Work in which you are often under pressure in physically risky, stressful, situations, which sometimes provide adventure and excitement. (Adventure)

Finding Your Skill Satisfiers

In Chapter 3 you learned that there are only eight basic skills. You identified which of those you have used in the past. Now is the time to choose which of those eight basic skills you enjoy using the most—and at what level. These preferences are sometimes called satisfiers because they indicate the kinds of activity that will give you satisfaction. We will soon look at jobs that involve use of these skills at the levels you would like.

Basic Eight Checklist

Check *H* (high), *M* (medium), or *L* (low) for each skill according to the following scale.

H = I would enjoy using this skill with a high level of ability as a major part of my job.

M = I would not mind using this skill with a moderate level of ability as an important part of my job.

L = I would prefer to use this skill only at an easy level or not much at all on my job.

Basic Skills	Check (√): H = Enjoy using M = Don't mind L = Prefer not
	Intelligence
1. I would like to concentrate and use my MIND on my job because I enjoy thinking, investigating, analyzing, planning, organizing, understanding, evaluating.	_____ H _____ M _____ L

2. I would like to use WORDS on my job because I enjoy reading, writing, speaking, listening, recording, discussing, directing, instructing, motivating.

Verbal proficiency

_____ H

_____ M

_____ L

3. I would like to use NUMBERS on my job because I enjoy measuring, computing, bookkeeping, budgeting, analyzing.

Numerical proficiency

_____ H

_____ M

_____ L

4. I would like to use my "mind's eye" for VISUALIZATION, because I enjoy visualizing lines on a flat surface or in three dimensions, comparing lines, figures, spaces, shadings. I can tell ahead of time how things will look.

Form/space awareness

_____ H

_____ M

_____ L

5. I would like to use my eyes to CHECK words and numbers because I enjoy detail, proofreading, catching errors, seeing slight differences, checking exactness and accuracy.

Clerical perception

_____ H

_____ M

_____ L

6. I would like to fill my eyes with COLOR because I enjoy choosing colors, remembering colors, using colors, blending colors, matching colors.

Color sense

_____ H

_____ M

_____ L

7. I would like using my FINGERS AND HANDS in my job because I enjoy making, moving, assembling, repairing, operating.

Finger/hand agility

_____ H

_____ M

_____ L

8. I would like to use my WHOLE BODY in my job because I enjoy carrying, lifting, moving, balancing, coordinating.

Body coordination

_____ H

_____ M

_____ L

Tallying Your Satisfiers

The Personality Mosaic, the Data, People, Things Indicator, the Work Qualities Inventory, and the Basic Eight Checklist all point to your own personal preferences, or *satisfiers*. They indicate the kinds of activity that will give you the most satisfaction on the job. Use the following tally sheet to record your satisfiers from these inventories.

Tally Sheet

1. *Personality Mosaic:* List your personality components from the Personality Mosaic on page 71, in order and with scores.

   1st ____ ____   2nd ____ ____   3rd ____ ____

   4th ____ ____   5th ____ ____   6th ____ ____

2. *Data, People, Things Indicator:* Indicate your "big three" ratings from the Data, People, Things Indicator on page 96.

Data	People	Things
H	H	H
M	M	M
L	L	L

3. *Work Qualities Inventory:* Circle the numbers of your "must have" work qualities from the Work Qualities Inventory on pages 96–97. Put an X on the numbers of the qualities you prefer to avoid.

1. Repetition	6. Business contact
2. Precision	7. Influencing
3. Intuition	8. Personal contact
4. Production	9. Prestige
5. Variety	10. Adventure

4. *Basic Eight Checklist:* Circle *H, M,* or *L* for the eight skills from the Basic Eight Checklist on pages 97–98.

1. Mental energy/Intelligence	H	M	L
2. Verbal proficiency	H	M	L
3. Numerical proficiency	H	M	L
4. Space and form awareness	H	M	L
5. Clerical perception	H	M	L
6. Color sense	H	M	L
7. Finger/hand agility	H	M	L
8. Body coordination	H	M	L

The Job Group Chart

Now comes the moment you've been waiting for—time to identify all the groups of jobs that have your satisfiers. Your future career will turn up *somewhere* on the Job Group Chart[3] in this chapter. The chart is subdivided into the following categories:

Personality Types: First, the chart is subdivided into jobs that are compatible with the six personality types—realistic, investigative, artistic, social, enterprising, and conventional—that you identified in the Personality Mosaic. The chart makes an even finer distinction, however, by subdividing each personality type into interest areas. Realistic, for example, is subdivided into mechanical, industrial, nature, protective, and physical performance areas. If you see yourself as a realistic type, you'll want to study each of these categories to find the ones that appeal to you the most.

Job Groups: The numbers 1 through 66 in the left-hand column and the descriptions in the chart refer to the 66 job groups identified by the Department of Labor. All the jobs in a group have similar characteristics. The jobs in a group generally attract people of similar personality types. They call for similar preferences regarding involvement with data, people, and things; they have the same work qualities; and they usually call for the same skills. An example of a job group is "engineering." There are many kinds of engineering—civil, electrical, mechanical, to name a few—but all engineers and engineering jobs have many characteristics in common.

Decimal Code: The decimal numbers in the next column refer to numbered items in the Department of Labor publication *Guide for Occupational Exploration,* which you may use in many libraries and state employment offices. The numbers 1 through 12 in the decimal code refer to the twelve interest areas identified by the Department of Labor.

Satisfiers: You will use the remaining columns to find your satisfiers. The high, medium, and low indicators are generalizations. They are only educated "guesstimates." Some applications are obvious; others may be arguable. The indicators are used here not as absolutes, but simply as guides to where your satisfiers are likely to be found.

By following the directions on page 108, you will discover which job groups possess your satisfiers. It is almost as important to *eliminate* groups or even whole interest areas as it is to zero in on job groups of interest. So, for example, if involvement with things is definitely not for you, the listing of realistic job groups can probably be crossed out. If you have no interest in the artistic area, cross that off too. Keep going through the twelve sections of the chart until you have narrowed down your choices. Then choose several job groups of interest to you within these sections. Keep on sifting. Now, turn to page 108.

The Job Group Chart
(See p. 108 for directions.)

R - REALISTIC JOB GROUPS

MECHANICAL

Basic Eight Skills

Job Group	Decimal code	D Data	P People	T Things	Work Qualities	1 Intelligence	2 Verbal	3 Numerical	4 Form/space	5 Clerical	6 Color	7 Finger/hand	8 Body
1. Engineering: Applying research of science and math to design of new products and systems.	05.01	H	L	H	2,3,4,5,6,7	H	H	H	HM	L	L	L	L
2. Managerial Work–Mechanical: Managing technical plants or systems.	05.02	H	ML	L	2,3,4,5,6,7,9	H	H	HM	HM	M	L	L	L
3. Engineering Technology: Collecting, recording, coordinating technical information.	05.03	H	L	H	2,3,4	HM	M	HM	HM	M	L	HM	L
4. Air and Water Vehicle Operation: Operating planes and ships to carry freight/passengers.	05.04	H	ML	M	2,3,4,6,9,10	H	HM	HM	HM	M	L	ML	M
5. Craft Technology: Doing highly skilled hand/machine custom work.	05.05	HM	L	HM	2,3,4,5	M	L	HM	HM	L	L	HM	M
6. Systems Operation: Caring for large, complicated mechanical systems like heating and power.	05.06	HM	L	M	2,4,5,6	M	M	M	ML	ML	L	ML	L
7. Quality Control: Checking and testing materials and products in nonfactory situations.	05.07	HM	L	HL	1,2,3,4	M	L	ML	M	L	L	ML	L
8. Land Vehicle Operation: Operating/driving vehicles that haul freight.	05.08	L	L	M	1,2,4	M	L	L	M	M	L	M	M
9. Materials Control: Keeping records of the flow and storage of materials and products.	05.09	M	L	L	1,2,4,6	M	M	M	L	M	L	ML	L
10. Skilled Hand and Machine Work: Doing moderately skilled hand/machine work	05.10	M	L	HM	1,2,4	L	L	ML	M	L	L	ML	L
11. Equipment Operation: Operating/driving heavy equipment such as in construction, mining.	05.11	L	L	M	1,2,4	M	L	L	M	L	L	M	ML
12. Elemental Work–Mechanical: Doing non-factory manual labor with machines, tools.	05.12	L	L	ML	1,2,4	L	L	L	ML	L	L	ML	L

The Job Group Chart continued

<table>
<tr><th rowspan="2"></th><th rowspan="2">Decimal code</th><th rowspan="2">D Data</th><th rowspan="2">P People</th><th rowspan="2">T Things</th><th rowspan="2">Work Qualities</th><th colspan="8">Basic Eight Skills</th></tr>
<tr><th>1 Intelligence</th><th>2 Verbal</th><th>3 Numerical</th><th>4 Form/space</th><th>5 Clerical</th><th>6 Color</th><th>7 Finger/hand</th><th>8 Body</th></tr>
<tr><td colspan="14">INDUSTRIAL (Factory Work)</td></tr>
<tr><td>13. Production Technology: Setting up/operating machines to produce goods in specific ways.</td><td>06.01</td><td>M</td><td>ML</td><td>H</td><td>2,4,6</td><td>M</td><td>L</td><td>M</td><td>M</td><td>L</td><td>L</td><td>M</td><td>L</td></tr>
<tr><td>14. Production Work: Doing hand/machine work to make a product; supervising/inspecting.</td><td>06.02</td><td>ML</td><td>ML</td><td>M</td><td>1,2, 4,6</td><td>M</td><td>L</td><td>ML</td><td>ML</td><td>L</td><td>L</td><td>ML</td><td>L</td></tr>
<tr><td>15. Quality Control: Testing, weighing, inspecting, measuring products to meet standards.</td><td>06.03</td><td>ML</td><td>L</td><td>L</td><td>1,2,4</td><td>M</td><td>L</td><td>L</td><td>ML</td><td>L</td><td>L</td><td>ML</td><td>L</td></tr>
<tr><td>16. Elemental Work–Industrial: Basic manual labor in production requiring little training.</td><td>06.04</td><td>L</td><td>L</td><td>L</td><td>1,2,4</td><td>I</td><td>L</td><td>L</td><td>ML</td><td>L</td><td>L</td><td>ML</td><td>L</td></tr>
<tr><td colspan="14">NATURE (Plants, Animals)</td></tr>
<tr><td>17. Managerial Work–Nature: Planning work for farming, fisheries, logging, horticulture.</td><td>03.01</td><td>H</td><td>L</td><td>HL</td><td>2,3,4, 5,6</td><td>HM</td><td>M</td><td>M</td><td>ML</td><td>L</td><td>L</td><td>L</td><td>L</td></tr>
<tr><td>18. General Supervision–Nature: Supervising on farms, in forests, fisheries, nurseries, parks.</td><td>03.02</td><td>H</td><td>M</td><td>HM</td><td>2,3,4, 5,6,9</td><td>M</td><td>M</td><td>M</td><td>M</td><td>ML</td><td>L</td><td>M</td><td>M</td></tr>
<tr><td>19. Animal Training and Care: Training, breeding, raising, showing, caring for non-farm animals.</td><td>03.03</td><td>HML</td><td>ML</td><td>M</td><td>1,2,3, 5,7</td><td>ML</td><td>ML</td><td>L</td><td>ML</td><td>L</td><td>L</td><td>ML</td><td>ML</td></tr>
<tr><td>20. Elemental Work–Nature: Doing basic physical labor related to farming, fishing, gardening.</td><td>03.04</td><td>L</td><td>L</td><td>ML</td><td>1,4</td><td>L</td><td>L</td><td>L</td><td>ML</td><td>L</td><td>L</td><td>ML</td><td>L</td></tr>
</table>

#	Job Group	Code													
21.	Safety and Law Enforcement: Administration, enforcing laws and regulations.	04.01	H	HML	ML	3,4,5,6,7,9,10	HM	HM	L	L	ML	M	L	L	L
22.	Security Services: Protecting people and property from crime, fire, and other hazards.	04.02	HML	L	ML	1,3,6,10	M	M	L	L	ML	L	L	ML	ML

PHYSICAL PERFORMANCE

#	Job Group	Code													
23.	Sports: Of all sorts; playing, training, coaching and officiating.	12.01	HM	ML	ML	2,3,7,9,10	ML	ML	L	L	ML	ML	L	H	H
24.	Physical Feats: Amusing/entertaining people with special physical skills and strengths.	12.02	M	M	ML	2,3,4,9,10	M	M	L	L	HM	L	L	HM	HM

I - INVESTIGATIVE JOB GROUPS

SCIENTIFIC/ANALYTIC

#	Job Group	Code													
25.	Physical Sciences: Research/development in physics, chemistry, geology, computer science.	02.01	H	L	H	2,3,4,7	H	H	H	H	HM	M	L	L	L
26.	Life Sciences: Studying functions of living things and how they relate to environments.	02.02	H	L	H	2,3,4,7	H	H	H	H	HM	M	M	HM	L
27.	Medical Sciences: Practicing medicine to prevent, diagnose, cure illnesses of people or animals.	02.03	H	H	H	2,3,5,7,8,9	H	H	H	H	H	L	M	HM	L
(1)	Engineering: Applying research of science and math to design of new products and systems.	05.01	H	L	H	2,3,4,5,6,7	H	H	H	H	HM	L	L	L	L
28.	Laboratory Technology: Doing laboratory work to carry out studies of various researchers.	02.04	HM	L	H	2,4	L	HM	HM	H	HM	ML	M	M	L
29.	Mathematics/Statistics: Using numbers and computers to analyze and solve problems	11.01	H	L	L	2,3,4,6,7	H	H	H	H	H	H	L	L	L

The Job Group Chart continued

A - ARTISTIC JOB GROUPS

ARTISTIC/CREATIVE

	Decimal code	Data D	People P	Things T	Work Qualities	Intelligence 1	Verbal 2	Numerical 3	Form/space 4	Clerical 5	Color 6	Finger/hand 7	Body 8
						Basic Eight Skills							
30. Literary Arts: Producing creative pieces from writing to publishing for print, TV, films.	01.01	H	L	L	3,6,7,9	H	H	L	L	L	L	L	L
31. Visual Arts: Doing artistic work, i.e., paintings, designs, photography for personal sale or for media.	01.02	H	L	H	3,4,6,7	HM	L	L	H	L	H	HM	L
32. Performing Arts–Drama: Performing in, directing, teaching, stage, radio, TV, film productions.	01.03	H	M	L	3,6,7,9	H	H	L	L	L	L	L	L
33. Performing Arts–Music: Playing an instrument, singing, arranging, composing, conducting music.	01.04	H	M	HL	3,6,7,9	HM	HM	L	HM	HM	L	H	H
34. Performing Arts–Dance: Performing, teaching, choreographing dance routines.	01.05	H	M	L	2,3,6,7,9	HM	HL	L	HM	L	L	HM	H
35. Craft Arts: Producing handcrafts, graphics, decorative products.	01.06	M	L	H	2,3,4	M	M	L	HM	L	M	HM	L
36. Elemental Arts/Amusement: Entertaining and doing novel routines at carnivals, circuses, fairs.	01.07	L	M	L	1,3,6,7	ML	L	L	ML	L	L	L	L
37. Modeling: Posing for artists; displaying clothing, accessories, other products.	01.08	L	L	L	1,7,9	ML	L	L	L	L	L	L	ML

S - SOCIAL JOB GROUPS

HUMAN SERVICES

Description	Code												
38. Social Services: Helping people deal with personal, vocational, educational, religious concerns.	10.01	HM	H	L	3,5,6,7,8,9	H	H	M	L	L	L	L	L
39. Nursing/Therapy Services: Providing diagnosis and therapy to help people get well.	10.02	HM	HML	M	2,3,5,6,7,8	H	HM	HM	M	ML	ML	ML	L
40. Child and Adult Care: Assisting with medical and physical care and services.	10.03	M	L	ML	1,2,3,5,6,8	M	M	L	L	ML	L	ML	L

ACCOMMODATING

Description	Code												
41. Hospitality Services: Touring, guiding, greeting, serving people to help them feel comfortable.	09.01	HM	ML	L	3,5,6,7,9	M	M	L	L	ML	L	L	L
42. Barber/Beauty Services: Hair and skin care to help people with personal appearances.	09.02	HM	L	H	2,3,4,5,6,7	M	M	L	HM	L	HM	HM	L
43. Passenger Services: Transporting people by vehicle; also instructing and supervising.	09.03	M	L	M	1,2,3,4,6	M	L	ML	M	L	L	M	M
44. Customer Services: Waiting on people in a routine way in a variety of business settings.	09.04	M	L	L	1,4,6	ML	ML	ML	L	ML	L	M	L
45. Attendant Services: Providing personal services to people at home or when traveling.	09.05	L	L	L	1,6	ML	ML	L	L	L	ML	ML	L

The Job Group Chart continued

S/E - SOCIAL/ENTERPRISING JOB GROUPS
LEADING/INFLUENCING

Job Group	Decimal code	Data (D)	People (P)	Things (T)	Work Qualities	Intelligence (1)	Verbal (2)	Numerical (3)	Form/space (4)	Clerical (5)	Color (6)	Finger/hand (7)	Body (8)
46. Educational/Library Services: Teaching, providing library services.	11.02	HM	HML	L	3,5,6,7,8,9	H	H	M	L	HM	L	L	L
47. Social Research: Studying people of various backgrounds both of the past and present.	11.03	H	L	L	2,3,5,7	H	H	HM	L	HL	L	L	L
48. Law: Counseling, advising, representing people/businesses regarding legal matters.	11.04	H	H	L	2,3,5,6,7,8,9	H	H	HM	L	M	L	L	L
49. Business Administration: Designing procedures, solving problems, supervising people in business.	11.05	H	HML	L	2,3,5,6,7,9	H	H	HM	L	M	L	L	L
50. Finance: Setting up financial systems; controlling, analyzing financial records.	11.06	H	ML	L	2,3,6,7,9	H	H	H	L	HM	L	L	L
51. Services Administration: Administering programs in an agency such as social, health, educational.	11.07	H	HM	L	3,5,6,7,8,9	H	H	M	L	M	L	L	L
52. Communications: Writing, editing, translating information for media—radio, print, and TV.	11.08	H	L	L	2,3,5,6,7,9	H	H	M	L	M	L	L	L
53. Promotion: Advertising, fund raising, sales, and public relations.	11.09	H	HM	L	3,5,6,7,9	H	H	HM	L	ML	L	L	L
54. Regulations Enforcement: Checking/enforcing government regulations, company policies, procedures.	11.10	H	L	L	2,3,5,6,7	HM	HM	M	ML	M	L	L	L
55. Business Management: Taking responsibility for operation and supervision of a business.	11.11	H	ML	L	2,3,5,6,9	HM	HM	M	ML	M	L	L	L
56. Contracts and Claims: Negotiating contracts, investigating claims.	11.12	H	H	L	2,3,5,6,7,9	H	H	M	L	M	L	L	L

Basic Eight Skills

PERSUADING

57. Sales Technology: Selling technical equipment or services including insurance. Also clerical work.	08.01	HM	M	L	2,3,6,7,9	HM	HM	HM	M	M	L	L	L
58. General Sales: Selling goods and services, wholesale/retail, to individuals, business, or industry.	08.02	M	M	L	2,3,6,7	M	M	M	L	M	L	L	L
59. Vending: Peddling, promoting items in public settings.	08.03	L	M	L	1,6,7	L	L	ML	L	L	L	ML	L

C - CONVENTIONAL JOB GROUPS

BUSINESS DETAIL

60. Administrative Detail: Doing secretarial/technical clerical work.	07.01	HM	ML	ML	2,3,5,6,7	HM	M	M	L	HM	L	L	L
61. Mathematical Detail: Keeping numerical records, doing basic figuring.	07.02	M	L	M	1,2,4,6	M	M	M	L	HM	L	L	L
62. Financial Detail: Keeping track of money-flow to and from the public.	07.03	M	L	ML	1,2,4,6	M	M	M	L	M	L	ML	L
63. Oral Communications: Giving information in person or by communication systems.	07.04	M	L	ML	1,2,4,5,6,7	M	M	ML	L	M	L	ML	L
64. Records Processing: Putting records together and keeping them up-to-date.	07.05	M	L	ML	1,2,6	M	M	ML	L	HM	L	ML	L
65. Clerical Machine Operation: Using various machines to record, process, and compute data.	07.06	ML	L	M	1,2,4,6	M	L	L	L	HM	L	HML	L
66. Clerical Handling: Keeping data in order by filing, copying, sorting, delivering.	07.07	L	L	L	1,2,4	ML	ML	L	L	M	L	ML	L

Finding Your Satisfiers in the Workplace

To use the Job Group Chart, transfer your satisfiers to the chart from the tally sheet on page 99.

1. Suppose you marked *H* (high) for data on the tally sheet; then circle every *H* in the Data column of the Job Group Chart, even in combinations such as (H) *ML* or (H) *L* or (H) *M*.
2. Under Work Qualities, circle the numbers that identify your "must have" work qualities—the same numbers you circled under Work Qualities on the tally sheet. If you feel positive about business contact on the job, for example, circle every 6 under Work Qualities. If you feel positive about personal contact, circle every 8, and so on, even if it appears with other numbers.
3. Transfer your skills from the tally sheet to the chart by circling the *H*'s or *M*'s or *L*'s in the appropriate columns. If you wish to work with your fingers and hands at a high level, for example, circle every *H* in column 7.
4. Go back and read *all* the job descriptions on the Job Group Chart. Circle the numbers (1 through 66) of any job group that interests you, whether it has your satisfiers or not.

Job Chart Follow-up

Some lucky people find the job of their dreams just by observing where their circles line up opposite one particular job group on the Job Group Chart. Perhaps the assessment results supported goals they had already established. Many people are surprised to find a good career choice they had never considered before. If you think you have already made your career choice, ask yourself these questions.

_____ Is this career clearly your own choice, or is it one recommended by others?
_____ Are you afraid to take a peek at other alternatives?
_____ Are you willing to keep an open mind by considering important factors that may change your decision?
_____ Can you support your choice with facts about your skills, interests, and values?

The majority of people are dismayed to find themselves definitely at sea in an ocean of many choices. If you are wondering why YOU don't have a nice, neat job title in hand, you may be tempted to give up. But if you keep on searching, you will have a great chance to learn more about yourself and the work world. You will be more willing to explore important supporting factors that go into a career choice, and you will have the joy of learning that many enjoyable careers would suit you equally well. All in all, the career search process is a confidence builder. Even those with a clear-cut career choice need to learn about the job market and how to connect with it.

Study the Job Group Chart line by line to find groups that look interesting. Some of your satisfiers may be more important than others. Try to be as flexible as possible. Maybe you have marked H or M on Color, for example, but could easily enjoy work in which color is irrelevant if all your other satisfiers are present. However, star any groups in which all your satisfiers are found. If your chosen job group falls within a personality orientation different from your top three, it may be possible to find ways to express your personality in certain aspects of the job. But it's important not to force the data to fit when it doesn't. You are the one who has to live with the job. A fairly close match in data, people, and things is important, and any group you're looking at with interest should match your "must have" work qualities. Then be sure the job group will let you use those of the basic eight skills you feel you must use for satisfying work.

Some people find the Job Group Chart too detailed. They would like to see the job chart, and hence the job market, simplified and summarized. Here is a short summary exercise to help you step back and take a better look at the process. An overview of the Job Group Chart will follow.

A Mini Career Search

Think about some activities that you enjoy so much that you forget time is going by Before you look at the score sheet and the interpretation that follows, circle the numbers of the statements below that apply to you.

I enjoy myself and lose track of time when I'm:

1. Having a friendly conversation with someone
2. Organizing my papers, files, and notebooks
3. Thinking up new ideas
4. Fixing something
5. Talking someone into doing a project
6. Keeping assignments up to date
7. Doing a puzzle
8. Tinkering with some gadget
9. Helping someone
10. Taking responsibility for every detail of an assignment
11. Reading to explore new things
12. Being physically active
13. Sharing my feelings
14. Completing a job as carefully as possible
15. Creating something different
16. Using my hands in some project

17. Getting people organized
18. Keeping track of my accounts
19. Discussing or reading some complicated idea
20. Doing physically daring things

People can live in and enjoy four different "worlds": people, paper, mind, or matter. Although they may enjoy a little of each, one or two favorites can be a clue to a satisfying career orientation. To find out which world you live in, circle on the following table the same numbers you circled on the "Mini Career Search." Then count the circles in each column to learn which is your world.

People	Paper	Mind	Matter
1	2	3	4
5	6	7	8
9	10	11	12
13	14	15	16
17	18	19	20

The twelve interest areas that represent the job market as a whole can be grouped into four "worlds": matter, mind, people, and paper. Each world relates to one or more of the six personality types: realistic, investigative, artistic, social, enterprising, and conventional.

The world of matter (or things) involves the five interest areas—mechanical, industrial, nature, protective, and physical performance—associated on the Job Group Chart with the realistic category of job and personality. The realistic personality gravitates toward jobs that deal with mechanical systems; factory or production work; heavy outdoor work with nature; police, fire, or other protective work; and physical performing activities such as sports and acrobatics. Some jobs in the world of matter give the *R* person with a social bent the opportunity to have the best of two worlds, things and people, by doing some management and supervision.

Social persons who score high in some material categories may wish to work with things only if they are also realistic types. Social persons already in thing-oriented jobs might wish to try management, supervision, or even personnel, training, or selling. In such social/investigative areas as the health field, they would work with both people and things. Realistic personalities with few social characteristics often find that a promotion to management status brings headaches they'd rather be without.

The mind world is for the logical, rational, investigative personality with a strong realistic bent who enjoys the physical/biological sciences and engineering. Purely investigative persons with little interest in the physical world usually take their inquiring minds into areas such as theoretical math or research in social sciences or business—that is, any area that requires little interaction with things or people.

CAREER FOCUS

World of Matter: Things/Body

- Mechanical
- Industrial (Factory Work)
- Nature (Plants, Animals)
- Protective
- Physical Performance

Generally involved with things from simple to complex. Little involvement with people unless supervising or managing. Use of data depends on complexity of job. Skills required are physical agility, coordination, strength—along with moderate intelligence and in some cases ability with numbers.

World of Mind: Ideas/Intellect

- Scientific/Analytic
- Artistic/Creative

Usually involves high to medium use of data. Little involvement with people except in medicine. Often deals with things or thinking about things. Skills required are generally above-average verbal and often numerical intelligence, and in some cases a well-developed sense of color, form, and spatial relationships.

World of People: Helping/Motivating

- Human Services
- Accommodating
- Leading/Influencing
- Persuading

Generally an ongoing involvement with people. Level of involvement with data increases with complexity of work. Usually little or no involvement with things except in jobs requiring physical contact. Requires a range of "people skills": facility in dealing with people, solving people problems, and providing human services.

World of Paper: Words/Numbers/Symbols

- Business Detail

Consistent use of data: words, numbers, symbols. Usually little involvement with people beyond what is required to process business details. Deals with things in terms of office machines. Skills required are moderate verbal and numerical intelligence, an eye for detail, and in some cases finger/hand agility.

Artistic persons use their intuitive minds in painting, sculpture, or crafts, if they have a facility with things. The more investigative types deal with music and writing. Some artistic persons with little specific "talent" give expression to their many ideas in a variety of other environments.

The world of people extends to the four interest areas—human services, accommodating, leading/influencing, and persuading—associated with the social cat-egory of job and personality. Jobs in these areas involve helping or motivating people. For new career seekers who would love to work with people, opportunities range from waiter to psychiatrist, from manager to mortician! Such jobs involve being with people all day: greeting people, waiting on them, taking charge of a group, solving business or personal problems. These jobs often require leadership to organize a group, show people what to do, and direct a project.

If you wish to work with people at a high level, consider earning a degree in business or one of the behavioral sciences. You will need to have or develop creativity and intuition if you work with people on any but the lowest level. If you are a social type in a realistic, investigative, artistic, or conventional job, look around your workplace for a job that will give you more contact with people.

The world of paper (which now includes the video-screen world) attracts con-ventional people who are careful about detail. If you have a realistic bent, you will enjoy paperwork that is related to machinery such as word processors or calculators. If you have a social bent, you will like gathering information from people and passing it on. If you are working in any other category, look for some ways to handle the data of your work environment.

People are attracted to jobs for all sorts of reasons besides interest in the job itself. We want people to like us. We'd like to feel important. We want to avoid competition, to please our parents, to look like the stereotypical male or female, to earn more money. We are influenced by the convenience and availability of jobs. All of these reasons tap into our value system. But can you find happiness in a career field that doesn't interest you? This all-important question must be balanced out with your values. If you pay attention to your strong interests, you will have fewer conflicts with your value system.

Just a Job or a Career?

Another thing to keep in mind as you choose a career is the degree of commitment you are willing to make. Do you want a career or just a job? A job might be defined as something one does to earn money, requiring little involvement beyond one's physical and mental presence performing in a routine way. Many people at all levels of intelligence and creativity use work in this way: some because their job is the only work they want or can get; others to support hobbies and creative activities for which there seem to be no work opportunities.

A career, in contrast to a job, can be seen as a series of work experiences that represent progression in a field. It is work that captivates much of one's total energy. A career is planned for, trained for, and involves the dedication of time and talent beyond the minimum required.

When two people are doing identical work, one may view it as "just a job" and another as "my career." Sometimes a person trains and sacrifices to achieve a career only to face disillusionment for some unforeseen reason and end up performing tasks mechanically, seeing no way out. Conversely, some people have been known to perform what society calls "menial" work with a level of dedication worthy of a professional.

Some work is almost impossible to do without a great deal of personal involvement. In our society, for example, "moving up" generally is an all-consuming activity. How much are you willing to sacrifice? For some, "success" has meant loss of family, health, friendship, and leisure. One can get caught up in work only to find that other values have slipped away. Others can pursue a career with great dedication and yet keep a balance.

How much involvement is enough for you? Sometimes your commitment to a career increases greatly when you become aware of your interests and skills and the way they relate to the world of work. Motivation and energy soar. Keep the question of commitment in mind as you consider your career choice.

Library Research

Library research enables you to survey the whole job market. Your most helpful guides will be the *Guide for Occupational Exploration* and the *Dictionary of Occupational Titles*. The McKnight *Worker Trait Group Guide* is another of the many helpful books about careers.[4] It is easy to handle because it lists only nationally important job titles. You can find these books in career centers, library reference rooms, and state employment offices.

Before you go to the library, list all the job groups that you would like to explore. Use the decimal code number from the Job Group Chart for easy reference. At the library, look up those numbers in the *Guide for Occupational Exploration*. As you explore the job groups, make a list of all the job titles you want to read about. Eliminate areas that don't interest you, but keep groups and titles on your list until you have explored each one. This process enables you to survey the entire job market without looking up *every* job title or even every job group.

Suppose you are interested in job group 55, Business Management, code number 11.11. In the *Guide for Occupational Exploration* you will find this information:

> Workers in this group manage a business, such as a store or cemetery, a branch of a large company, such as a local office for a credit corporation, or a department within a company, such as a warehouse. They usually carry out operating policies and procedures determined by administration workers, such as presidents, vice-presidents, and directors. Some managers own their own businesses and are considered self-employed. Managers find employment in all kinds of businesses as well as government agencies.

This paragraph is followed by answers to some important questions: What kind of work would you do as a business manager? What skills and abilities do you need for this kind of work? How do you know if you would like or could learn to do this kind of work? How can you prepare for and enter this kind of work? What else should you consider about these jobs? This information is followed by a list of all the job categories in the Business Management group:

11.11.01   Lodging
11.11.02   Recreation and Amusement
11.11.03   Transportation
11.11.04   Services
11.11.05   Wholesale-Retail

Each of these listings is subdivided into specific job titles, each identified by a nine-digit number. Under Wholesale-Retail, for example, you will find: Manager, Retail Store 185.167.046. If this job interests you, you can find a description of it in the *Dictionary of Occupational Titles* just by looking up the nine-digit number, 185.167.046. The section will include other, similar job titles so that you can explore a variety of jobs.

Remember that titles for the same job differ from one company to another. But if you know what general functions you want to perform, and if you spend enough time with these books, you will have an overview of the whole job market.

By now you should have your job chart well marked. You've noticed in which of the twelve interest areas your circles tend to cluster and which of the 66 job groups offer your most important satisfiers. Whenever your likes and skills point toward the same job group, you've hit the bull's eye on the career target.

The Career Target

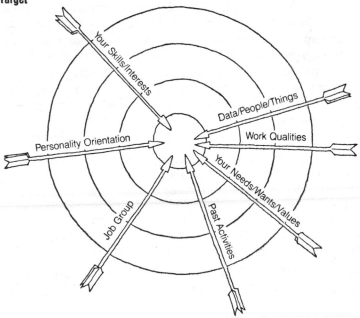

At this point you might be feeling a little scared/anxious/uncertain/confused. These are all normal feelings for anyone on the verge of a *great discovery*! Keep going! Don't be overwhelmed if you find that several jobs look good to you. Some people are comfortable in a number of areas. Sometimes a person needs more experience with work before making a decision. Give yourself more time if you need it. Don't decide to decide without seeing clearly.

There are still other things you can look at to help your decision along. Finding out about projected job market trends for your areas of interest can be helpful here. But one of the best ways to decide is to get some "inside information," through work experience, group tours of work places, or interviewing people who work in your area of interest. The rest of this manual will give you some help with these concerns.

Making a good career decision is a growth process, and growth takes patience. You can't make a flower grow by pulling on it.

1. Job Groups Expanded

This listing, arranged by decimal code, expands each of the groups from the Job Group Chart. Before you do any more research on interest areas and job groups, circle the decimal codes of the subgroups of interest to you at this time.

Summary List of Interest Areas, Job Groups, and Subgroups

---

01   ARTISTIC/CREATIVE

01.01   Literary Arts
01.01-01 Editing
01.01-02 Creative Writing
01.01-03 Critiquing

01.02   Visual Arts
01.02-01 Instructing and Appraising
01.02-02 Studio Art
01.02-03 Commercial Art

01.03   Performing Arts: Drama
01.03-01 Instructing and Directing
01.03-02 Performing
01.03-03 Narrating and Announcing

01.04   Performing Arts: Music
01.04-01 Instructing and Directing
01.04-02 Composing and Arranging
01.04-03 Vocal Performing
01.04-04 Instrumental Performing

01.05   Performing Arts: Dance
01.05-01 Instructing and Choreography
01.05-02 Performing

01.06   Craft Arts
01.06-01 Graphic Arts and Related
         Crafts
01.06-02 Arts and Crafts
01.06-03 Hand Lettering, Painting, and
         Decorating

01.07   Elemental Arts
01.07-01 Psychic Science
01.07-02 Announcing
01.07-03 Entertaining

01.08   Modeling
01.08-01 Personal Appearance

02   SCIENTIFIC/ANALYTIC

02.01   Physical Sciences
02.01-01 Theoretical Research
02.01-02 Technology

02.02   Life Sciences
02.02-01 Animal Specialization
02.02-02 Plant Specialization
02.02-03 Plant and Animal
         Specialization
02.02-04 Food Research

02.03   Medical Sciences
02.03-01 Medicine and Surgery
02.03-02 Dentistry
02.03-03 Veterinary Medicine
02.03-04 Health Specialties

02.04   Laboratory Technology
02.04-01 Physical Sciences
02.04-02 Life Sciences

**03   NATURE (PLANTS,
        ANIMALS)**

**03.01   Managerial Work: Plants and
           Animals**
03.01-01 Farming
03.01-02 Specialty Breeding
03.01-03 Specialty Cropping
03.01-04 Forestry and Logging

**03.02   General Supervision: Plants
           and Animals**
03.02-01 Farming
03.02-02 Forestry and Logging
03.02-03 Nursery and Groundskeeping
03.02-04 Services

03.03   Animal Training and Service
03.03-01 Animal Training
03.03-02 Animal Service

**03.04   Elemental Work: Plants and
           Animals**
03.04-01 Farming
03.04-02 Forestry and Logging
03.04-03 Hunting and Fishing
03.04-04 Nursery and Groundskeeping
03.04-05 Services

04   PROTECTIVE

04.01   Safety and Law Enforcement
04 01 01 Managing
04 01 02 Investigating

04.02   Security Services
04.02-01 Detention
04.02-02 Property and People
04.02-03 Law and Order
04.02-04 Emergency Responding

05   MECHANICAL

05.01   Engineering
05.01-01 Research
05.01-02 Environmental Protection
05.01-03 Systems Design

11 LEADING/INFLUENCING *continued*	11.10-04 Immigration and Customs 11.10-05 Company Policy	11.12-03 Booking 11.12-04 Procurement Negotiations
11.09 Promotion 11.09-01 Sales 11.09-02 Funds and Membership Solicitation 11.09-03 Public Relations	**11.11 Business Management** 11.11-01 Lodging 11.11-02 Recreation and Amusement 11.11-03 Transportation 11.11-04 Services 11.11-05 Wholesale/Retail	**12 PHYSICAL PERFORMANCE** **12.01 Sports** 12.01-01 Coaching and Instructing 12.01-02 Officiating 12.01-03 Performing
11.10 Regulations Enforcement 11.10-01 Finance 11.10-02 Individual Rights 11.10-03 Health and Safety	**11.12 Contracts and Claims** 11.12-01 Claims Settlement 11.12-02 Rental and Leasing	**12.02 Physical Feats** 12.02-01 Performing

2. Ranking Your Interests

Rank the twelve interest areas from the Job Group Chart in order of importance to you:

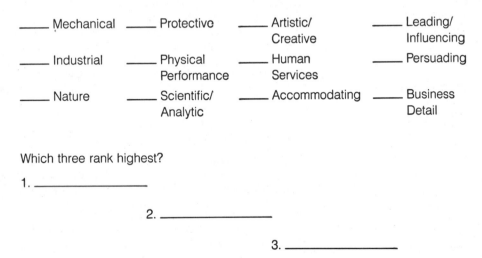

_____ Mechanical   _____ Protective   _____ Artistic/
                                    Creative

_____ Leading/
         Influencing

_____ Industrial   _____ Physical
                     Performance

_____ Human
         Services

_____ Persuading

_____ Nature   _____ Scientific/
                    Analytic

_____ Accommodating

_____ Business
         Detail

Which three rank highest?

1. _____

2. _____

3. _____

3. Numerical Analysis (Optional)

If you like numerical data, record the total number of circles that you have placed in each of the twelve interest areas. (Count your circles under Data, People, Things, Work Qualities, and Basic Eight Skills.) If you then divide each count by the total possible number of circles and multiply by 100, you will get percentages, which you can then compare.

Interest Area	Your Total Circles		Total Possible Circles		Percentage
Mechanical	_____	divided by	197	× 100 =	_____ %
Industrial	_____		68		_____ %
Nature	_____		78		_____ %
Protective	_____		41		_____ %
Physical Performance	_____		42		_____ %
Scientific/Analytic	_____		103		_____ %
Artistic/Creative	_____		136		_____ %
Human Services	_____		63		_____ %
Accommodating	_____		92		_____ %
Leading/Influencing	_____		205		_____ %
Persuading	_____		51		_____ %
Business Detail	_____		129		_____ %

Number the interest areas in order from highest to lowest. Does this order agree with the ranking above? If not, which order seems more accurate? _____

_____

4. Tentative Job Group Choices

List three or more job groups you'd like to explore further.

Job Group Number   Job Group Decimal Code   Job Group Title

_____   _____   _____

_____   _____   _____

_____   _____   _____

5. The Match Analyzer

Match your satisfier information from the tally sheet (p. 99) with the characteristics of your chosen job group(s) on the chart. This exercise will point out areas of agreement and areas of possible job dissatisfaction. Circle any significant mismatches.

Tally Sheet Data	*Job Group Chart Data*	*Job Group Chart Data*
	Group No. _____ Title _____	Group No. _____ Title _____
Personality Type _____	Personality Type _____	Personality Type _____
Data ___ People ___ Things ___	Data ___ People ___ Things ___	Data ___ People ___ Things ___

Work Qualities	*Work Qualities*	*Work Qualities*
_____ 1. Repetition	_____ 1. Repetition	_____ 1. Repetition
_____ 2. Precision	_____ 2. Precision	_____ 2. Precision
_____ 3. Intuition	_____ 3. Intuition	_____ 3. Intuition
_____ 4. Production	_____ 4. Production	_____ 4. Production
_____ 5. Variety	_____ 5. Variety	_____ 5. Variety
_____ 6. Business contact	_____ 6. Business contact	_____ 6 Business contact
_____ 7. Influencing	_____ 7. Influencing	_____ 7. Influencing
_____ 8. Personal contact	_____ 8. Personal contact	_____ 8. Personal contact
_____ 9. Prestige	_____ 9. Prestige	_____ 9. Prestige
_____ 10. Adventure	_____ 10. Adventure	_____ 10. Adventure

Skill Levels	*Skill Levels*	*Skill Levels*
_____ 1. Intelligence	_____ 1. Intelligence	_____ 1. Intelligence
_____ 2. Verbal	_____ 2. Verbal	_____ 2. Verbal
_____ 3. Numerical	_____ 3. Numerical	_____ 3 Numerical
_____ 4. Form/space	_____ 4. Form/space	_____ 4. Form/space
_____ 5. Clerical	_____ 5. Clerical	_____ 5. Clerical
_____ 6. Color	_____ 6. Color	_____ 6. Color
_____ 7. Finger/hand	_____ 7. Finger/hand	_____ 7. Finger/hand
_____ 8. Body	_____ 8. Body	_____ 8. Body

6. Researching a Job Group

a. Discuss the job group of most interest to you.

_____

_____

_____

b. Look up the job group in the *Guide for Occupational Exploration*; then summarize the kind of work you would do.

_____

_____

_____

c. Summarize skills and abilities you would need for this kind of work.

_____

_____

_____

d. Summarize clues that tell you whether you would like or could learn this work.

_____

_____

_____

e. Summarize the training you would need and the usual methods of entry into this field.

_____

_____

_____

f. List job titles you'd like to explore further.

_____

_____

_____

7. Researching Job Titles

Look up one job title in the _Dictionary of Occupational Titles_. Summarize what you find.

_____

_____

_____

8. Your Expectations

Now that you've researched the job market, answer this important question: Do you want a career or "just a job"? Explain your answer.

_____

_____

_____

Five

The Job Market:

Facts, Trends, and Predictions

any people are so overjoyed when they have picked a job title or two that they can hardly wait to start job hunting. But sophisticated career searchers will first investigate the job trends in their chosen field to see where they're heading. Second, they will research a variety of workplaces to find some that are right for them. Third, they will talk to people who are currently working in these fields and visit their workplaces. Then they will make a careful decision and begin the job hunt.

In this chapter you will look at job trends and predictions, along with some guidelines for uncovering alternatives. In the next chapter you will learn how to examine the subtleties of the workplace and find out how to do that research.

Charting the Future

Job seekers are sometimes advised to "find a need and fill it." During your career search you may often find yourself wondering, "Who needs me out there?" The truth is, there is no really accurate way to predict the future needs of the job market.

Statisticians and futurists collect facts about past events to discover present trends. Understanding these trends enables them to make predictions (which are only educated guesstimates) about the future—including *your* job future. But although the trends affect your future, you will also affect the trends. If you are in tune with yourself and your deepest values, you will make wise choices and connect with others like yourself who share your aspirations. They are likely to hire you, or start a business with you, or do business with you. You will start your own trend!

Five global explosions will be affecting the job market of the 1980s and beyond—explosions in population, science, technology, information, and global consciousness.

Population: The number of people has been increasing so fast that the time required for population to double has dropped from 1 billion years to 1,000 to 200 to 80 to 35 years. There have never before been so many people. Supplies of resources and energy seem stretched to the breaking point. How will all these individuals survive, much less find enrichment?

Science: About 90 percent of all scientists who ever lived are alive today. They have split the atom and pursued its parts into quarks and beyond. They have unleashed forces unimaginable a century ago—the power to re-design the human race and its companion creatures and even to re-design the structure of matter itself and then with the touch of a button to destroy it all. Misunderstanding such power gives birth to fear. Understanding it gives birth to even greater fear.

Technology: In a relatively few short years, modern technology has reached almost every corner of civilized life. Until the nineteenth century, the speed of transportation never exceeded 20 miles per hour. Now, the speed record for a jet-powered automobile exceeds 730 miles per hour, and spaceships travel at more than 149,125 miles per hour.[1] More than half of the energy consumed over the last 2,000 years has been consumed in the last 100 years. The time it takes for technology to apply scientific discoveries to the real world has shortened from centuries to a few years and in some cases months. Chemical pollution of the planet increases fear pollution in the minds of earthlings as we strive to understand what technology has wrought.

Information: The average adult is bombarded by enough words and ideas every day to cause sensory overload. In 450 years, the publication of new books has increased from 1,000 a year to more than 1,000 a day.[2] In ancient times, it took years for ideas and information (data) to travel from place to place. Two California Indian tribes living in villages ten miles apart spoke completely different languages! Today we can process and transmit vast amounts of information in the twinkling of an eye. But despite the quantity of information instantly available to us, discovering facts is as hard as it ever was. Truth and accuracy are not necessarily conveyed in direct proportion to the speed of transmission.

Global Consciousness: The explosions of population, science, technology, and information—all interrelated, all the result of great social change, all creating vast problems—are giving rise to a fifth explosion: our awareness of ourselves as inhabitants of a global village, all breathing the same air, drinking the same water, drawing sustenance from the same earth. Astronaut Russell Schweickart described our tiny planet as seen from outer space.

It is so small and so fragile, such a precious little spot in the universe . . . you realize that everything that means anything to you—all of history and art and death and birth and love, tears and joys, all of it—is on that little blue and white spot out there which you can cover with your thumb.[3]

Although these explosions are bringing exciting changes, the trends in population, science, technology, and information are rapidly creating problems. Willis Harmon, senior economist at SRI International, says that global consciousness will be the trend that provides solutions. All of these trends will affect your work life. "Future shock" is a term coined by Alvin Toffler to describe the effects of increasingly rapid change on our slow-to-catch-up psyches. If you understand the trends, you won't find yourself a victim of future shock. You'll be a shock absorber, instead. You won't find yourself out on a limb clinging to an obsolete view of the world or to an obsolete job. You'll develop the skills necessary for living in a fast-paced world—flexibility, the ability to learn, and the ability to use information wisely. You'll understand the need for a set of enduring values, which will enable you to maintain a broad sense of direction without being swept away by fads or trends. And, most important, you'll build a flexible, satisfying career with opportunities for growth.

Trends and the Job Market

As competition increases along with the world's population, flexibility will become ever more important. The fifteen-year "baby boom," between 1946 and 1961, added 60 million people to the U.S. population, compared to 40 million born in the previous fifteen years. This group, born into unprecedented affluence, has affected diverse areas of life such as education, the crime rate, and entertainment, and its impact will continue to be strong. By the year 2025, for the first time more than half of the population of the United States will be over 60.

Terry Kirkpatrick of the Associated Press says of the baby-boom people, "They will be remembered as the generation that stood in line." Now in their twenties and thirties, they are competing for everything—loans, housing, education, jobs, promotions, raises. And although they are having smaller families, their numbers are creating a modest need for teachers, child-care workers, and all the goods and services that children require.

There are now 100 million Americans in the work force. From 1980 data supplied by the U.S. Bureau of the Census, we can predict that the U.S. labor force will grow by 25 million, or about 1.6 million per year, between 1980 and 1995. Over the next ten years, greater numbers of workers in the midmanagement age bracket, 35 to 45, will increase competition for promotions. Also increasing competition are women, minorities, and older workers who decide to work past age 65.

In 1950 one person in twelve was over 60; the ratio will be one in seven by 2025. The number of older people will increase only slightly until the year 2000, and then it will increase by 40 percent worldwide. More elderly people will need medical and support services, adult education, travel arrangements, and all the other goods and services appropriate to older, affluent, and active people. Fortunately the rate of population growth is slowing down, which will result in a need for older workers to stay in the work force. Nevertheless, the world population is expected to increase 50 percent, from 4 billion to 6 billion, by the year 2000.[4]

Six billion people will impose heavy demands upon the earth's natural resources. The United States has a history of overpowering nature and using or abusing its resources, all in the name of "progress." As America became the world leader in manufacturing, poets immortalized the power of its flaming steel mills, its thundering railroads, and its amber waves of grain. The American automobile, mass produced by union labor on an assembly line, symbolized a dream of universal affluence, a happy marriage of science and technology. Then in the 1980s, Germany and Japan were competing in steel and auto making, American railroads were in disarray, U.S. farmlands were eroding at a rapid rate, and labor unions were losing their power.

While our natural resources dwindle, applied and theoretical sciences and engineering are booming as we strive to develop alternative substances for the manufacture of things. Science and technology have given us an affluent, leisurely lifestyle undreamed of fifty years ago. Yet many advances and solutions to old problems seem to create new problems. Environmentalists warn of acid rain, the greenhouse effect, and meltdowns at nuclear plants. Many Americans are concerned about the possibility of nuclear war. With technologies operating on massive scales, human error can be disastrous. Technology is sometimes in conflict with biology.

Against this background, a quiet but powerful revolution is spreading throughout the United States. It seems that the silicon chip is king, computers reign, and robots rule. Electronics technology, growing out of a period of tremendous scientific achievement, is here to stay, is the wave of the future, is touching us all. Smart machines are changing not only the face of the workplace but its body and soul as well. Science and technology together have given birth to a new era of information processing. Formerly makers of things, we are becoming a nation of data processors—we collect data, sort it, control it, and pass it on.

Every job requires data of some kind, but with each passing year, more workers are processing data and fewer are manufacturing material goods. The 1980 census shows only 19 percent of the population in manufacturing, and this figure is expected to drop below 10 percent by the mid-1990s. Over 75 percent of the U.S. population is working in the information and service sectors, which continue to grow rapidly. The information sector provides jobs for word processors, computer operators, programmers, systems analysts, software producers—all involved with science and technology and with entertainment, the arts, and business as well. The service sector contains jobs in which people "wait on" or serve other people and things in work that ranges from nursing the sick to repairing robots, from feeding the poor to feeding data into computers.

Changes in the structure and content of work are creating new industries that require new kinds of skills. How will great numbers of workers retrain? Which "old" industries will be revitalized? Which should we let go?

John Peers, inventor of the talking computer concept and director of the Robotics

THE FAR SIDE/ Gary Larson

Reprinted by permission
of Chronicle Features, San Francisco

Institute, predicts that manufacturing will return—automated, efficient, and profitable—by the end of this century.[5] Computer-controlled robots are already online in a growing number of factories. In short, we are experiencing the birth of a new social phenomenon—an information society in which data seems to surpass things and sometimes even people in importance.

Information is like a child's riddle: It's not only renewable but expandable: it's never scarce, doesn't wear out, uses few resources and little energy to produce, can be kept while given away. Its use requires new concepts of work; its applications to every phase of life are just beginning to be appreciated.

What has happened to the people component of the data-people-things trio?

Some are running mightily to stay in place; some are falling by the wayside in future shock; and some are taking night courses in computer programming. The need for skilled labor in an information society is tremendous. Ironically, after a period of high unemployment, we will have 1.5 million fewer 16-to-24-year-olds in 1990 than in 1980 and severe shortages of people with technical skills. Service workers also will be in demand in the next decade.

Overall, projections show an economy using smart machines and thus fewer *resources*, an economy in which two-paycheck couples will have more savings but fewer children, and thus an economy with more *capital* to build businesses, but an increasing shortage of *skilled labor*, the third essential component in employment. This adds up to a good outlook for specially skilled job seekers.[6] In the long run, then, automation should create more jobs but of a different sort.

With computers extending the capacity of our brains and robots giving us brawn, the work of the future should be ideal: Boring and repetitive tasks, dangerous and dirty tasks, can be taken over by smart machines, and "steel-collar workers." New-age secretaries will manage and process data in electronic offices, already present in many companies. More people will be wearing white collars and being creative in their jobs. The reality, however, may be less than ideal if we apply the old concepts of mass production to the new technology.

What place will education have in this scientific, high-tech, information society? College degrees have been declining in value largely because increased numbers of people are obtaining them. But a degree will still have greater earning power than a high school diploma. And a high school graduate will have job opportunities that a dropout will not have.[7] One study, for example, has shown skilled workers earning one and one half as much as those working in jobs that require little reading ability.[8] Degrees will still make employment, upgrading, promotions, and raises more attainable, although many degree holders will be "underemployed," or working in jobs that require less than their abilities, at least through the 1980s. Without knowledge and training, survival in the 1990s will be more difficult.

Unemployment: Options and Strategies

As a result of population increases, scientific and technological developments, and the emergence of the information society, full employment in the old sense may never be seen again. At some time in 1981, one out of five Americans was unemployed. The demise of many old industries and the growth of many new ones is causing a dislocation of workers of enormous magnitude. Patricia Westfull, writing for the *Insider*, says that it is theoretically possible that all the goods and services the world needs could be produced by only 2 percent of the population. Robots and computers are moving into place—*our* place.

New job skills are needed to fit in with the new technology. There are many proposed solutions: Slow down the change; increase the availability of part-time

If I have to keep going to school, all the best jobs are going to be snapped up.

HERMAN by Unger

Copyright 1977
by Universal Press Syndicate

work for those who want it; retrain people as automation takes over. We clearly aren't ready to implement such large-scale changes. The resulting unemployment is frightening to many.

Facts and a sense of history are of little comfort if you are presently unemployed or see a possible layoff in the immediate future. Job hunting in a tight job market with your benefits running out, the mortgage payments due, and applications producing rejections can undermine the strongest ego. Now is the time to become job-wise. Work out a plan of action to avoid sitting at home, reading the want ads, and feeling terrible. First, review both the you-data collected in this book and the job market information in the Job Group Chart and related resources. Second, follow the job-hunting techniques described in the next two chapters: Update your résumé; renew your contacts; and collect letters of recommendation. Third, join or start a support group. Fourth, work out a daily schedule of things to do that include not only the above tasks but other important "business of living" tasks like exercising and visiting friends. Also consider temporary work, part-time work, "just any job," and negotiating to share a job.

As stressful as unemployment is, if you can avoid panic and keep a level eye out for opportunities, you may find them in unlikely places. Take the steps you can take comfortably. Be money-wise and always have a plan for lean times. Consider what you really *need* to survive and look for sources to fund your needs. Have a garage sale and get rid of excess baggage. Plant a garden of basics to save on food bills. Start a small co-op to buy food wholesale. There are many people who could share resources with you. Look at your expanded activity lists from Chapters 1 and 3 and check off things you can do now to earn needed cash.

Bartering creatively can bring astonishing results. One artist bartered stained-glass windows for expensive dental work. One young man with no money or place to stay bartered lawn care at a veterinary clinic to get shots for his much-loved dog, while a neighborhood soup kitchen and some friends saw him through some rough times. Connie Stapleton of Middletown, Maryland, asked a service-station manager if he had any work she could do in exchange for repairs for her car. When that brought a negative response, she asked what he liked least about his job. He said, "Collecting bills!" She now makes collections in exchange for free car care.*

Twenty-five percent of all unemployed people lose their jobs through plant closings, by one Department of Labor estimate. One in four of them never returns to work, according to Dr. Lou Ferman, director of the Institute of Labor and Industrial Relations at the University of Michigan. Some workers are buying out their companies. Some are proposing the manufacture of alternative products:

> As an alternative to closings and spiraling military stockpiles, unions are look-ing at encouraging workers to propose new products and systems. They would use the same skilled labor and machinery. In England, workers at Lucas Aerospace designed over 250 marketable and socially useful products ranging from a kidney machine to a road-rail vehicle for use in Third World countries. The company resoundingly rejected the plan and chose to close the plant. However, the programs there and elsewhere are being studied by U.S. union leaders.[9]

In employee-owned companies, productivity increases along with product reli-ability. More and more companies now have stock option plans for employees.

Even if such large-scale, risky ventures aren't for you, get together with others to share resources: physical necessities, ideas, job leads, and support. Call your local school career center for ideas. If you are unemployed, keep busy with courage.

A layoff can be a liberating experience—if one doesn't grow too hungry—and a good time to reevaluate a career and make changes. Unemployed people have started businesses, often on a shoestring, found rewarding partnerships, created satisfying new careers. Many people have moved from the corporate complex to small-business ownership. From designing gas guzzlers to designing sandwiches in

---

*If you are interested in bartering, you can read Stapleton's book, co-authored with a *Washington Post* columnist, Phyllis C. Richman—*Barter: How to Get Almost Anything Without Money* (New York: Scribner's, 1982).

Courtesy of Mal Hancock

their own delis, from making hardware to making beds in their guest cottages by the sea—many laid-off persons are "so glad they made the change" as a result of unemployment.

People have created "new ways to work," such as job sharing, alternating male/ female roles in child and house care, and "flextime." When people cut down their work involvement, they free up jobs for others. In California, an organization called New Ways to Work, while exploring work issues and providing resources, is helping people present themselves to employers in unique ways. The sponsors feel that "there are just not enough jobs to go around unless the work is shared." Job sharing is a good way for two people to find part-time employment, especially when child care or other commitments preclude full-time work. Not all employers are convinced of the worth of these ideas, however, so their impact on employment statistics is very small. Creative solutions are needed to the worldwide problem of unemployment. In France, a Minister of Leisure Time has been appointed to deal with the underlying causes of problems of unemployment in a technological age.*

*Le Chef Madame de Service, Ministère du Temps Libre, Service de l'Information, 116-118 Avenue du Président Kennedy 75775, Paris, Cedex 16, France.

Global Consciousness

A consideration of facts can help us to see trends and predict some outcomes. But just as we begin to understand the implications of a particular trend, we notice a minitrend, or a countertrend emerges. The population pendulum swings from baby boom to zero population growth and then back to mini–baby boom. We plan for the huge but long for the small. We've seen the sexual revolution, the women's movement, radical changes in lifestyle, increasing rates of divorce, religious movements both away from established religion and toward older, even more established religion. Each of these challenges our deepest values and makes us feel like strangers in a strange land.

We live in a "new world" that seems to get "newer" every day. We are all people in transition. The speed of change is captured by John Peers, who has said that "We live three days a day compared to the 1950s. We do in one day what couldn't be done in a week in 1900, in a lifetime in the 1600s."

In *The Third Wave,* Alvin Toffler helps us to view the current accelerated rate of change from a broad, historical perspective. He speaks of three giant waves. The first wave, slow and long-lasting, brought about the change from a food-gathering, nomadic life to a food-raising, agrarian lifestyle. Some peoples are still making that transition. The second wave, faster and of far shorter duration, about the last three hundred years, has seen farm life yielding to industrial, urban life. Before much of the world was able to industrialize, the third wave began rushing in, bringing with it the information society.[10]

Not everyone is swallowing all the advances in science, technology, and information processing in one gulp, however. There is a growing global consciousness—an awareness that thoughtless, unplanned growth harms the planet and that what happens in Chile or Bangladesh affects us all. Thoughtful women and men are looking at their lives and trying to make wise choices based on concern for people and our planet.

In our affluent, consumer-oriented society, success has tended to mean a job rewarding enough to support a comfortable, suburban lifestyle. But there are alternative ways of defining success. Some people, for example, measure success in terms of their ability to simplify their lives. Some may try to return to nature and reject much of what technology has to offer. Others, more moderate, are like the Amish, who choose to live a nineteenth-century lifestyle, and Thomas W. Foster, writing in the *Futurist,* has said that "Amish society, a relic of the past, could become a model for the future."[11] But many groups are trying to foster the use of appropriate technology that they believe could lead to a better life.

Here are some elements of an ideal lifestyle and sustainable society based on conservation and the wise use of technology. Most products would be recycled. Factories would run on renewable, nonpolluting energy sources. The raw materials and by-products of manufacturing would not damage the environment. Machinery and products would be more durable, simpler, easier to repair, and less expensive to replace. More products would be produced near the consumers, saving fuel and decreasing the cost of transportation.

Things are manufactured for one of two reasons: either because we really need and want them, or because the manufacturer hopes to create a demand for them and make a profit. At the checkout counter of the supermarket, we "vote" on each product and the way it was made, packaged, and distributed. When we buy the product, we vote in favor of each company involved in its production. We endorse the company's ethics and approve its advertising.

With our undiscriminating support, big business is growing even bigger, but not always better. Agribusiness and nonfood conglomerates have been buying up farmland and establishing a worldwide food network that eliminates the small farmer and many of the rural poor, who flock to the cities to find work but often find grinding poverty instead.[12]

The number of Americans living in urban areas has increased steadily throughout the last 150 years. But there is a trend that may indicate a longing for a "Small is beautiful" lifestyle in a healthy world: The 1980 census shows that the number of Americans living in urban areas increased only 0.1 percent in the 1970s, compared to 3.4 percent in the 1960s. More people are moving to rural areas, and fewer are leaving. The U.S. Department of Agriculture reported a 17 percent increase in the number of farms in New England, some carved out of larger farms by part-time farmers.[13] In 1982, to reserve land for small farmers, Nebraska passed a law restricting the sale of farmland to large corporations.

A company in San Jose, California, is importing the British concept of the minicondominium. These 440-square-foot studio apartments are a departure from the American Dream of a house with a two-car garage in the suburbs. Minicondos may be the only homes many people can afford in these days of inflation, recession, and high interest rates. Many people enter into shared ownership and appreciate their escape from the struggle to maintain a home and yard alone.

Add minicars to minihomes, minifarms, minicities, minicomputers, and minibusinesses, all for the minifamily. About 88 percent of all new jobs in America in the last five years were created by companies with 20 or fewer employees.[14] Small companies have the added advantage of being less alienating. These minitrends foretell the future. According to Toffler, everything will come in small, variable parts, "de-massified and diversified," instead of large homogeneous clumps.

Industrialized society required obedience to authority, repetition, and mass production. Information systems require more autonomy, responsibility, commitment, flexibility, and creativity. The social-investigative-artistic personality types will be in demand.

As things become less important to those who have enough, emotional, intellectual, and altruistic wants can surface to a greater degree. There may be more being and less doing, more cooperating and less competing, more communicating and less achieving, more listening and less producing, more sharing and less grabbing. If robots and computers take some of the tedium and danger out of work, we might look forward to a more enriched life on all levels.

If we can "telecommunicate" sometimes instead of commuting to work and school, we will use less energy in transportation and also less personal energy. We need to consider such new ideas that are sometimes dismissed at first as unrealistic and impractical. James Benson of the Council of Economic Priorities, for example, recently estimated that in the Nassau-Suffolk area of Long Island, New York, a low-cost energy package aimed at installing insulation, storm windows, and solar hot water systems could provide 270 percent more employment and 206 percent more energy over a 30-year period than the same amount of money spent to construct and maintain nuclear power plants.[15]

In *The Third Wave,* Toffler notes that as second-wave institutions crash about our heads, we tend to see only decay and breakdown. "Yet social decay is the compost bed of the new civilization. In energy, technology, family structures, culture, and many other fields, we are laying into place the basic structure that will define the main features of that new civilization."[16]

Because of the trends, countertrends, and minitrends, it is important to know what *you* believe in, so that as you begin to choose your future, you can put your energy to work in a job that is consistent with your values and that has a positive impact on the world. But in the meantime, predicting the job market becomes increasingly difficult as these movements occur ever more rapidly. It is awesome to visit automated warehouses, power plants, and other work sites where silent computers initiate, direct, and terminate complex and heavy work. But watch for the countertrend: Increasing costs of automation and high unemployment are causing some employers to delay investing in this technology. Some are hiring low-cost human labor instead.

Nobody can predict the future with absolute certainty. And few people want to acknowledge trends or listen to predictions that seem totally out of harmony with their view of the world. Not many people in the 1950s and 1960s believed that we would ever have an energy shortage. And many people still don't see the connection between pouring a harmful chemical down the drain and the pollution of their own water supply. But major trends have a tremendous impact on the job market and on the quality of our lifestyles.

As you consider a "thought-full" career and lifestyle decision, you can remember that trends are trends because people choose them. Your own life and work will have an effect upon the earth and its people. *You* will be a "futuremaker."

Fast-Growing Jobs for the 1980s and 1990s

Now that we have examined some long-term trends, you realize that job openings in manufacturing and agriculture are decreasing throughout the United States. Many fast-growing jobs can be found in the service industries. After studying trends in employment, the Department of Labor published lists of jobs that are expected to be among the fastest-growing occupations until 1990.[17] Labor market predictions are based on dated statistics and random samples—not on 100 percent of the population—yet they are surprisingly accurate.

Fast-growing does not always mean easy-to-get. The availability of jobs is affected by competition, geographical limitations, educational requirements, and the state of the national economy. Jobs that have a high salary potential and few openings are in demand; and competition for them may be fierce. This category includes positions in advertising, commercial art, fashion merchandising, industrial sales, personnel, and public relations. If you are interested in such work, check the number of jobs available in your area. Local trends may be more important than national trends. Talk to people and consult the state employment office to learn the dynamics of your job market. Figure 5-1 is a listing of fast-growing jobs related to the six personality types—realistic, investigative, artistic, social, enterprising, and conventional. Perhaps you will find a job that you would like in the listing.

Researchers Marvin Cetram and Thomas O'Toole[18] went out on a limb to predict the following fast-growing, strange-sounding new jobs for the 1990s:

Battery technician	Holographic inspection specialist
Bionic-electronic technician	Housing rehabilitation technician
Computer programmer	Industrial laser process technician
Energy technician	Industrial robot production technician
Genetic engineer	Materials utilization
Geriatric social worker	Paramedic
Hazardous waste management technician	

An ad by Champion International Corporation[19] suggests the following even stranger future job titles:

Android physiologist	Laser dentist
Artificial intelligence tester	Microastronomer
Computer psychiatrist	Oceanic/space hotel manager
Cyberg mechanical engineer	Planetary geologist
Deep sea mining engineer	Quarkologist
Epizoothic therapist	Tectonic statistician
Fusion engineer	

According to Alvin Toffler, the "big four" growth areas are electronics, space, oceans, and gene research, application, and technology. Moreover, the energy-producing industries will need more workers worldwide—mining, chemical, and petroleum engineers; metal workers; offshore rig construction workers; synthetic fuel plant construction workers; and biotechnologists. Satellite-based telecommunications and the construction and maintenance of earth stations will be big business. Information technology will bring financial, library, and entertainment data into every home. There will be an increase in small businesses. Money management, sales, and franchising will be important.[20] These trends should mean new jobs for men and women of each personality type.

Figure 5-1 The Fastest Growing Jobs, 1980 to 1990

REALISTIC

Automobile mechanics
Automobile repair service
  estimators
Automotive painters
Bricklayers
Business machine repairers
Cement masons and terrazzo
  workers
Coal mining operatives
Computer service technicians
Construction inspectors
  (government)
Dental laboratory technicians
Dispensing opticians
Drywall installers and finishers
Electrical sign repairers
Food counter workers
Guards/security
Hotel housekeepers and
  assistants
Insulation workers
Janitors
Lithographers
Television and radio service
  technicians
Tilesetters
Truck drivers
Waiter/waitress
Waiter's assistants and kitchen
  helpers

INVESTIGATIVE

Actuaries
*Architects
*Economists
*Engineers:
  Aerospace
  Agricultural
  Biomedical
  Ceramic
  Civil
  Electrical
  Industrial
  Metallurgical
  Mining
  Petroleum
Engineering and science
  technicians

INVESTIGATIVE

Geologists
Geophysicists
Landscape architects
Medical laboratory workers
Podiatrists
*Programmers
Systems analysts
Urban and regional planners
Veterinarians

ARTISTIC

Actors and actresses
Models
Radio and television announcers
  and newscasters
Technical writers

SOCIAL

Child care attendants
Claims representatives
Correction officers
Dental assistants
Dental hygienists
Dietitians
Electro-cardiograph technicians
Electro-encephalographic
  technologists and technicians
Elementary school teachers
Employment interviewers
*Health services administrators
Licensed practical nurses
Medical assistants
Medical records administrators
Nurses' aides/orderlies
Occupational therapists
Occupational therapy assistants
Optometric assistants
Physical therapists
Physical therapists' assistants
Radiologic (x-ray) technologists
Registered nurses
Respiratory therapy workers
Sales clerks
Speech pathologists and
  audiologists
Surgical technicians

ENTERPRISING

Automobile sales workers
Hotel managers
*Lawyers
*Market research analysts
Real estate agents and brokers
*Securities sales workers
Travel agents

CONVENTIONAL

*Accountants and auditors
Bank clerks
*Bank officers and managers
Bank tellers
Bookkeepers
Cashiers
Computer operating personnel
Court reporters
General clerks
Hotel managers' assistants
Legal assistants
Medical records technicians and
  clerks
Receptionists
Secretaries
Tax preparers
Typists

Source: "The Job Outlook in Brief," *Occupational Outlook Quarterly* (Washington, D.C.: U.S. Department of Labor, Bureau of Labor Statistics, Spring 1982), pp. 7–33; Max L. Carey, "Occupational Employment Projections," *Monthly Labor Review* (August 1981), p. 48.

*Jobs that have a high salary potential.

Personality Types in the Job Market

Understanding the relationship between your personality mosaic and job trends can help you make a wise career decision. You've seen that specific jobs can be related to each type of personality. Now, we will consider general characteristics of, and outlook for, jobs that seem to fit each type.

Realistic Type

Jobs for the realistic type generally involve handling things, using body skills, and dealing with the data required. Examples range from various trades and crafts to professional sports. Careers in sports, of course, are extremely competitive and limited to the most talented. Since realistic personalities provide food, clothing, shelter, and transportation, such jobs are basic, necessary, and highly visible. Although automation and imports will increase in some areas, the employment outlook ranges from good to excellent for many jobs in the realistic category, especially for those that are service oriented.

If you belong to this personality group, you might consider indoor or outdoor jobs in industry or with the public utility companies. You may need special vocational training, although on-the-job training is sometimes available. In the building trades, you may be required to join a union as an apprentice. Cutbacks in government spending have limited the number of outdoor jobs available to people who like to work with nature.

Volunteering is a way to get training and work experience in some of these jobs. Sometimes realistic persons build unique and creative careers by cooking, tailoring, or cabinetmaking at home.

Investigative Type

Jobs for the investigative type are high-data jobs and, except for jobs in health care, have little involvement with people. They usually require above-average intelligence and verbal or mathematical skills. Except for the technical area, most jobs require at least a four-year college degree. Most jobs in this area require *thinking about* things, rather than handling things, but they are nevertheless thing-oriented.

Many investigative jobs in the sciences are not directly "productive" because they deal with "pure research." When there are no products or direct services to be sold for profit, funding tends to be less abundant. Engineers and medical researchers are generally well paid, however, because they do research that applies directly to practical problems. Hence more jobs are available in these categories. In fact, there are good job possibilities in all investigative occupations except pure research. Investigative types who are not science or technically oriented will apply their investigative talents to other areas.

Artistic Type

Most jobs for the artistic type require special talent along with special training. They are usually high-data, high-things jobs, with no deep involvement with people. Artistic persons enjoy creating new things but often dislike the mass producing and marketing aspects of earning a living because business pressure often militates against creativity. Many highly creative people also find it hard to work in structured settings doing work for others, such as architecture, advertising, and various other design jobs. Since artistic jobs tend to be highly competitive, the artistic type should plan alternatives. New developments in electronic media will provide opportunities for some creative people.

Social Type

Social-personality careers deal primarily with people and the data necessary to do the job. Workers should be good with people, concerned with people's problems, or at least comfortable providing services. Many people have a strong desire to do socially useful work, such as caring for children or solving problems of the disabled and the elderly.

The need is great, yet many of the jobs in the social services area are government funded and are now scarce because of tax cutbacks. Some government jobs in human services defeat the purpose of helping people: Workers in some settings are drained by large numbers of clients with serious and chronic problems. With little support, few resources, and yards of red tape, the worker needs strong motivation to succeed. People with good business sense and enough funding start private practices.

Health care has been a growing field, but growth is now slowing. In many localities entrance into training programs is limited. Traditional health care also requires thing involvement and tends to be conventional. People with social concerns find that their special talents can be used in a variety of settings, however, because all employers hire people and need to solve employee problems.

Enterprising Type

The enterprising type is usually a person of energy, courage, and confidence who loves the "game" of selling, persuading, risking, and motivating. Enterprising personalities, by their very natures, seem to have the inner drive to "connect" with the people and events that help them get ahead. And there is always a need to organize and sell goods and services in the world of things and data. Purely enterprising types are out there, already involved.

Generally, men have been socialized to strive for success with courage and confidence—whether they like it or not—but women have been socialized for a commitment to people instead of accomplishment. The most effective person for these enterprising jobs achieves a balance between striving to accomplish and being sensitive to people.

Many jobs in this category require both "drive" and "good people skills"—the social and enterprising types combined. Those who have or can develop both traits will usually be successful. These are all high-data jobs requiring intelligence and good verbal skills.

Conventional Type

Conventional-personality careers require steadiness, orderliness, and accuracy in dealing with data. They require tolerance for paperwork and at times involve business contact with people and the use of machines. Workers who favor this orientation rarely seek promotions and additional responsibility. Experience may build their confidence and give them the courage to advance, but generally they do well in a supportive role.

There are many careers that demand the steadiness and order of the conventional personality. Since we have become a nation of data keepers and processors, jobs in this area are abundant, visible, and usually easy to find.

SIAs: The Hard Cases

The realistic, conventional, and enterprising types and combinations of these have the easiest time launching careers: the realistic because their jobs are concrete and visible, the conventional because they tend to follow established patterns, and the enterprising because they are willing to take risks. Generally speaking, the SIA personalities—social, investigative, artistic, or some combination of these—have a harder time choosing and launching a career. People who work with ideas or feelings have no tangible product to show their employers.

But all SIA personalities gravitate toward work in which they can deal with people to solve problems by creating new systems. This need may arise in just about any work setting with any group or type of workers. SIA jobs call for transferable skills, such as analysis and communication. Satisfying jobs in this area are usually on a highly competitive, professional level. A college education is almost a must for the successful SIA personality. The beginner will need some supporting work-specific skills that relate to the workplace. If you are applying to a computer firm, for example, know something about data processing. If you plan to get a four-year liberal arts degree, take electives in such subjects as business, technology, or health. Or obtain a two-year vocational degree at a community college before transferring to a university.

The social and investigative person with conventional rather than creative characteristics enjoys working with people to solve problems by following established guidelines. Guidelines are provided in personnel and labor relations work, probation and law enforcement, health care, and sales. Travel agents and bank clerks are often required to investigate and state rules for customers.

Regardless of your personality type, analyzing your transferable skills in depth and zeroing in on your strengths are important steps in choosing a career. Consider various careers that utilize the same skills and offer similar satisfiers. No one can guarantee you a job after you have invested many years and dollars training for it. How much are you willing to risk? How motivated are you? Have you looked for ways to use your training in alternate choices?

If you need some help in being your own futurist, you will find that the *Occupational Outlook Handbook,* published by the U.S. Department of Labor, is one of the best beginning references to explore trends. Generally available in any library, the handbook provides a good overview of 800 of the most popular careers in the United States. It outlines the nature of the work, average earnings, training requirements, and places to write for further information, along with the projected employment outlook. No matter what the trends, it's always wise to have some alternate choices and to keep your options open.

Brainstorming Alternatives

Choosing a career is no problem, you think. You have decided on *the* career. Ever since high school when Mr. Yesteryears turned you on to the Peloponnesian Wars, you have wanted to be a history teacher, just like him. You could hear your students sighing "Wow, I never knew history could be so great!" Slowly into your fantasy seeps the news that there are hundreds of unemployed history teachers. The bubble bursts.

But wait. All is not lost. Have you considered alternatives? Think over the various elements that make up a career. For example, where in the world are you willing to go to teach history? Germany? Australia? Does Alaska need you? The Peace Corps?

List all the functions of a history teacher (or whatever career you are exploring). Check the functions you think you'd enjoy. Do you like history, or appearing before an audience, or both? What can you do with a history background besides teaching high school or college students?

Consider developing a unique lecture series on a topic of current interest—such as the architectural history of Victorian homes in Dubuque—to present to community groups. Consider tutoring, learning to be a docent, working as a tour guide, working as an historian for a state park department, getting involved in politics.

If you can get along without teaching, consider developing a tour series on tape or by map—for example, a walking tour of Atlanta—writing news articles about historical subjects such as the Indians of the upper Michigan Peninsula, working in a library or book store and specializing in historical books "on the side," or planning historical tours.

Perhaps, after thinking it over again, you will decide that teaching is more important to you than history. Consider teaching other subjects (check school districts for local trends); volunteering in schools, recreation centers, senior citizen centers; working as a teacher aide; teaching small classes at home in cooking, macramé, vegetable gardening, or house plant care; teaching these or other subjects to community groups such as the Parent-Teacher Association or Girl/Boy Scouts.

With a little work some of those activities can be parlayed into a lucrative business, but others cannot. A job must fulfill the needs of other people to such an extent that they will part with money to fulfill those needs. For people who would like to teach and earn a more secure living, an often overlooked area is industry. Larger industries, especially, have training programs/orientations for new employees and in-service training for continuing employees. Someone must be "teacher" in these industrial settings.

THE FIRST THING
to do in life is to do
with purpose
what one proposes to do.
PABLO CASALS

Working in marketing and sales, public relations, or personnel, including such areas as job development or affirmative action, can involve you in many situations similar to teaching: giving site tours, helping people find employment, and working with other people problems that arise.

Go back to the Data, People, Things Indicator and the Job Group Chart and consider the factors that are important to you. Consider related jobs again and *brainstorm, brainstorm,* with friends, relatives, neighbors, acquaintances, strangers, anyone who will give you five minutes of their time and a dip into their experience pool. For just about any career that you can choose, there are alternatives that give you most of what you would enjoy from a job.

If you still want more than anything to be a history teacher, if your motivation for that one career is unusually high, don't be afraid to face the competition. Develop some unique skills by getting involved in some of the above alternatives to get super-good at history and teaching. Keep open to alternatives, but keep to your chosen goals.

Here are some other ideas to give you a start in your career:

■ Volunteer experience can be extremely valuable in skill development. It wouldn't do to stay in the back room and lick stamps, however, unless licking stamps is your goal. Pinpoint the skills you would like to develop. When you volunteer, ask for experience doing these things: public relations, fund raising, supervising people, organizing materials, activities, and such. Be specific.

- Be sure to review your volunteer experience for skills you've already developed: writing good letters, directing membership drives, and so on. Be very specific about your accomplishments.

- Don't overlook entry-level or support-service job skills, such as typing and cashiering, to gain access to businesses of interest to you. You can often then work into jobs closer to your interest field in places from art galleries to auto shops by beginning "at the bottom."

- Take skill courses that can help you gain access to jobs. For example, most banks train tellers on the job but might prefer to hire someone with training in accounting or computers.

- Use your main career interest as a hobby while you work at something else to support yourself. Who knows where it will lead? Walter Chandoha pursued a business degree while maintaining an interest in photographing cats. He has been a professional animal photographer for more than ten years now and is doing better than he ever dreamed.[21] Maybe his business background has been a help!

- Investigate training programs in various industries and government agencies.

- Consider earning extra money, perhaps at home, through cooking, hobbies, and crafts or teaching them. For example, think about:

Catering, special food services	Aprons
Cake decorating	Embroidering shirts, jeans
Picture framing	Sewing alterations
Dried flower arrangements	Knitting
Sculpture	Crocheting
Shadow boxes	Painting
Macramé	Furniture re-finishing
Weaving	Stained glass
Hand puppets and dolls	Decoupage
Doll clothes and jewelry	Pet care

- Consider teaching recreation skills:

Dancing	Riding
Yoga	Swimming
Music	Bridge
Exercise	Tennis
Skiing	Golf
Massage	

Advertise your skills and classes through friends, supermarket bulletin boards, local community groups. Donate samples and demonstrations.

Here are some careers to do at home:

Typing, perhaps in a medical, technical, scientific, or legal specialty
Word processing
Bookkeeping
Computer programming
Translating
Telephone wake-up service
Singing messages
Designing:
    Stationery
    Business cards
    Party favors
    What else?
Recycling:
    Clothes
    Furniture
    Household appliances
Income tax service
Tool/gadget repair and maintenance

Consider direct selling for companies such as Avon, Tupperware, Cutco, and others of good reputation. Write for member list and information. Enclose a long, stamped, self-addressed envelope to: Direct Selling Association, Suite 610, 1730 M St. N.W., Washington, DC 20046. Write for free *Tips on Work at Home Schemes* and *Tips on Mail Order Profit Mirages* from the Council of Better Business Bureaus, Inc., 1150 17th St. N.W., Washington, DC 20036. Request *Small Business Bibliography No. 3, Selling by Mail Order,* and *Free Management Assistance Publications* from the U.S. Small Business Administration, P.O. Box 15434, Fort Worth, TX 76119, or pick up copies at any local field office. Ask advice from friends who have sold such items as cosmetics or cleaning products.

Consider temporary employment. One of the local agencies can provide a way to survey businesses, make contacts, make money on your own schedule.

Keep your options open. The narrower your "satisfaction band," the less likely you are to achieve satisfaction. In other words, the more options the better.

When you have done everything you can but end up with a job you don't care for, you still have some choices:

- Watch for opportunities within the business
- Re-train at night or get further training
- Create your own career within a career—some people have found exciting things to do in apparently the dullest and most stifling of situations.

Some people create so much joy within themselves—despite facts, trends, and predictions—that they are happy anywhere. Perhaps that joy, after all, is the key to success.

Self-Assessment Exercise

Predicting Your Future

1. Does future shock affect you? If so, how?

   _____

   _____

   _____

2. Will your career probably be in manufacturing, service, or information? _____

3. Describe the general job prospects for your personality types.

   _____

   _____

   _____

4. What does the *Occupational Handbook* (or other job outlook reference) say about the jobs you are considering?

   _____

   _____

   _____

5. If you find that few job openings are predicted for your career area, what will you do?

   _____

   _____

   _____

6. What effect would a college degree have on your job prospects? On salary? Job satisfaction?

_____

_____

_____

7. List your tentative job choice and several alternatives.

_____

_____

_____

8. How will the work you choose to do affect trends in society?

_____

_____

_____

9. How will your lifestyle affect trends in society?

_____

_____

_____

10. What positive contribution will your career make to society?

_____

_____

_____

1. Name ten specific changes happening around you as a result of the five major trends.
2. How have these trends affected the world during your lifetime?
3. Which problems resulting from these trends concern you the most?
4. How can your career contribute to the solution for these problems?
5. What does John Peers mean when he says, "We live three days in one compared to the 1950s. We do in one day what couldn't be done in a week in 1900, a lifetime in the 1600s"? Give examples.
6. Give present-day examples of first-, second-, and third-wave jobs.
7. Can we afford to let all our manufacturing go overseas? To become totally an information and service society?
8. Is training everyone for the high-tech/information society desirable in the long run? If not, what are the alternatives?
9. If you could repair or build things by directing distant robots from your living room, what kinds of goods or services would you like to provide?
10. In what ways do technology and modern life conflict with biology?
11. If we could provide goods and services through automated electronic systems, might cities and their business activities become obsolete? Describe how.
12. How would you cope with a reduced work week and a slightly diminished paycheck?
13. What contribution does each personality type make in the job market?
14. Fantasize a third-wave world in 2025 in which all robot-made products are durable and beautiful. People purchase only goods and services that enrich their lives. Many people provide some basic needs for themselves. Many work at home via microchip devices. How would the world be different? Would there be more unemployment or could everyone find work? What kind of work? How could people use their leisure time? What resources would be conserved? How would you feel about that world?
15. Can you choose your future? How? Describe it.

Six

Workplaces and Work Styles:

Scanning the Subtleties

eciding on a career is a big step. But even with a job title in mind, you still need to decide on the type of place where you can do what you enjoy. You have many choices, but you may be surprised to learn that there are only seven categories of workplaces: business, industry, education, communication/entertainment, health, government, and military. If you're still unable to choose a job title, just being able to pick one of these seven is a huge step in narrowing down your choices. Let's look at each of these broad categories.

Business includes every desk from an executive suite to a tiny space in the back of an auto repair shop. Business is not limited to office buildings: It occurs wherever two or more people get together to trade goods or services. Its workers range from the retail clerks in your neighborhood record shop to the shipping tycoon who has private offices around the world, from one person working at home to a complex international organization. Labor relations, personnel, contract negotiations, consulting, accounting, marketing, and hundreds of other functions make up the work of the business world and its many support systems.

The enterprising and conventional types are most at home in business, but all types can find expression here: the social personality in dealing with people and their problems, the artistic person in advertising or creating new designs, the realistic in managing products and production, and the investigative in research and problem-solving. Choosing business, then, will narrow down your choices yet leave the door open to a variety of careers.

To facilitate the flow of goods and services, business involves data: writing it, reading it, typing it, data/word processing it, and filing it. General clerical skills will enable you to enter the field of business in positions such as filing or shipping clerk. When you feel the need for more training, you can attend workshops and seminars or take college work at the A.A. or B.A. level. Or you might go directly to college

153

to earn a B.A. in business, in a field such as accounting or marketing. Even with a B.A. degree, however, most people must start near the bottom of the ladder and work up—unless there is a serious shortage of personnel.

Industry can be defined loosely as a concern with products, not with people or paper (if you exclude the "business end" of industry). Repairing cars, flying planes, pouring concrete, and raising wheat are industries in this sense. Even the artist making clay pots at home is involved in industry. Working with machines and tools and tangible materials attracts the realistic person to industries of all kinds.

Education offers many careers besides teaching in schools and colleges. Computer companies hire specialists to develop learning programs, while business and industry carry on employee training programs of all sorts. People who teach cooking or crafts at home or at community centers are also part of education.

The enterprising and social personalities enjoy the task-oriented interaction of teaching, leading, and motivating others. Realistic personalities enjoy teaching such subjects as physical education and shop, while the artistic types drift toward humanities and fine arts, crafts, and design classes. Investigative interests are needed for scholarship and research, while conventional personalities do well in teaching "the basics." In fact, all personality types can be found in education—it helps to be a "jack of all trades" when teaching.

The communication/entertainment workplace ranges from circus tents to TV studios, but opportunities tend to be more limited than those in any other area because this field is highly competitive. In order to succeed here, you need exceptional ability, great quantities of luck, and lots of courage. Artistic personalities are naturally attracted to communication and entertainment but may be unsuccessful unless they possess some of the qualities of the enterprising type (or possibly a good agent). But with the incredible rise of the information society, opportunities will open up for the technically talented, word wise, or number nimble.

Health suggests a hospital or doctor's office, but in fact health care workers find employment also in business, industry, schools, and military settings. The investigative person with a good social orientation will enjoy the challenge of helping people solve their health care problems. This area expands rapidly when specialization trends and technological advances continue but slows when recession and unemployment pinch health care budgets. Several hundred job titles are involved in the delivery of health care.

Government employs people of all types in every setting from agricultural stations to hospitals. One must usually pass a test to become employed at the federal level (and often at state and county levels, too). The test may combine an oral interview and a written examination with points added for years of education, military service, and past work experience. Any type of personality can find satisfiers in one of the great variety of government jobs. Your state employment office has information about these civil service jobs.

Traditionally, a government job implied security but low pay. In recent years the pay has increased, along with the number of jobs. But now the taxpayers' mood prevails. Low pay and insecurity have entered the picture for many employees of the government.

Military operations and procedures appeal most readily to realistic and conventional personalities, but here again, people of all types can find opportunities of many varieties, from cooking to hospital laboratory work to sophisticated industrial research and design. For those so inclined, the military provides a good living with training in a variety of skills.

And finally, some people conclude that no job in existence will give them enough of their satisfiers. They decide to create their own careers to serve an unmet need in society. You may be one of these creative folk.

Which of these categories seems to fit you? Choosing a workplace focuses your career exploration and can even get you started on a basic college curriculum or training program.

Wanted: Rewards on All Levels

Workplaces provide pay and benefits, which supply basic needs and some of the wants on your agenda. But work also brings intangible rewards on many levels. Self-esteem, prestige, caring relationships, and opportunities to actualize one's unique potential are powerful motivators that draw people into the work world.

You will find that workplaces have personalities just as people do. Some are austere, rigid, demanding; others are lavish, casual, and easygoing. They reflect various combinations of the six personality types and tend to attract people who enjoy being together. Before you choose a workplace that matches your unique need/want/value/personality combination, consider these areas of reward: possibility of climbing the career ladder, fringe benefits, and some emotionally subtle satisfiers, including a supportive atmosphere, autonomy, and compatible values.

The Career Ladder

You may find it rewarding to match your satisfiers with one of the levels in the career ladder in Figure 6-1. The chart identifies four levels that can be found in many institutional work settings. In some settings, such as the military, the structure is rigid. In others, the levels are less formal and less evident.

All workplaces, no matter what size—a lawyer's office, a large catering service, a hospital, or an international manufacturing corporation—have similar structures. A small staff might consist of the boss, who has many management functions, and one assistant who does the rest. Some places "contract out" certain jobs like data processing, accounting, income tax, and maintenance service. As more workers are added to the staff, specialization usually increases.

The fewer the workers, the more likely each worker will have more interesting

Figure 6-1 The Career Ladder

Position	Responsibility	Education	Support staff
Top level			
Top management and professionals, such as Presidents Board members Doctors Lawyers	The decision-makers, who are responsible for nearly everything. There is more independence at this level.	Ph.D., D.D., M.D., M.B.A., etc. Technical and professional expertise	Operates at all levels to provide auxiliary services such as Personnel Finance Communications/ Graphics Legal counsel Research Purchasing Marketing Data Processing Secretarial/Clerical Maintenance
Middle level			
Middle management and professionals, such as Department heads Engineers Nurses Teachers Product managers	Shares responsibility with the top level and enjoys some independence.	M.A., M.B.A., M.S., B.S., B.A., etc. Middle-level expertise	
Lower level			
Lower management and technicians, such as Supervisors Lead persons Legal assistants LVNs	Responsible for a small part of decision-making. May supervise others.	A.A., A.S., vocational, or on-the-job training	
The workers			
Basic production and service work, such as Trades, crafts Assemblers Machinists Waiters/waitresses	Responsible for a particular function. Entry level jobs, often repetitive work.	High school, apprenticeship Usually *some* training or experience is needed.	

and varied work with more responsibility. A medical assistant in a doctor's office may do billing, typing, a little family counseling, public relations, tax work, and research and never know what each day will bring. In a larger place, entry-level workers can expect to do a more limiting job, whether it is putting lettuce leaves on a thousand sandwiches, or soldering a link in a thousand electronic circuits, or word processing a thousand letters.

So size and complexity of the workplace can be a very important factor in job choice. In a larger place a specific position may be subject to more limitations; however, possibilities for change, including moving both over and up, are greater. In a smaller place work may be more varied and responsibility greater, but options are narrowed. Generally, the higher you climb on the career ladder, the higher your salary. Usually education and training increase as the level of involvement increases. But we have all heard of the self-made man (and now the self-made woman). Where do you fit in this scheme of things? How far up the ladder do you wish to be? (It is lonely at the top but exciting and challenging. And not everyone can get there. It is comfy at the bottom but often not so rich or interesting!) If you know where you want to be a few years from now, you will not limit yourself by neglecting present opportunities or choosing dead-end jobs.

Don't Overlook Benefits

Benefits are not just a minor attraction. They may represent a considerable though hidden part of your pay. Health care, for example, can include dental and vision care in addition to hospital care. Ten paid holidays and three weeks vacation with pay, use of a company car, expense accounts, education subsidies, and even use of vacation resorts are just a few of the benefits offered by some companies.

If a company is very sensitive to personal needs, its managers may include fringe benefits that help with the ever more complex "business of living." This term refers to the endless, and absolutely necessary, tasks each person must perform in regard to: (1) financial matters, such as banking, taxes, insurance, real estate, and other investments: (2) medical/dental care; (3) personal care, including food, clothing, and shelter; (4) child care in all of these categories; and (5) education—"keeping up with your field." Concern about such problems drains energy, awareness, and creativity.

Some large corporations have begun to hire people to assist workers with these problems. For instance, some places have doctors or nurses for short-term consultation, financial services such as credit unions, courses for work improvement, and even increased recreational activities and dry cleaning pick-up and delivery.

The Emotional Contract

Most workers want to feel that they are valued not only for the work they do, but also for themselves as persons. When you are hired in a workplace, you agree to an unspoken, unwritten "emotional contract" that is almost as real as a legal document. It pertains to the way you will be cared about and respected, how personally supportive the atmosphere is, how fairly you will be treated. It's the kind of thing you pick up from people who work there, from the environment, suggesting that emotional rewards will be forthcoming. Your work life will be more satisfying if you choose an environment with just enough support for you. On the other hand, some people have exaggerated expectations about the place of work and co-workers in their emotional lives.

Sometimes the interpersonal characteristics of a job can change. One newly divorced mother enjoyed working in a small savings and loan office. An older woman gave her much understanding; the boss was great, and the younger workers a delight. But the boss, who had decided to work harder at "moving up," began to be more restrictive, even to the point of pressuring workers to stay overtime without pay. The older woman was being "phased out" as the company had decided to hire a "security guard/teller." The work atmosphere of the job changed from fun to funk. (The latest word from this office is that it's back to fun again: The now experienced working mother has become the manager.)

No matter how carefully you plan your career, at some time you are likely to have a job that does not supply all of your needs and wants. Cultivating a reasonable amount of independence and a moderately thick skin can protect one against the ups and downs of the work world. At the same time, be aware of your particular needs and aim for a match.

Autonomy Dimensions: Who's Boss?

An emotionally supportive environment usually leads to an attitude of responsibility and trust between employer and employee, which allows the worker a certain amount of autonomy. People appreciate having some say in what happens to their souls and bodies during the work day. Alienation is less prevalent when people feel involved in decision-making. Some autonomy can do a lot to ease systems pained at all levels, global to personal. Employees can make the really major decisions, like who will go to lunch when, who can have the most computer time, and how many times a day you can use the copier. These are the decisions that affect personnel personally, where it hurts, in the every day.

The *minor* decisions include whether to expand company operations into Pakistan, invest a million in a new widget/gidget, or buy a shipping line. The majority of workers will be touched by these types of decisions only in that less sensitive spot called "the long run," which is not today. What directly affects *me now* has a high-level priority.

Erving Goffman wrote in *Asylums* that just by reason of sheer numbers, institutions tend to become dehumanizing.[1] But large size doesn't always connote depersonalization. Within many a large organization, one can discover small, cohesive, caring groups of people looking out for each other's interests. This kind of support would not be found even in a small place if it is run by a tyrannical leader.

Barbara Garson studied three workplaces in New York. She reported that Fair Plan Insurance Company and Reader's Digest showed extremely restrictive policies for workers: no talking to other employees while working, no personal phone calls about family emergencies, and other rigid rules. In contrast, the report described the accounting office of a community college where five older women worked very hard to complete their tasks but managed to fit in noon parties, trips to the hospital to visit sick family members, and other personal ventures. No want ad or job description will ever deal with these "fringe benefits."[2]

Since the number of workers with college degrees is increasing, and since they are often underemployed, they are likely to challenge old-style management techniques. When their survival needs are fulfilled, they focus on the emotional need for self-esteem, prestige, and recognition as well as the intellectual need to use their minds creatively. And often, altruistically, they are more aware of the needs of people and planet.

Much management training today concerns the creation and use of decision-making teams. More worker involvement increases productivity, especially when supported by profit and benefit sharing. Communications skills are the key to effectiveness in today's management. The openness required to encourage trust requires constant encouragement and much sensitivity to human needs. This approach involves risk but the majority of people (even small children) act responsibly when given a chance. The momentum is in this direction. Only a prolonged economic depression or other disaster will change it.

The alternative, an arbitrary use of power, can stifle growth and initiative and defeat the ultimate goals of the workplace. But workplaces tend to be conservative. "Work is hard work" and is a serious enterprise mainly geared to profit and/or public service. Shared decision-making means we have to *think, adapt, relate, create,* which takes *time* . . . and *time* is *money.* What is more, some workers would like to keep the status quo and not get too involved. Joe Rodriquez, age 36, a ten-year Ford employee took part in an experiment at Saab Engine Plant in Sweden designed to maximize worker involvement in decision-making. Said Joe, "If I've got to bust my ass to be meaningful, forget it. I'd rather be monotonous."[3] Thus, tension arises between employers' needs to get on with it and their dependence on worker goodwill to get the job done. It will probably always be so. There is need for the right balance. But the human potential is there waiting to be tapped by creative, positive leadership in cooperation with workers. It's a lofty goal, perhaps, but one worth aiming for.

Flexible Time Experiments

One important facet of autonomy is flextime. Most people need *some* structure in their lives, even though they might like to think of themselves as free spirits. Work is the basic organizing principle for most people. But for the past 40 years, the nine to five, 40-hour work week has been virtually set in solid concrete. Now that tradition is slowly changing.

Some experimentation with new work schedules is taking place. Flextime, for example, allows workers to work for any eight hours between specified times, such as 7 A.M. to 6 P.M. Absenteeism drops and productivity rises. People can take care of "the business of life" in their off-hours when others are still at work to serve them. Those whose biorhythms make them either early or late risers are accommodated. Four ten-hour days per week is a variation on flextime that has yielded similar good results. Some companies are even experimenting with three twelve-hour shifts, enabling college students to work three week-end nights and still attend classes.

Job sharing enables people to choose shorter work hours while getting the job done with a partner. Some companies allow people to work at home on their own time. While such flexibility may add to the work and cost of management, research shows that absenteeism drops and productivity rises.

How important are these things for you? Single parents, especially, carry burdens that demand attention not always amenable to an nine to five schedule. One woman engineer noticed several male colleagues consulting on what she assumed was their project. On closer inspection, she found these newly divorced males discussing the merits of the crockpot for the working parent.

Not everyone could slow down and enjoy leisure even if more were available. For some, work is life. Instead of getting in touch with other facets of their personalities, the total technologist eschews social gatherings; the confirmed clerk avoids art. In the extreme, a highly successful person could be leading a life impoverished on many levels.

And yet many more people could be employed if some people worked fewer that 40 hours per week, 50 weeks per year. The loss of income might be offset in many ways (even financially): saving energy and resources, enjoying a more enriched life, having more time for the business of living.

Today one out of six Americans works part-time regularly and by choice. Over 2 million part-timers are professionals, managers, and administrators.[4] In 1981 a Louis Harris survey of American Families found 28 percent of all working men and 41 percent of all working women perferring part-time work over full-time or volunteer work or work at home. Percentages were highest in the over-55 age group.[5]

Corporate Values

You will invest time and energy getting started on just the right job. What would you do if you found your employer was involved in some illegal, unethical, or immoral actions that clash head-on with your value system? And suppose you further found that you were expected to participate either actively or by keeping quiet.

Such dilemmas can usually be avoided by doing a little research ahead of time. Investors are pulling their money out of companies that make faulty products, pollute, treat employees poorly, or practice fraud. A "social screen" has been developed by the U.S. Trust Company of Boston for use in advising concerned investors. They gather information from a number of sources: annual reports, Securities and Exchange Commission reports, findings of the Investor Responsibility Research Center, the National Labor Relations Board, the Council on Economic Priorities, Inform, and the Interfaith Center on Corporate Responsibility, among

"Night work! You mean when it's dark?"

HERMAN by Unger
Copyright 1977
by Universal Press Syndicate

others. They use the following questions to test and grade the social performance of corporations or other issuers of securities:

- Do they produce and market safe, pure products?
- Do they produce in ways that respect and preserve the natural environment?
- Do they provide a safe, healthy work environment?
- Do they provide equal employment opportunities for women and minorities?
- Do they have fair labor practices and allow the participation of workers in management?
- Do they operate nuclear power plants or provide products for those plants?
- Do they operate under and depend upon a repressive government—in particular, South Africa?
- Do they depend upon military weapons contracts?
- Are they willing to disclose information that gives us answers to all of the above questions?

As a concerned potential employee, ask around about the integrity of a company. The question "Can a company do well when doing good?" (be both ethical and profitable) has been answered with a resounding "yes." It's important to find a company whose values match yours.[6]

Alternatives to Nine-to-Five

As we watch the frantic activity in the work world we've created, a disturbing question arises. What is happening to the individual in the workplace? Many work situations prove far from ideal.

First, subtle changes have separated us from natural things. We drive and park along heavily concreted wastelands. Many people work in buildings without windows, far from sunlight and breezes.

We work on schedules that don't accord with our natural rhythms. We are continually caught in a time bind in an increasingly complex world of ever longer commutes, more complicated personal business transactions, more involved main-

Listen, if you want to eat in the office, BRING SANDWICHES!

HERMAN by Unger

tenance of homes and gadgets. Most people work on a rigid schedule with little leeway for personal needs.

Many people are convinced that such stress even causes death. In the book *Type A Behavior and Your Heart,* Friedman and Rosenman deal with behavior characteristics of the heart-attack-prone individual. We see a profile of the striving American doing six things at once and all the while fearing failure.[7]

Our biology tries to catch up with our technology. We have much evolving to do to learn to blend with technology without losing our identities. Yet it would hardly be feasible to give it all up. We need technology. How about "biorhythmic technology"—moderated and more humane?

Second, work takes time. It can occupy a large part of a day, a week, a year, a lifetime. For many people the forty-hour week and the fifty-week year are the center of life. Flexibility for many is nonexistent and leisure, hard won. But John

Kenneth Galbraith says, "Only if an individual has a choice as to the length of his working week or year, along with the option of taking unpaid leave for longer periods, does he or she have an effective choice between income and leisure."[8]

Many people feel that work uses too much prime time. Work plus family demands and the "business of living" leave one with little time for other enriched choices. Studs Terkel quotes a steelworker who says, " If I had a twenty-hour work-week, I'd get to know my kids better, my wife better. Some kid invited me to go on a college campus. On a Saturday. It was summertime. Hell, if I have a choice of taking my wife and kids to a picnic or going to a college campus, it's gonna be the picnic. But if I worked a twenty-hour week, I could do both. Don't you think with that extra twenty hours people could really expand?"[9]

Many workplaces creak with rigidity. For example, most employers are fearful of letting people leave work early when they are caught up. To avoid such struggles, the 40-hour week has become sacrosanct and is further regulated by professional and union rules about who does what when. Thus, it is reported that the workers in a little state office in one small midwestern town, when they occasionally finish all assigned work at 4 or 4:30, don hats and coats and sit in their darkened office until 5 o'clock. Probably they use the time to worry about children at home alone and what to have for supper.

A secretary at one of the world's largest corporations sits at her desk at 11:30 A.M. facing a day with little or no work because of a slowdown. Asked if she is permitted to go home early in such a case, she is horrified. "Never, in a company like this!" With a spectacular view of San Francisco, its bay, ocean, and bridges all around, she sits surrounded by little portable walls, seeing nothing, doing nothing. To knit or read a good book—even a book on how to be a better secretary— would violate a taboo. What a strain to fear being seen without work lest one's job disappear!

In order to relieve worker boredom, management psychologists have tried to diversify tasks, but such measures have limited value when the tasks themselves remain repetitive and dull. Psychologists have also attempted to give workers more autonomy by including them in the decision-making process. Robert Schrank, a Ford Foundation work specialist, believes that such attempts are likely to be fruitless. Schrank, who has worked on an assembly line himself, points out that every detail is predetermined in a modern production line. The workers cannot introduce variations.

Schrank suggests that workers, especially blue-collar people, be allowed time to socialize on the job, if they can still complete their work on time. He uses the word "schmooze" to describe the amenities that professional and white-collar workers enjoy: time to make a phone call, talk with co-workers, take some extra time off at lunch. "Schmooze time" would relieve some of the boredom inherent in many production jobs. Schrank believes these minor privileges would be more rewarding to the worker than diversified tasks or other current attempts at motivation.[10]

The late Hal Boyle of Associated Press estimated that most people who spend eight hours in their offices could get their required work done in two hours.[11] And Tony Shively (pen name, Thorne Lee), writer and philosopher, says, "The average person is only capable of four productive hours of work a day. The rest is spent filling time. Society often demands more of a man's nature than he can give." In a walk through many workplaces, one can observe people finished with their four essential hours. One of James Michener's characters advises a young man in *The Fires of Spring,* "A lot of nonsense is spoken about work. Some of the finest men I've known were the laziest. Never work because it's expected of you. Find out how much work you must do to live and be happy. Don't do any more."[12]

Some people long to find alternatives to the nine-to-five corporate world and end up creating a variety of new work styles: full-time and part-time entrepreneurs, intrapreneurs, worksteaders, and prosumers involved in creative careers.

Self-Employment

Have you considered creating your own work environment by starting your own business either at home or outside? What services does your locale need that you might provide? A unique system to find out has been designed by the Council for Northeast Economic Action in conjunction with the First National Bank of Boston. Dr. Judy Appelt, a geographer with the project, can tell if a certain type of business will succeed. We have had few such ways of making good predictions for the beginning entrepreneur.

The person with a product or service to offer and the energy to "do it all" can find great satisfaction in being an entrepreneur. Molly Bauer who owns Communi-Speak, a firm that teaches people to speak more effectively, attributes a large measure of her success to having a good business advisor. Jessica McClintock, designer/owner of Gunne Saxe Fashions, cautions, "Hire a helper only when you're ready to drop." There is no question that beginning a business can be hazardous to your health on many levels. But from the farmer in a communist country marketing vegetables on the side to the weekend do-it-yourselfer remodeling the American kitchen, self-interest is a powerful motivator in getting work done.

But rather than investing a fortune, you can start small by investing in a simple business card at $3/hundred.* Then begin handing them out to friends and relatives, charging little or nothing for your services. Despite all our media efforts, the best advertisement is word-of-mouth by satisfied customers. Be sure to check local zoning and licensing laws before business starts booming or if you intend to use dangerous materials. Learn business before starting a business!

Worksteads

People who do work at home—typing, translating, editing, and now data entry— are "worksteaders." Either working for a company or on one's own, it is now

---

*A catalog is available from Walter Drake and Sons, Inc., 94 Drake Bldg., Colorado Springs, CO 80901.

SMALL BUSINESS RESOURCES

American Women's Economic Development Corporation
The Lincoln Building
60 East 42nd Street
New York, NY 10165

In Business—For the Independent, Innovative Individual
Box 323
18 S. Seventh Street
Emmaus, PA 18049 $14

Journal of Small Business Management
International Council for Small Business and Bureau of Business Research
West Virginia University
Morgantown, WV 26506

National Association of Women Business Owners
500 N. Michigan Avenue
Chicago, IL 60611

U.S. Small Business Administration
P.O. Box 15434
Fort Worth, TX 76119

possible to do much of our work at home by computer. Telecommunications can bring people within sight and sound of each other though they are hundreds of miles apart. One production plant was kept running all week-end even though the human in charge was ten miles away. Equipment thousands of miles away in outer space can be operated and repaired from the earth by remote control. The Japanese have an experimental farm run by computerized robots. Who knows what goods and services will be produced from the "electronic cottage" of the future? Here's what some "worksteaders" say:[13]

There are a whole bunch of soft industries that are information oriented or technologies that have no pollution whatsoever. . . . These kinds of industries could be right in our neighborhoods. . . . I've always lived where I work.
—Peter Ziegler, Earth Lab Institute

If a person is going to leave a job to work at home, he needs a very clear attitude about how he is going to live. I set up a rather modest goal of the kind of security I wanted to have before I left the law firm. I don't buy expensive clothes, for instance. I enjoy cooking so I don't go to restaurants much. If you have a place to live, where you can also work, you can get along on very little. The rest of life doesn't really take too much money if you have a place to be.—George Hellyer, Attorney

The Intrapreneur

An intermediate step between the cold, cruel corporation and the cold, cruel world on one's own is the "intrapreneur." *Intrapreneur* is a term coined by Gifford Pinchot III, a consultant to such companies as Exxon. It means contracting one's services to a company as a company employee. It takes little if any capital and involves less risk than entrepreneurship. Even a small work section within a company could do this. A typing pool could set up its own pace and system in return for a lump sum payment.[14] Look around your workplace for a possible intrapreneurial opportunity.

Third Wave Prosumers

. When a truck driver with a college degree was asked what he intended to do with his education, he replied, "I will practice living. I will develop my intellect, which may incidentally contribute to the elevation of the esthetic and cultural levels of society. I will try to develop the noble and creative elements within me. I will contribute very little to the grossness of the national product."[15]

Some prefer not to contribute to an economy that they feel encourages mindless consumption of goods, wastes energy and resources, and contributes to a poor quality of life. These nonconformists, called "prosumers" by Alvin Toffler, are riding in on the Third Wave. Do-it-yourself and self-help tasks, bartering, and sharing are all parts of their diversified lifestyle.[16] The psychologist, who helps people grow at the office, may come home to a small farm and grow vegetables for self and for sale. A veterinarian's varied work schedule includes part-time work spaying dogs and cats at an animal shelter, along with researching, writing, and private consulting. He and his artist wife grow many of their own vegetables and repair their own car. Richard and Susan Pitcairn are Third Wave Prosumers. Their book *Natural Health for Dogs and Cats* reflects their caring lifestyle.[17]

Prosumers Pat and Bill Cane live a largely self-sufficient lifestyle, raising goats and making French cheese. Chickens and a bountiful garden supply food for table and barter. A monthly nine-course gourmet meal for a group of friends provides their basic expenses. While Pat barters beautiful stained glass for a variety of goods and services, Bill writes. In *Through Crisis to Freedom,* a book about life transitions, he says, "In crisis, you are somehow enabled to get in touch with sources of life deep inside yourself—sources you never knew were there. And then mysteriously, like the blades of grass, you begin to know how to grow."[18] These new, "old" lifestyles aren't for everyone, but are options in a nine-to-five world for those willing to take the risk. Many people lived this way years ago. In the technological future, we may be able to do less work and enjoy more of life's good things.

Most people, especially males, begin work after graduating from high school or college and keep at it until age 65. Even the most exciting of career fields can pall after many years. Steps must often be taken to keep up one's motivation. Going back to school, looking for promotions, changing positions or companies, looking for a unique approach to one's job, finding enriching hobbies, fostering personal growth on all levels, all help to keep up one's energy. Some industries have experimented with leaves of absence for social action projects and part-time or full-time educational leaves, either paid or unpaid.

For some people the opportunity to work after age 65 is most welcome. To others retirement (as early as possible) means liberation to do other things. We are just barely beginning to consider the possibility of integrating work and leisure. Some husbands are taking time off while wives work; some people are "easing into retirement" with reduced schedules. Total involvement in work, then, may not be essential in an affluent, information society.

Most workers have experienced the two extremes—either total work or no work—instead of a balance of the two. But in 1969 we passed the era of full employment based on a forty-hour week. Now we need creative schemes that will enable education, business, industry, and government to train more workers for fewer hours of work per week. The cost will be great, but the benefits might be even greater. In a work-oriented society, where the unemployed feel inadequate, crime and mental illness increase when the unemployment rate is high. The quality of life is diminished. Taxes must be increased to pay for welfare and related problems, including law enforcement and health care. With productivity sagging nationally and unemployment plaguing us, creative life/workstyle options are fast becoming a necessity.

Creative Careers

As you interview people and observe them on their jobs, look for those who have taken an ordinary job and brought it to life in a creative way, sometimes within a very structured bureaucracy. "Store manager" with its attendant duties may sound formidable or dull. But Monique Benoit of San Francisco, well known for her community involvement, loved to shop in expensive antique shops and boutiques. She also cherished her independence and loved to travel. She managed to satisfy a number of divergent needs by creating her own job. She carefully composed a letter and sent it to managers of her favorite stores. She offered to "shop sit" if they had to be away from the store for business or personal reasons. She received a good response and subsequent offers of part-time employment.

"Susie Skates" indulges in her favorite sport while delivering messages. "Flying Fur" delivers pampered pets around the country, while "Sherlock Bones" searches for missing pets. From Rent-a-Yenta, Clutter Cutter, and Rent-a-Goat, to Mama's Llama's, Rent-a-Thief, and Sweet Revenge, people create careers with imagination instead of capital.

Here are a few other creative, though not always lucrative careers: house sitting, shop sitting, pet sitting, providing travel/transportation companions, creative child sitting that includes instruction in a craft or hobby, shopping for the elderly, transportation for the elderly and disabled, photography at special events, house calls on sick plants, giant cookies, tasty diet candy, exercise groups for the elderly, masquerading servants at parties, teaching do-it-yourself auto repair. People are making money doing all of these things.

The Ins and Outs of Workplaces

Begin *now* to collect information about workplaces. First, get a view from the outside by reading about them and eliminating those that don't match your needs and wants. Then the next step is the information interview, getting the inside story about careers and companies by talking to people "on site."

Many places provide information about companies. Most local librarians love to help people and take pride in knowing where to find data. Most libraries have a business reference section. Texts like Standard and Poor's or *Thomas Register* may be more technical than you need or want. Look for books like *Everybody's Business: An Almanac,* the irreverent guide to corporate America by Milton Moskowitz, Michael Katz, and Robert Levering. *Who's Who in Commerce and Industry* will give you key names. Business and professional journals in your field provide a wealth of information. Your Chamber of Commerce has information about all the businesses in your town. College career center libraries, placement offices, and state employment offices are often stocked with material about companies. Some companies have public relations departments that send information if you write or call. The Yellow Pages of your phone book are a gold mine of ideas because just about every business in your area is listed there according to what they do. If you read the business section of your local newspaper regularly, you will know who is doing what and where in the work world in your area. The applicants best prepared for a job interview are those who not only know the company they want to work for, but also have a broad knowledge of the work world. Knowing some of the basics about a company, an industry, and its competition, gives you confidence when job hunting.

Information Interviewing

After the library research, many people still feel that some pieces are missing from the puzzle. Some are disappointed because many jobs described in occupational guides sound dull. But those descriptions are the "bare bones" of the job. You can bring flesh and blood to those skeletons by visiting workplaces and interviewing people about what they do. So from here on in, it's important to be out—out talking to everyone about their jobs, out observing work environments.

How often have working friends given you a blow-by-blow description of life at Picky Products, Inc.? If you've worked for a company, you have information about it that's not easily available to an outsider. You know the people who are likely to help beginners; you know how tough or easy the supervisors are, how interesting or boring the work is—what it's *really* like!

So a key part of the career search process is interviewing people about their jobs and observing them in their workplaces to get that inside information. You want to answer two questions: One, is this a job you would really like? Two, is this a place you would like to work? So unless you are an experienced and sophisticated job seeker with a broad knowledge of jobs, it is important to gather as much first-hand information as you can before you choose a career and perhaps plan courses and get a degree. The job may require education or special training. Why not find out all you can before spending time, energy, and money on training for a job you may not like? You can also eliminate misconceptions about the preparation you need in order to be hired.

If you feel timid about approaching a stranger, begin by interviewing someone in your family, then a friend or neighbor, about his or her job. Ask people you know for names of willing interviewees. It's amazing how you can usually find someone who knows someone who knows someone. . . . Your college alumni office is often in touch with graduates in different fields. An instructor in a particular field of interest may know someone "out there" who will talk to you.

If you feel uncertain about going to an interview alone, ask a friend to introduce you, or ask someone with a mutual interest to go along. Invite the people to be interviewed out for coffee or lunch after you visit their workplaces—always ahead of time by appointment—at their convenience. If you want things to go smoothly, do not drop in on a busy person unexpectedly.

Use the information interview sparingly, not casually. Wait until you have done all your homework carefully and have some idea of your direction. Most people are sincerely interested in helping information seekers but sometimes they cannot afford the time. Don't feel discouraged if you are refused an interview.

Also seek someone close to the level at which you are applying. Don't ask to see the president of a company if you are searching out information about safety engineering. Rather, find a person who is a safety engineer, or industrial technologist, or technical supervisor.

Following your skills and interests may lead you into work environments that range from serene to frenetic. As a writer, for example, you might find yourself either researching in a library or risking your life as a war correspondent. The work environment, then, is another dimension that should be considered as you choose your career. There are many things you thoroughly enjoy but might hate if you had to do them under pressure—a thousand times a day—in a hot, crowded, noisy, and otherwise unpleasant place—for an irritable boss with ulcers! You may enjoy cooking but be fairly certain you would not enjoy serving a million hamburgers every day. You might not like cooking regularly for any large group, even in the most elegant setting. You can find out by visiting various kitchens, talking to the cooks, and observing what they do. Barbara Rosenbloom and Victoria Krayer, owners of a charcuterie in Berkeley, showed one visitor the huge pots of heavy paté that had to be mixed, emptied, and cleaned. The visitor learned that cooking is sometimes physically demanding.

Find out whether the company you are interested in (or one like it) gives tours. In some cases you can spend a whole day observing someone doing a job you might like.

Become *career aware!* Talk to everyone: Ask friends, relatives, and colleagues what they do and if they can introduce you to someone in your career field of interest. Read the newspaper, especially the business section. Don't be afraid to call or write to people who seem interesting. Ask them to tell you more about what they do, or congratulate them on some accomplishment or promotion. Let them know if you are sincerely interested in some aspect of the company. People appreciate positive feedback.

Remember, when you talk with people in your career field of interest, you are gathering all their biases. Each person likes and dislikes certain things about the job. Each one will give you a different view. Keep your antennae out to receive the emotional content of their messages. And then weigh all these messages against *your* good feeling and reasoned judgment.

There are other ways to meet people in your field of interest. Many professional groups welcome students at their meetings and have special rates for student/lay participation. The Society of Women Engineers is one of these. The *Occupational Outlook Handbook* lists names and addresses of such organizations. Throughout the United States, the American Society for Training and Development has chapters that hold monthly meetings and annual conventions. At such meetings you can meet people who have access to local business information and contacts. The Chamber of Commerce and other community organizations hold regular luncheons with speakers. In social settings like these, it's possible to make contacts easily and explore possibilities for on-site visits. At workshops or classes in your career area of interest, speakers and participants can share information with you both formally and informally.

Much of your success will come from keeping your eyes and ears open. Begin to wonder what just about everyone you meet is doing. Almost every media news item is about people's doings. Which activities attract you? How can you learn more about these activities? Keep on looking, listening, and asking questions—it's your best source of information. Eventually you will be talking to people who are doing work you would like to do. Something will "click" as you begin to share experiences and enthusiasms. You will make a network of friends who later may wish to hire you.

At first many people hesitate to call a stranger in a large company—or even an acquaintance in a small one. One student, whose talents were apparent to everyone but herself, was terrified at the prospect. She grimly made the first phone call. To her amazement, the interview was delightful—that is, until she was advised to explore a graduate program at a nearby university. She forced herself to see the department head that same day. Another warm reception! Another success! Elated, she rushed out to call her career counselor from the nearest phone booth. She was chuckling, "Here I am, 35 years old, and as excited as any kid over talking to two human beings!"

Another student, given the same class assignment, simply didn't do it. She had been a psychology major with a love for art, but changed to business which seemed more "practical," although it didn't seem to fit her creative "people" needs. Then she discovered organizational development and told someone about it—who knew a management consultant who uses graphic arts in his work. Her reluctance to interview vanished as possibilities began to open up.

Perhaps not everyone you meet will be helpful. You may meet a "Queen Bee" or a "King Pin"—someone who has made it and is unwilling to help others. Sometimes people are just having a bad day, are truly too busy, or they have yet to learn what all self-actualizing people know: "The more you help others, the more successful you'll be." But if you don't give up, you will find warm-hearted people who understand your needs, your confusion, and YOU! Keep on searching for those who are sensitive to *YOU*.

When people have spent time with you, follow up with thank-you notes. This courtesy will be appreciated and help employers to remember you when you begin the job hunt.

Work Experience

Probably the best way to get the "inside story" is to get a little first-hand experience in the work environment—even if you have to volunteer. Try your school or state employment placement office for positions at different workplaces. Or sign up at a temporary employment agency—one with a good reputation—and research many people at many companies while you earn some money. Get acquainted with people in the cafeteria, for example, and watch the bulletin boards for job announcements.

With some actual work experience, a young person who "loves animals" may find working at the local vet's office is exciting or that dealing with sick animals and worried owners is traumatic. On the other hand, every job will gradually (or quickly) demonstrate some unpleasant aspects. Basically, work is often hard work. One must function within the economic and time parameters of an organization. When both time and money are in short supply, deadlines and shortages create pressure.

Human relations can require much of your energy as you seek to accommodate to the various personalities you meet at work. Sometimes a change in yourself can make a vast difference. You can learn to communicate more effectively, assert yourself in a tactful way, grow in self-confidence, become more considerate and understanding of the problems of others. It will usually be necessary to strike a balance: not make a "federal case" out of every annoyance, yet be able to make changes in a situation that clashes sharply with your sensibilities.

Sometimes asking for a change of work can alter your outlook and change the environment. For example, could you answer questions at the information window part of the time instead of answering the phone all day? A change to another department or to a slightly different job often means a new start. You might learn to manage time or the flow of work activities more efficiently, making the job more enjoyable.

Even if one workplace doesn't work as a place for you, the career itself may still be a good choice. Try to separate the job from the place and people, if you can.

As you become familiar with the workplace, your confidence will grow. By the time you are ready for an interview, you will understand the job and its problems. You will know the latest techniques in your trade or profession. You will know people in the field who may recommend or even hire you. Remember: The Department of Labor has estimated that 70 to 80 percent of all jobs are acquired by word of mouth.

The information interview process puts you in the hiring network. It can be an adventure. It can be very profitable. With your new-found self-confidence, the first job interview will be "duck soup"—not sitting duck!

Self-Assessment Exercises

The following exercises will help you to decide what kind of workplaces and work styles you prefer, and then to locate those that match these preferences.

1. Where Do You Fit In?

a. If you can identify the category and size of workplace you would like, you have greatly narrowed down your choices. Check your choices on the appropriate lines.

Check one or more:	Small	Medium	Large	Inside	Outside
Business	———	———	———	———	———
Industry	———	———	———	———	———
Education	———	———	———	———	———
Entertainment/ communication	———	———	———	———	———
Health	———	———	———	———	———
Government	———	———	———	———	———
Military	———	———	———	———	———

b. At this point in your search, how far up the career ladder do you think you want to go?

_____

c. Do you want a traditional nine-to-five career, or would you prefer an alternative work style? Check your preference here:

_____ Career creator   _____ Third Wave prosumer

_____ Entrepreneur   _____ Traditional career

_____ Intrapreneur   _____ Worksteader

d. Describe an alternative work style that interests you.

_____

_____

_____

e. Look in the Yellow Pages for businesses in your field of interest. List three such businesses here:

_____

_____

_____

2. Researching Workplaces

Using the resources of your library, state employment office, school career center, and company public relations department, research a workplace in your career area. The following guidelines will help you in your search.

Name of workplace _____

Organization

Divisions _____

_____

Locations _____

_____

Products/services _____

_____

Number of employees _____

_____

Job functions _____

_____

Performance

Past history _____

_____

Present market _____

_____

Yearly earnings _____

_____

Future projections _____

_____

Stability _____

_____

Competitors _____

_____

Other factors

Reputation/integrity _____

_____

Environmental record _____

_____

Social concern _____

_____

3. Workplace Checklist

Interview friends and relatives about their employers and the environments they work in. Visit workplaces. Observe your own workplace. Rate one workplace on the following checklist:

a. Check (√) good, fair, or poor in the columns on the right.

b. Rank your top ten priorities, from 1 to 10, in the column on the left.

Company name: _____ City, state, zip code: _____

Address: _____ Phone number: _____

	Good	Fair	Poor
Management style			
___ Positive	___	___	___
___ Respectful	___	___	___
___ Honest	___	___	___
___ Trusting	___	___	___
___ Reasonable	___	___	___
___ Objective	___	___	___
___ Committed	___	___	___
___ Receptive	___	___	___
___ Cooperative	___	___	___
___ Open	___	___	___

| | Good | Fair | Poor |

Good Fair Poor

Environment

_____ Location/setting _____ _____ _____

_____ Appearance of buildings _____ _____ _____

_____ Work stations _____ _____ _____

_____ Cafeteria _____ _____ _____

_____ Restrooms _____ _____ _____

_____ Equipment _____ _____ _____

_____ Colors _____ _____ _____

_____ Light _____ _____ _____

_____ Furnishings _____ _____ _____

_____ Safety _____ _____ _____

_____ Compatible co-workers _____ _____ _____

_____ Order/confusion _____ _____ _____

_____ Friendly/unfriendly _____ _____ _____

Use of skills/interests

_____ Encourages growth/responsibility _____ _____ _____

_____ Supports efforts _____ _____ _____

_____ Acknowledges achievements _____ _____ _____

_____ Provides transfers/promotions _____ _____ _____

_____ Offers educational options _____ _____ _____

Salary/benefits

_____ Salary _____ _____ _____

_____ Medical/dental _____ _____ _____

_____ Promotes health _____ _____ _____

_____ Life/disability insurance _____ _____ _____

_____ Vacations/holidays _____ _____ _____

_____ "Business of living" time _____ _____ _____

_____ Child care _____ _____ _____

_____ Profit sharing _____ _____ _____

_____ Moving/travel expenses _____ _____ _____

_____ Flextime _____ _____ _____

_____ Retirement benefits _____ _____ _____

	Good	Fair	Poor

The community

_____ Recreational, cultural facilities _____ _____ _____

_____ Medical/dental facilities _____ _____ _____

_____ Acceptable schools _____ _____ _____

_____ Transportation _____ _____ _____

_____ Cost of living _____ _____ _____

_____ Other amenities _____ _____ _____

c. Complete this statement: I would (or would not) like to work there because

_____

_____

_____

4. Workplace Values

a. Rank these corporate values in order of importance to you as a potential employee:

_____ Produce and market safe, useful, and pure products

_____ Use production methods that respect and preserve the natural environment

_____ Provide a safe and healthy environment for work

_____ Make equal opportunities available for women and minorities

_____ Maintain fair labor practices

_____ Allow workers to participate in management

b. Would you turn down a job because of violations of any of these issues?

Yes _____   No _____

5. Information Interview

Interview workers in a career field that interests you. Write the results of one such interview either here or on a separate sheet of paper.

Name   Company

Job Title   Address

Phone Number   City, State, Zip

Here are some questions you might ask:

a. Why did you choose this field?

_____

_____

b. How did you get your job?

_____

_____

c. What do you really do all day?

_____

_____

d. If you could redesign your job, what parts would you keep? What parts would you get rid of?

_____

_____

e. If you had it to do all over again, what would you do differently in your career?

_____

_____

f. What is the outlook for the future in this field?

_____

_____

g. What are the requirements for the job: training, certificates, licenses, degrees, tools and equipment, union membership?

_____

_____

h. Will your company have openings in this field in the near future?

Yes _____ No _____

i. Whom would you recommend that I interview for a different perspective?

_____

Name   Company

_____

Job Title   Address

_____

Phone Number   City, State, Zip

 Group Discussion Questions

1. What have you learned about various workplaces?
2. What insights did you gain from information interviewing?
3. What factors prevent workplace environments from improving?
4. In what ways is your household a workplace? Consider goods and services, management, finances, maintenance, communications, personnel, labor negotiations, your degree of commitment, emotional climate, skills you use, and functions you perform. Does your household respect the rights of its members and care for the natural environment?
5. Ask for career information from members of your group. Trade resources.

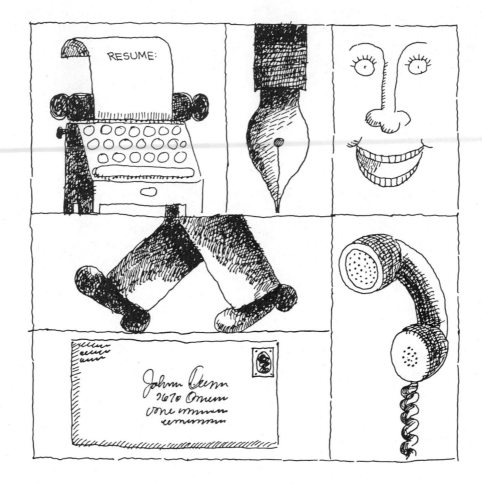

Seven

The Job Hunt:

Tools for Breaking and Entering

You have thoroughly assessed your needs, wants, shoulds, values, and interests. You have envisioned your ideal lifestyle. You have researched your skills so thoroughly that you now have a marvelous list of your own accomplishments. You have begun to collect words to describe yourself. You have looked over the whole job market and found many jobs that would suit you well. You have interviewed people, researched companies, explored workplaces. You have considered the "job versus career" issue, the career ladder, possibilities for future goals, creative careers, and owning your own business. You have zeroed in on a job title or two and some companies where you have contacts. In short, you are ready, at last, for the job hunt!

Job hunting is often a full-time job. And like work, it is often hard work. Résumés, networks, letters, applications, phone calls, and interviews can make your head swim. The challenge and excitement of a career search may wear thin as you travel this long and sometimes weary road. Keeping your wits about you and keeping up your courage are two essential skills.

Some people find it helpful to join a support group or start one at this time. Friends can be a source of ideas and emotional support if and when the going gets tough. Ask for help and understanding. It also helps to keep several options open—developing possibilities on your present job, taking a course or two, inching toward starting your own business—while you interview in several different areas.

Networking

Many employers use want ads and employment agencies, and many people walk through these doors to find jobs. Use all the help you can get. But be aware that

183

private employment agencies are like used car dealers: Some are reliable, and some are only there to put bodies behind the wheel and collect a fee. Some are downright dishonest. They put phony ads in the newspaper to attract clients, use excessive flattery to get your signature on a contract—and then forget about you. They may be able to collect their fee even if you find a job on your own, without their help. Check with people who have used the services. Read the fine print before you sign over a big chunk of next year's paycheck for a job that may not be right for you.

If you have followed all the steps in the career search process, you should be able to do your own job hunting. Now get into the hiring network and take charge of the hiring process. Perhaps someone you've contacted in your information interviewing is just waiting for your résumé and application in order to hire you. Sending out dozens of résumés to personnel departments is the least effective strategy, especially if you are looking for a job in a competitive field. You may get a nibble or two but not too many people are hired this way. Here is where your information interviewing will pay off to get you into the hiring network.

Networking is a new "old" word. Whatever it's called—the buddy system, the old boys' network, or the new girls' network—the fact is that employers have always passed jobs along to people they know. An estimated 80 percent of all jobs are filled by word of mouth even though they may be advertised. People are networking when they shake hands and exchange business cards—something that many men do automatically and women are learning to do. Men talk business everywhere—in the hallways, over coffee, in the men's room. These casual conversations may sound trivial, but they strengthen the links in the old boys' network.

Where do you stand in the networking game? If you are new at creative job hunting, the inner circle may look like a closed circuit that doesn't include you! But think again. How often have you or people you know heard about a job opening from a friend? And bring it close to home. Suppose you want to hire someone to do work of great importance to you: take care of a child or ailing parent, fix your much needed car, clean the house that contains everything you own. No doubt you feel safer when you ask around and get a referral from a friend. All employers feel better when they hire someone they know or someone recommended by a trusted friend or colleague. If you have already done information interviewing, you'll have a good start on networking. Use the same process and the same contacts to find out about job openings and how to approach a particular workplace. These insiders can offer you both the inside story and moral support.

Even if you haven't developed a network of personal contacts, call on as many companies (or clients) as you can and apply for possible openings. Make contacts instead of staying at home alone and reading the want ads all day. Now is the time to keep your energy up. Plan a schedule: Exercise, eat well, get plenty of rest, and talk to as many positive people as you can. In a tight job market it's important to keep up your courage. Remember that rejections are part of the game and don't mean you're unacceptable. Chances are, you are just one of many good candidates.

Later the company may offer you a job different from the one you had in mind. If the company is a good one, it may even be worth taking a different job just to get inside where promotions are more accessible. No one ever said the job hunt would be easy! Work on your résumé, schedule your time, set goals, and keep moving.

The Résumé

A résumé is a summary of personal information relevant to the job you seek. A good résumé marks you as a serious job seeker. Much has been written about the résumé. Some see it as a sacred cow—the most important item to use in presenting oneself; others say preparing a résumé is a worthless exercise. Still, many employers require them, so job hunters, an obliging lot, will continue to oblige.

Writing a résumé can be very rewarding even if you never use it. It forces you to state clearly how your education and experience relate directly to the job you are seeking. Sample résumés are shown in Figures 7-1 through 7-4 and in the Appendix.

Now is the time to decide whether you want a chronological or functional résumé. If your work experience was fairly continuous and can be stated concisely in reverse order, make it chronological. If your experience was not continuous or consisted of a number of scattered activities or many small jobs, a functional résumé may be best.

When your résumé is finished, type it up correctly. Then plan to have it copied on good off-white, gray, or beige tinted paper. Once copied, it will look very sharp even if you've erased or used "white-out." If you plan to mail it, prepare a carefully typed, matching envelope addressed to the correct person. For a final touch, use a handsome commemorative stamp. You want your résumé to get a second look, rather than the usual 30-second glance.

Some people send a résumé with an individual letter addressed to a specific person in a company. Sometimes the résumé is attached to an application, or requested after an application has been received. The general idea is to give the employer a preview of you, before an interview takes place. Always have your résumé handy, and bring a copy to the interview.

There is no one and only way to write a résumé, but there are some good basic guidelines to follow: (1) be brief, (2) be clear, (3) be neat, (4) be honest. The best résumé describes your qualifications on only one page.

A reasonable résumé should rarely require two pages. It should state, succinctly, your education and work experience that specifically relate to the job for which you are applying. It is easiest to read in outline form with plenty of "white space," with good spelling, punctuation, and grammar, and well typed and reproduced. Although it is important to be truthful, a résumé isn't the place for true confessions. Emphasize your good points! Ask experienced friends to read and criticize your

RÉSUMÉ FORMATS

1. Name, address, home phone, business (or message) phone

   List this information prominently at the top of the page. Be sure to give useful phone numbers: A prospective employer should know where to reach you, day or evening.

2. Position objective

3. Qualifications in brief

   Highlights of your experience and skills.

4. Experience summary

   The type of presentation may be chronological, functional, or a combination of the two.

   Chronological:
   Begin with your most recent job and work backward.

   > March 1982: Company, Job Title
   > June 1980: Company, Job Title (If it seems helpful, add a brief, concise description of what you did.)

   In this type of résumé, you may wish to include a section on community service, military service, or whatever applies (see Figures 7-1, 7-4, and the Appendix).

   Functional:
   The information is arranged by areas of competence, expertise, or effectiveness, such as public relations, management, organization, program development, sales.

rough draft, but have confidence in your own judgment about what is right for you.

You may spend from 12 to 15 hours writing a good résumé, but writing it will help you to recognize your own qualifications. There are an almost infinite number of ways to describe you. Doing a résumé means picking a winning combination that exactly fits the job you are seeking. Yes, it's true! You *do* need a separate résumé for each job title and sometimes even for each company! If you have been developing a list of file cards for each job, a résumé will be not only easier to do but easier to adapt.

Start with the lists you made of all your favorite activities and skills in Chapters 1 and 3. The basic eight skills empower you to do many different things in many different settings with data, people, and things because the skills are transferable. The key question to answer when you go job hunting is, "What can you *do*?" The most important words to use on your résumé are action verbs that tell what you've

List functions that are related to your position objective.

Follow each category with businesslike action words such as "planned" and "classified"; then give a summary of the type of things you accomplished. You may either list employers and dates at the end or note them on the company's application form (see Figure 7-2).

Combination of chronological and functional:
If this format suits your experience, be sure that special skills relevant to your position objective are highlighted (see Figure 7-3).

5. Educational background (This could go before work experience if it is more relevant.)

The purpose of listing educational background is to indicate general and specific training for a job. A person who has little or no educational training would omit this item.

College: Degrees, majors, dates, places. If you received no degree or you are presently attending college, give the number of units completed, major, date, place.

High school: List diploma if you have not attended college.

Also include: Relevant workshops, adult education, vocational training—either in summary form or in chronological order.

6. Personal paragraph

You may wish to include a statement describing personal attitudes toward work that make you a valuable and unique employee (see Figures 7-3 and 7-4).

done and therefore *can do.* Action verbs have an impact when they are relevant to the job you want. Collect businesslike nouns, adjectives, and adverbs to use with the action verbs. A woman who worked for a sanitation district said she "gave messages to the guys in their trucks." On her résumé this phrase was translated to "communicated by radio with personnel in the field."

As you polish your résumé, try to make each statement very specific. Here are four different versions of the same sentence, which becomes more concrete with each revision:

1. Designed a program . . .
2. Designed a marketing program . . .
3. Designed an *effective* marketing program . . .
4. Designed an effective marketing program that resulted in a 60 percent sales increase

Figure 7-1 Chronological Résumé of a College Student

```
                        KEVIN DONOVAN
                        643 Eagle Drive
                      Dubuque, Iowa 52001

                        319-555-6789
```

JOB OBJECTIVE:

   CUSTOMER SERVICE – Management Trainee

QUALIFICATIONS IN BRIEF:

   Learn quickly, easily oriented to job routine. Possess ability to deal
   effectively with the public and flexible enough to work alone or in a team
   effort. Good driving record. Not afraid of hard routine work. Primarily
   interested in a swing shift to allow time to further my educational goals.

WORK EXPERIENCE:

   K-MART, Dubuque, IA   1982 to present
   Customer Service/Bagger

   Help customers with merchandise, stock shelves in warehouse, maintain
   appearance of the store, bring carts from parking lot into building, and
   bag merchandise from checkstands.

   DUBUQUE GYMNASTIC ASSOCIATION, Dubuque, IA   1981
   Gym Instructor

   Sold memberships and equipment, outlined programs for participants, gave
   tours of the facilities to potential customers and guests, balanced monies
   and accounts daily, answered phones, and was responsible for maintaining a
   smooth operation of the gym facilities, adding a professional tone.

   S & S WELDING, East Dubuque, IL   1980
   VAN'S FURNITURE AND MATTRESS CO., Dubuque, IA   1979
   Warehouse Worker

   Moved furniture, paint, and equipment; helped with inventory control; and
   assisted customers in making proper selections.

EDUCATION:

   LORAS COLLEGE, Dubuque, IA   1981 to present
   Major: Business/Liberal Arts

   DUBUQUE HIGH SCHOOL, Dubuque, IA   1977-1981
   College Preparatory

REFERENCES. Provided upon request.

BETTY A. BUG
5403 W. Monroe Street
Chicago, Illinois 60644
312/555-9829

POSITION OBJECTIVE: Employee trainer in industry

QUALIFICATIONS IN BRIEF:

   BA in English, Mundelein College, Chicago, 1973; six years elementary
   teaching; fluent in Spanish; demonstrated skills in instruction, supervision, communications, human relations.

EXPERIENCE SUMMARY:

   INSTRUCTION: Planned, organized, presented language and mathematics
   instructional material to elementary students; developed instructional
   modules to solve specific learning problems; developed computer programs
   for instruction, instructional audio-visual material, used equipment such
   as Apple II, overhead and movie projectors, audio and video cassettes; did
   extensive research in various curricula; member of curriculum development
   committee; introduced new motivational techniques for students. Conducted
   staff inservice workshops.

   SUPERVISION: Supervised student groups, teacher interns, and a classroom
   aide; evaluated students, peers, and programs; moderated student activities.
   Interviewed, trained, and evaluated support personnel, volunteers, and
   teacher interns.

   HUMAN RELATIONS: Did effective problem solving/conflict resolution
   between individual students and between student groups; initiated program
   of student self-governance; acted as liaison between families of diverse
   cultural, ethnic, and economic backgrounds and school personnel/services;
   conducted individual and group conferences to establish rapport with
   parents and discuss student progress. Represented agency to the community.

   COMMUNICATIONS: Presented new curriculum plans to parent groups; sent
   periodic progress reports to parents; developed class newsletter.

CURRENTLY EMPLOYED: Austin Elementary School, Chicago, Illinois

REFERENCES: Provided upon request.

Helen B. Bell
432 Spruce Street
Junction City, Kansas 66441
913-555-7035

POSITION OBJECTIVE:

    Office Manager with accounting responsibilities.

EXPERIENCE:

    Successful Accounting Work: Managed payroll, payroll taxes, accounts
receivable, accounts payable, bank reconciliation, and executive
credit card expense account; acted as full-charge bookkeeper through
monthly and annual profit and loss statements.

    Supervision and Management: Directed office functions such as secre-
tarial, accounting, customer relations, sales, employee performance,
and schedules.

EMPLOYERS:

Kindergarten Supplier, USA, Inc., Wichita, KS Accountant	2 years
Electra Corporation, Wichita, KS Receptionist	1 year
Ridgeway Company, Topeka, KS Accountant/Secretary	2 years
Rod's Van & Storage Company, Topeka, KS Accountant/Secretary	2 years
Humphrey Motor Company, Junction City, KS Accountant/Secretary	9 years
Scott Stores, Junction City, KS Bookkeeper	1 year

PERSONAL PARAGRAPH:

    The accounting field with its attendant and complex problems is fascinat-
ing and thoroughly involving for me. I am interested in ensuring smooth
flow, efficiency, and accuracy of accounts in a moderately sized, growing
company.

Figure 7-4 Résumé with a Personal Paragraph   **191**

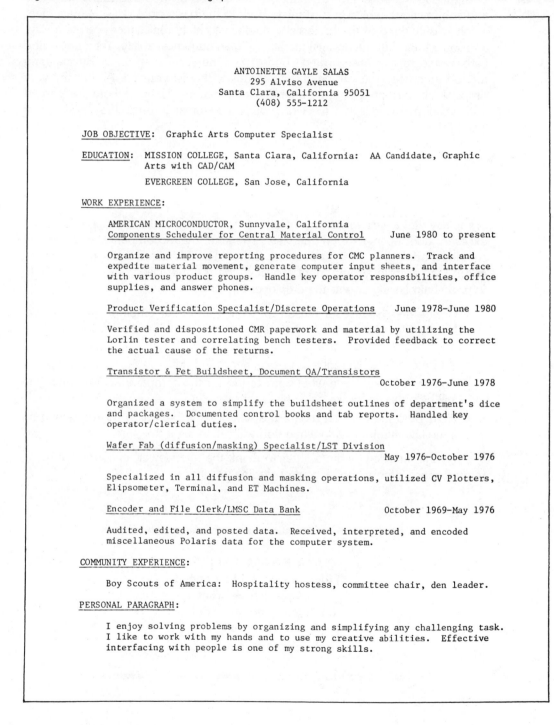

ANTOINETTE GAYLE SALAS
295 Alviso Avenue
Santa Clara, California 95051
(408) 555-1212

JOB OBJECTIVE: Graphic Arts Computer Specialist

EDUCATION: MISSION COLLEGE, Santa Clara, California: AA Candidate, Graphic
Arts with CAD/CAM

EVERGREEN COLLEGE, San Jose, California

WORK EXPERIENCE:

AMERICAN MICROCONDUCTOR, Sunnyvale, California
Components Scheduler for Central Material Control   June 1980 to present

Organize and improve reporting procedures for CMC planners. Track and
expedite material movement, generate computer input sheets, and interface
with various product groups. Handle key operator responsibilities, office
supplies, and answer phones.

Product Verification Specialist/Discrete Operations   June 1978-June 1980

Verified and dispositioned CMR paperwork and material by utilizing the
Lorlin tester and correlating bench testers. Provided feedback to correct
the actual cause of the returns.

Transistor & Fet Buildsheet, Document QA/Transistors
                                          October 1976-June 1978

Organized a system to simplify the buildsheet outlines of department's dice
and packages. Documented control books and tab reports. Handled key
operator/clerical duties.

Wafer Fab (diffusion/masking) Specialist/LST Division
                                          May 1976-October 1976

Specialized in all diffusion and masking operations, utilized CV Plotters,
Elipsometer, Terminal, and ET Machines.

Encoder and File Clerk/LMSC Data Bank   October 1969-May 1976

Audited, edited, and posted data. Received, interpreted, and encoded
miscellaneous Polaris data for the computer system.

COMMUNITY EXPERIENCE:

Boy Scouts of America: Hospitality hostess, committee chair, den leader.

PERSONAL PARAGRAPH:

I enjoy solving problems by organizing and simplifying any challenging task.
I like to work with my hands and to use my creative abilities. Effective
interfacing with people is one of my strong skills.

Many-faceted skills such as management can be divided into many functions and subfunctions, which in turn relate back to the basic eight skills. Management involves only three of the basic skills: medium to high intelligence, verbal ability, and sometimes (but not always) medium to high numerical ability. Yet many action verbs would apply: advise, arrange, budget, communicate, control . . . By analyzing the job functions, you will be able to complete the list yourself. All but the very simplest jobs contain a large number of such functions. Many of them are learned and developed with some level of proficiency simply through the "business of living."

Cover Letters

Some say that a well-written cover letter (see Figure 7-5 and the Appendix) is an excellent door opener for an interview. The letter that accompanies your résumé should be brief, clear, neat, and honest. It should be addressed to a specific person, and it may amplify an important aspect of the résumé. Use your cover letter to form a chain linking you to the employer:

- *Connecting:* State your reason for writing and your employment objective. Mention the person who referred you to this employer or the source of the reference, such as a classified ad.
- *Add more links:* Describe your experience in brief.
- *Solder the links:* State what you can do for the company and tell how you will help this employer solve his or her problem.
- *Hold onto the chain:* Prepare the way for the next step by requesting an interview and indicating when you will call to set it up.

After the interview, write a letter to thank the interviewer, encourage a reply, request more information, accept or decline an offer.

I AM RATHER
like a mosquito in a nudist
camp; I know what
I ought to do, but I don't
know where to begin.
STEPHEN BAYNE

Letters of Reference

Be prepared to supply the names of people who have written or will write letters of reference for you. Do not name someone as a reference unless that person has agreed to be contacted. The people you ask should be professional people, former employers—individuals who are acquainted with your work skills. Some college placement offices keep letters of reference, a current résumé, and transcripts on file for their graduates and send them out to prospective employers for a nominal fee.

When you apply for a job, the usual procedure in regard to references is to provide names if they are requested or to bring copies of letters along to the interview. If letters are on file at a college placement office, have them sent to the prospective employer either right before or soon after your interview. But if the competition is fierce and you are almost certain this is a job you want, it may be appropriate to ask a couple of key people to write letters or even make phone calls to the person who may hire you. Ask a teacher or counselor who knows your skills, an acquaintance in the company to which you are applying, or some other professional acquaintance known to the interviewer or to the person you will be working for to speak on your behalf. But understand that this is not the usual procedure and should be used with discrimination.

The Application Form

The application form provided by the company may determine the employer's first impression of you. It must look sharp. Carelessness or sloppiness may cause you to be eliminated. Be sure to fill out an application as clearly, completely, and neatly as possible.

Try to obtain two copies ahead of time. (Sometimes companies will mail them to you by phone request.) Use one copy for practice and keep it for your file. Type, or at least print, very carefully and completely but succinctly.

Applications vary from one company to another, but each form requires an accurate record of past work experience and education. Prepare a mini-file containing all relevant information. Check it carefully for accuracy. You will need names, addresses, and dates for both education and work experience. Obtain this information now if you do not have it. Employers often verify these facts, and they should check out. The more careful you are, the better you look. Be clear if you are asked what you did. Know exact job titles, the types of machines you've used, and the salary range you are interested in. Here are some helpful hints to remember.

- Read the *whole* application form before beginning to fill it in. Follow all directions, and note the fine print.

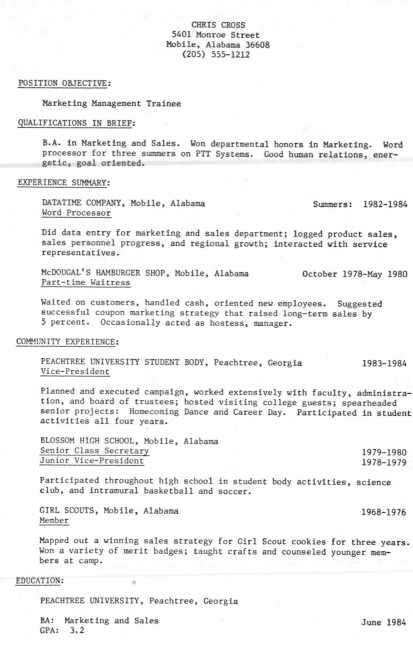

CHRIS CROSS
5401 Monroe Street
Mobile, Alabama 36608
(205) 555-1212

POSITION OBJECTIVE:

Marketing Management Trainee

QUALIFICATIONS IN BRIEF:

B.A. in Marketing and Sales. Won departmental honors in Marketing. Word processor for three summers on PTT Systems. Good human relations, energetic, goal oriented.

EXPERIENCE SUMMARY:

DATATIME COMPANY, Mobile, Alabama   Summers: 1982-1984
Word Processor

Did data entry for marketing and sales department; logged product sales, sales personnel progress, and regional growth; interacted with service representatives.

McDOUGAL'S HAMBURGER SHOP, Mobile, Alabama   October 1978-May 1980
Part-time Waitress

Waited on customers, handled cash, oriented new employees. Suggested successful coupon marketing strategy that raised long-term sales by 5 percent. Occasionally acted as hostess, manager.

COMMUNITY EXPERIENCE:

PEACHTREE UNIVERSITY STUDENT BODY, Peachtree, Georgia   1983-1984
Vice-President

Planned and executed campaign, worked extensively with faculty, administration, and board of trustees; hosted visiting college guests; spearheaded senior projects: Homecoming Dance and Career Day. Participated in student activities all four years.

BLOSSOM HIGH SCHOOL, Mobile, Alabama
Senior Class Secretary   1979-1980
Junior Vice-President   1978-1979

Participated throughout high school in student body activities, science club, and intramural basketball and soccer.

GIRL SCOUTS, Mobile, Alabama   1968-1976
Member

Mapped out a winning sales strategy for Girl Scout cookies for three years. Won a variety of merit badges; taught crafts and counseled younger members at camp.

EDUCATION:

PEACHTREE UNIVERSITY, Peachtree, Georgia

BA: Marketing and Sales   June 1984
GPA: 3.2

REFERENCES: Provided upon request.

West Mill Hall
Peachtree University
Peachtree, GA 30214

April 11, 1985

Ms. Jill Jones
Director of Marketing
PTT Corporation
Dogwood, AL 36309

Dear Ms. Jones:

As a word processor at Datatime Company last summer, I had occasion to meet with customer representatives from your company. I was impressed with both your product and your personnel. This June I will receive my bachelor's degree in marketing and sales from Peachtree University. I would like to be considered for a position in marketing with PTT.

I am an energetic, enthusiastic person with a commitment to whatever I take on. My involvement in student affairs led me to plan and execute a successful campaign for student body vice-president. In this capacity I met and negotiated with faculty representatives and board of trustee members and hosted visiting guests of the college. My senior project in marketing won departmental recognition while my 3.2 GPA put me on the dean's honor list.

With these qualifications I feel that I can make a positive contribution to PTT. I look forward to meeting your campus recruitor, A. J. Lupin, next month to explore a marketing trainee position.

Sincerely yours,

Chris Cross

Chris Cross

- Print with a pen or, better still, type answers.
- Fill in all blanks. Use N/A if question does not apply to you.
- You need to obtain a social security number if you do not have one. Have it available. Some companies ask for a driver's license as identification. (Revocation or denial of a driver's license can be a clue to some physical or mental problem.)
- Your reason for interest in the position should state an advantage to the employer. Research the company and know what you can do for it.
- An arrest is not a conviction. Arrests need not be mentioned.
- Provide accurate names and addresses of those who have given you permission to use their names as references. Have original reference letters available, plus copies to leave if requested.
- Re-read the application with care.
- Sign the application.

The Interview

Although it has been denounced by some as a barbaric custom and by others as "proven ineffectual," the interview is likely to remain an employer ritual for some time to come. Usually an employer interviews persons whose applications, letters, or résumés have proven interesting, or someone who has made a personal contact or been referred.

An interview is a "structured conversation" between an employer or delegated interviewer and a prospective employee. Its purpose is to exchange information. The interviewer needs to find out if the interviewee has the qualifications necessary to do the job. The applicant needs to make sure that he or she understands the job, the company, and what is expected.

The interviewer may be a department head, project director, or even a series of people familiar with various aspects of the job. A group of staff members may act together as an interviewing committee. In a small business you may be interviewed quite casually and briefly by the owner. A large corporation employs professional interviewers. Reputable companies want their interviewers to present a positive image. They want you to leave with a favorable impression of the company, to feel that you were treated well. Interviewers want to do a good job too—by hiring the best person. Their jobs depend on it!

Like a good English composition, the interview usually has a beginning, a middle, and an ending. Introductions and casual conversation begin the interview and are designed to help you feel at ease.

After a few minutes, most interviewers will guide you to the purpose of the meeting and will then begin inquiries about your qualifications. A good interviewer will also give you information along the way to help you make your decision. The interviewer will discuss

- Job duties
- Hours/overtime
- Salary/benefits
- Vacation/sick leave
- Opportunities for advancement
- Company policies and procedures

Some interviewers also give you a tour of the workplace. Depending on the level for which you are being considered, an interview might be over in fifteen minutes or last several hours. Most information can be exchanged in 30 or 45 minutes. Interviewers bring these meetings to an end and usually give information about when you will be notified. They usually are seeing other people, sometimes many others.

An interview is not a time for game-playing or for one person to try to trap the other. It will be counterproductive for both parties if they deceive each other. The interviewer will end up with an employee who "doesn't fit." The worker will be dissatisfied.

However, there are some guidelines you can follow to help you appear at your best. Knowing what to expect ahead of time and preparing well can be important for a successful interview. A successful interview, however, might be one in which you *don't* get the job. In some cases, the interview turns up the information that a hire would not be good for either you or the company. In that instance, the interview has accomplished it purpose.

Getting Prepared

When you are meeting someone you wish to impress, common sense and courtesy are your most reliable guides. Lean slightly toward the conservative in dress and manner if you have any doubts along this line. A genial, positive, low-key manner and sense of humor are valuable assets. Generally let the interviewer set the pace and "be in charge." Don't try to take over unless the situation clearly calls for tactful assertion (for example, if you have had little chance to state your abilities).

The very best preparation for an interview is practice. Practice talking to people about their jobs; practice calling for appointments to see people in order to ask for career information. If you have done information interviewing and networking, you will be used to sharing enthusiasm about the career of your choice, and this enthusiasm will come naturally at the interview. Go to interviews even if you think you might not get a job, and then honestly assess your performance.

More immediately, do homework on the company you are approaching. Many have brochures; many are listed in standard library references. A call to the public relations department can sometimes result in a wealth of material. Talk to people,

INTERVIEW OVERVIEW

Get Ready

Check: The company (from reference section of library, public relations department of firm, contacts, friends):

- Location
- Products/services
- Potential market
- Earnings
- Policies
- How you fit in

Check: Important items you wish to cover:

- Your strengths
- Your experiences
- Your interests

Get Set

Check: Items for your application:

- Social security number
- References (personal and professional)
- Name of person to notify in case of accident
- Details of past experience:
  - Name of company
  - Full address and phone number of company
  - Dates worked
  - Salary
  - Job titles
  - Supervisors
  - Duties, projects, skills
  - Education (dates, majors, degrees)
  - Military experience (if any)
- Copies of résumé and, if relevant, examples of work

Check: Exact time, date, location (building and room), availability of parking

- Name of interviewer (and its pronunciation)
- Go alone

Go

Check: Your appearance:

- Neat, clean, conservative outfit
- No gum, no smoking, no fidgeting
- Sit comfortably straight, at ease

Check: Your attitude:

- A serious job seeker
- Definite goals
- Willing to work and work up
- Reasonable approach to salary, hours, benefits, or other aspects of the job
- Uncritical of past employers, teachers, co-workers
- Evidence of good human relations
- Sense of humor
- High personal values
- Wide interests, openness, flexibility

Check: Your manner:

- Confident, not overbearing
- Enthusiastic but not desperate or gushy
- Courteous, attentive
- Good voice, expression
- On-target answering questions
- Shake hands firmly
- Leave promptly after the interview

ask questions. Try to see how you best fit in. Know the important facts about the job and, if possible, the salary range. Prepare to bring any relevant examples of your work, such as sketches, designs, writings.

In some career areas, salaries are nonnegotiable and not an issue—the teaching profession and unions are such examples. In others they *are* negotiable. In such cases the interviewer may ask what salary you expect. If you have no idea of the range and were not able to find out ahead of time, ask. Unless you are a superstar, don't ask for the top of the range, but don't undervalue yourself either. Know the minimum you'll accept—and know your worth. Place yourself somewhere in the middle and leave it open to negotiation. Also, you might ask for a salary review in six months or so.

Don't be afraid to ask about salary and benefits such as medical, dental, disability, and life insurance, vacations, and retirement plans if these are vitally important. A better way is to check all this out before the interview. Ask the personnel office for brochures on their benefit plans. Also feel free to ask when you will hear the results of the interview if you aren't told.

Follow up the interview with a thank-you letter and then a phone call after a week or so if there is no word—unless you have been given a different time line. Sometimes, there is a delay in hiring someone after an interview. Several months might go by because of changes inside the company. A key employee may decide to quit or retire, for example; or an employer may decide to fill another position first; or a complex reorganization may take more time than planned. Tactfully keep in touch with your contact in the company or with the personnel department until you are certain there is no opening for you.

Interview Behavior

As a job seeker, you should approach each interview by being yourself, being true to yourself, and trusting your own judgment about the style that suits you best. You can build self-confidence by practicing ways of talking and listening effectively and by learning to answer an interviewer's questions. Here are some key points to practice.

- *Good eye contact:* Don't avoid this form of personal contact. If you like your interviewers, your eyes will communicate warmth and liking.
- *Appropriate body language:* Be relaxed and open, interested and attentive. Notice how bodies speak! Become aware of ways in which your body sends messages of boredom, fear, enthusiasm, cockiness, nervousness, confidence.
- *Appropriate voice melody:* Try to come across with vitality, enthusiasm, and confidence. Remember that low tones convey confidence and competence; high tones convey insecurity.
- *Active listening:* Indicate that you have heard and understood what the interviewer has said. For example, if the interviewer mentions tardiness as a problem, say, "It must be difficult to have employees who are late all the time. I can assure you that I'll make every effort to be on time."

■ *Good choice of words:* If you do your interview homework and practice, the right words should come easily. Much of what you "say" will of course be conveyed by your manner, not by your words.[1]

Practice Questions

You will be asked questions about your previous work experience and education, your values, and your goals. You may possibly be asked questions about your family life and leisure activities, but very personal questions are not appropriate in an interview.

Questions dealing with factual information should not be a problem if you have done your homework. Have on hand your own file of all education, previous jobs, and other experience, with correct dates, place names and addresses, job titles and duties, names of supervisors and other relevant information in case these might slip your mind. Usually this information is on the application. The interview centers on clarification of points on the application and résumé.

If you have been working regularly and successfully in your field for a period of years, the interview will be mainly a chance for you to tell what you have done. If you are a young graduate, the discussion may focus on your education, interests, and casual jobs.

If you have been in and out of the job market or have had problems in the past, the interviewer will want to explore the reasons. Be relaxed and not defensive. Look upon the interview as a chance to make a fresh start. Assure the interviewer that you will not be a problem, but a solution. You can do the job. All the questions in the interview are different ways of asking, "Can you do the job?" It's not fair to expect to be hired if you can't do the job well. If you keep that clearly in mind, you will be able to support your answer, "Yes, I can do the job," with all sorts of relevant data.

Practice answering questions until you feel comfortable. Prepare concise answers so you won't ramble. Omit inappropriate personal information and especially any negative information about your past job and employers. Some people get carried away and start talking about their childhood, personal problems, and all sorts of irrelevant data that wear interviewers out and hardly charm them. Before the interview, tape record your answers and replay them or at least practice them out loud, either alone or with someone who will give you honest feedback.

Here are some typical, commonly asked questions, along with answers for you to consider.

Tell me something about yourself. This request could be followed by a dismayed silence as you race your mental motor trying to find something to talk about. If you are prepared, you will hop in happily with the reasons you feel that your skills, background, and personal attitudes are good for the job and how you see your future with the company. You will seldom have a better opportunity than this to tell about yourself.

Why are you leaving your present job? (Or: Why did you leave your last job?) If the circumstances of your leaving were unpleasant or your present conditions are unbearable, these personal problems will be the first things to pop into your mind—but they should be the last things you discuss. Everyone leaves a job for more than one reason, and negative reasons can be made positive. If your boss was oppressive, co-workers disagreeable, or the job was too difficult, a move can provide opportunity for growth in a variety of ways. It's difficult for anyone to improve on a job when feelings are all negative. Some possible replies are:

- "I seemed to have reached a point where there was little potential for growth."
- "I have learned my job well and would like to try new dimensions of it in a growing [or larger, or innovative] company."
- "I decided to change careers, and I just got my degree."
- "I left to raise a family, and now I am ready to return to work permanently."
- "I moved [the company reorganized or merged or cut back or slowed down]."

Your application indicates that you have been in and out of the work force quite often (or haven't worked in some years). What were you involved with in those periods of unemployment? Here the interviewer has several concerns. One is that you might be likely to leave after being trained for this job. Another is that your skills might be rusty. Be prepared to give assurance that you plan to stay with this job and that your qualifications are such that you can handle it. Knowing your abilities and what the job demands can clarify this subject for you.

What are your weaknesses, and what are your strengths? Smile when they ask this one. Have a list that you have memorized about what you do best, such as "I work well with other people on a team basis." If the job you are applying for matches your personality type, your weaknesses will be in areas not important for the job. On a conventional job (C), for example, artistic strengths (A) would get in the way. So you might say, "I'm not very creative. I prefer to follow a set routine." Or if the job calls for machine work *(R)*, you might say your communication skills *(S)* aren't the best. Whatever personality type the job calls for, weaknesses of the type that is opposite on the hexagon can be turned into plusses!

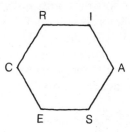

Do you have any physical limitations that may interfere with your performance? If you do not, there is no problem. If you *do* have a physical limitation or a past history of serious illness, be prepared to show that it will not interfere with your work. A doctor's statement might be helpful here.

Imagined situations that test a person's knowledge of the job may begin with questions like, "What would you do if . . ." The quality of your solution is not nearly as important as your attitude. A calm approach is a best bet. It's better to cushion your statements with answers like, "One of the things I might consider would be . . ." If you commit yourself to a process of what you *would* do, and it isn't one *they* would like or consider, you are in an awkward position. Give your answer a cushion of several possible choices.

How did you get along with . . . This question can be asked regarding supervisors, co-workers or subordinates, or even teachers. If you generally get along with people, say so. If you had a problem with someone, there is usually no need here to tell the whole tale. Simply say that occasionally you've had to work out difficulties with people. Be positive, not blaming or complaining.

Would you accept part-time or temporary work? Employers are more inclined to hire for full-time work from a part-time or temporary employment pool than to take a person from the outside. If you want a temporary job and are offered a permanent position, however, consider the cost of training you only to have you leave. It takes most employees at least several months to begin to earn their pay. If you plan to stay with the company, ask if a temporary or part-time job may result in a permanent hire before you say yes. "No" is a better answer if you really wish temporary or part-time work and you are offered a permanent, full-time position.

Why do you think you would like to work for our company? When most individuals look for a job, they are more interested in getting a good job than in being particular about where they work. It comes across that they don't care about the company. One of the most important things you should do before you go to an interview, or ask for one, is find out all you can about the company. Identify some positive things about policies, procedures, or products that you can discuss with interest. Do your homework—so that you will have work to come home from.

How long do you expect to work for us? The truth is that a company will not keep employees past their ability to use their skills. And you are not going to work for a company past the time that it is good for you. The best answer might be, "As long as it is good for both of us."

Do you have any questions about the company or the job? An interview doesn't have to be one-sided. Be ready for this question by preparing some questions of your own ahead of time to show your interest. Employers, down at the bottom of their company hearts, believe the myth that good people are hard to find. If asked, a good person is always one that is really interested in the company and in the job that they do. So this is an ideal time to relate your interest, enthusiasm, and commitment to the company and the job.[2]

Questions to resolve honestly ahead of time:

- Are you willing to/can you
  Move (or travel)?
  Work overtime?
  Take a temporary or part-time job?
- Do you have plans for
  Your next job?

Here's one! Sophisticated, attractive, well-groomed, typing experience—
too bad we can't type.

BOBBY SOX by Marty Links

Your next few years?
Starting your own business?
Changing fields?

Sometimes you may be asked questions that startle you. If you feel unprepared, it's wise to say, "I need a few moments to think about that." Then take a few deep breaths, relax, and begin confidently. If it should happen that you still "draw a blank," be prepared to deal with the situation. Possibilities: "Maybe we could come back to that later," or "I really should be prepared to answer that but I'm not." It's a learning experience, and you learn that you can keep cool.

Know your successes and failures, your strengths and weaknesses. Be prepared for some difficult ("Whew!") questions if you have ever been convicted of a crime or fired for serious problems, or if you have a poor work record. Take a deep breath, relax a minute, look at the interviewer, and say in your own words something like this: "Yes, I made a mistake [or have done poorly in the past] but I learned my lesson, and I'm determined that it won't happen again." Then stop. Do not keep on explaining. If you sound confident and not defensive, the interviewer will be more likely to accept your answer.

Perhaps you can include some recent experience as evidence that you've made some changes in your life. Again, you need to reassure the interviewer that you are capable of doing the job.

You might be startled by inappropriate questions that appear to have nothing to do with job qualifications, or even illegal questions that indicate discrimination. The interviewer should not ask questions about age, race, religion, nationality, or disabilities unless the answers are job-related. Also inappropriate are questions that discriminate between males and females, for example, questions about family planning, child care, or pregnancy. Even questions about education may be discriminatory if not related to job performance.

Decide in advance how you will answer such questions if they are asked. If the issue is not really important, you might prefer to answer the question rather than risk alienating the interviewer with a refusal. If you'd prefer not to answer, you might say, "I wasn't aware that this was a requirement for the job," or "Can you explain how this question relates to the job?" One can appeal to the law in obvious cases of prejudice; in less serious instances, a good sense of humor and respect for others can be enormously helpful. Don't win the battle and lose the war!

Nelva Shore, a California employment specialist says, "It really doesn't matter much what questions are asked as long as you can talk!" Be ready to talk positively about yourself, your goals, and your reason for applying. Practice talking. There is no other way. One woman who stood out in an interview later told about how she had practiced sitting down in front of a mirror; she practiced talking out loud, answering questions, eye contact, voice melody, every phase of the interview until she felt totally at ease. Her enthusiasm came through unspoiled by anxiety. You can learn these skills too.

Send a thank-you letter after the interview (see Figure 7-6). It's a good chance to call attention to your interest in the job and to refer to your skills again.

After you are hired, you may be asked to supply such items as a birth certificate, proof of citizenship, a photograph, and proof of age. Have these items ready if you feel they might be required.

Job Offers: Too Many or Too Few?

You probably will not get a job offer during your first interview. In competitive fields, people interview for many months before they find jobs. But suppose you

Figure 7-6 Thank-You Letter Following an Interview   **205**

411 Park Lane
Rutland, VT 05701

November 20, 1983

Ms. Margaret T. Caitan
Title Insurance and Trust
Winooshi, VT 05404

Dear Ms. Caitan:

It was a pleasure meeting with you on Friday. Thank you for the opportunity to interview for a sales position.

I was pleased with what I learned about Title Insurance and Trust and your approach to sales. Your attitude toward professionalism in sales reflects my view completely.

I am excited about the possibility of working with you and hope to be considered to fill one of the positions available.

Sincerely,

Marie Mello

Marie Mello

get a job offer—or two or three—in this early phase of your career search. Maybe you had planned to do personnel work, but the welding shop would welcome you! Beware of such decisions. You can easily get carried away with excitement and leap into the first job that comes along.

Some jobs sound rewarding in terms of personal growth opportunities, but the salary is so low you could not live on it without making sacrifices. Another job pays very well, but the work sounds dull and disagreeable. You might even be offered a temporary job; it would fulfill your immediate needs, but you'd be back on the job market in six months or so. Should you accept one of these less desirable jobs just to get hired or to get experience?

Now is the time to review your needs, wants, and values and become very clear about what you want the job to do. Perhaps your goal is just to get into a special company that you've chosen. Taking a job you don't particularly like could give you this chance. Many companies promote from within before they open jobs to outsiders.

If you aren't hired for the job you really want right away, you may be only one of many well-qualified applicants. In a competitive field it can take six months or more of continuous job hunting to find a job. Whether you should take a less desirable job depends on how long you can afford to wait and continue the search. If you job-hunt for many months without a nibble, you may need to consider alternatives: other careers, new training, other opportunities in your present position, additional paid or volunteer experience that might be useful in a different kind of job.

Choosing may be difficult because you have in mind a portrait of the perfect workplace. But when you actually go job hunting, you will find that perfection doesn't exist. You need a job because the rent is due and you have car payments to make. Sometimes physical realities rule out waiting until you find a perfect match.

You may have to start at the bottom and work up to the job you want. Suppose you are a business major with a fresh degree from a good university, and you are offered a job as a mail clerk. Or you have a master's degree in computer programming, but you are offered a job as a computer operator. You may feel such offers are beneath your dignity. But before you ride away on your high horse, consider these facts: One major oil company makes a practice of hiring as mail clerks new grads who are candidates for all management and public relations jobs. Many excellent companies promote from within. In so doing, they have a chance to look you over before entrusting a more important job to you. And you have a chance to network inside and explore possibilities before getting too entrenched. Be wary of turning down a job that fails to meet your expectations. Ask some company employees what the offer means. Ask the interviewer what the growth potential of the job is and whether you might be given a performance review in three to six months for a possible promotion.

Job hunting is full-time work, which requires that you keep involved at all times in some part of the process. The more exacting your requirements, the longer you will job hunt and the more often you will be turned down. But if you can accept some frustration as a normal part of the job-hunting process, you will not be discouraged. Keep in mind a clear picture of the place you would like to work in so that you will recognize it when you find it. Focus on the changes you can make to begin to experience more satisfaction in the workplace.

Self-Assessment Exercises

1. The Job Hunt Begins

  a. Begin your résumé.

    Write a rough draft of some items you will use.

    Name: _____

    Address: _____

    Home phone: _____ Work phone: _____

    Position objective: _____

    Qualifications in brief: _____

    _____

    _____

    Experience summary: _____

    _____

    _____

    _____

    _____

    Education: _____

    _____

    _____

Personal paragraph: _____

_____

_____

_____

Special notes (honors, works published, organizations, etc.):

_____

_____

_____

    b. Write a cover letter to accompany your résumé.

    c. Fill out a sample application, such as Figure 7-7 (pp. 209–10).

2. Practicing an Interview

Some interviewers use a rating scale to grade your performance on various points of importance to them. Figure 7-8 shows a scale used by recruiters who come from various workplaces to interview students on the campus. Role-play an interview. Then rate yourself or ask someone to rate you on your interview skills.

Here are some what/how/why practice questions.

Work Experience

What were your major responsibilities on your last job?
What did you like most about that job?
What did you like least about that job?
What problems did you face? How did you overcome these problems?
What did you learn on your last job?
How do you feel your last job used your ability?
Why did you leave your last job?
What impressions did you leave behind on your last job?
Why do you want to work for us?
What do you feel you can contribute?

The same questions could be asked of someone with recent military experience.

Education

What were your favorite courses (workshops, seminars)?

Why did you choose your major?

How would you rate your instructors?

What activities and clubs were you in? How did you participate?

How did you finance your education?

What further education are you planning?

Yourself and Your Values

How do you get along with people (supervisors, co-workers, instructors)?

What are your transferable skills?

What are your work-specific skills?

What are your personal-responsibility skills?

What are your strengths?

What are your weaknesses?

How important is money to you?

How well do you work on your own?

How many days did you take off last year for sickness and personal business?

How do you feel about overtime? Flexible hours? Part-time work? Temporary work? Travel? Moving to a new location?

What do you do when a co-worker is behind schedule?

Goals

What do you see yourself doing in five years?

How do you plan to get there?

What areas of growth and development do you plan to work on?

What salary would you like to earn?

Family/Leisure

What are the most important qualities in your family?

What do you do in your leisure time?

What books have you read lately?

What newspapers and magazines do you read regularly?

What kind of vacations do you enjoy?

Tell me about yourself!

Figure 7-7 Sample Application Form

HEWLETT **hp** PACKARD
1501 Page Mill Road, Palo Alto, California 94304

PLEASE FILL OUT COMPLETELY.
ANY OMISSION OF INFORMATION MAY DELAY PROCESSING

EMPLOYMENT APPLICATION

HEWLETT-PACKARD IS AN EQUAL OPPORTUNITY EMPLOYER AND ALL APPLICANTS ARE WELCOME.

PERSONAL INFORMATION

NAME: _____   Social Security No.: ____ – ____ – ____
       Last   First   Middle

Address: _____
       No.   Street   City   State   Zip

Telephone No. _____   Message No. (If necessary): _____
     (Area Code)   Number   (Area Code)   Number

Other name(s) under which you have worked: _____

Have you ever applied for employment at HP?:   Yes ☐ No ☐   If "yes", Location: _____   Date: _____

Previously employed with HP?:   Yes ☐ No ☐   If "yes", Location: _____   Date: _____

Names of relatives employed here: _____   Relationship: _____   Location at HP: _____

How were you referred to HP? _____

If not a U.S. citizen, please name type of visa: _____

Have you ever been convicted of a felony?: Yes ☐   No ☐   If "yes", give date, place, offense, and outcome: _____

Previous convictions do not exclude an applicant from consideration for employment.

Are you between the ages of 18 and 70? Yes ☐   No ☐. All applicants under the age of 18 must submit a work permit.

TYPE OF WORK APPLYING FOR

CHECK:
☐ Electronic Tech. ☐ Machinist ☐ Tech. Maint. ☐ Stock ☐ Custodian
☐ Shop Helper ☐ Computer Op. ☐ Assembly ☐ Office ☐ Other _____

State specific type of job in the area you checked and your qualifications: _____
_____

Shift(s):   Day _____   Swing _____   Grave _____   Hours: Full-time _____   Part-time _____

Do you have any physical condition which may limit your ability to perform the job(s) applied for? ☐ Yes   ☐ No

OFFICE	SHOP	OTHER
Typing Speed _____ WPM	List tools and machines you feel qualified to use without further experience.	What specific skills or abilities do you have?
Shorthand Speed _____		_____
Office Machines _____	_____	_____
_____	_____	_____
Keypunch/Data Proc.: _____	_____	_____

EDUCATION

CIRCLE LAST GRADE COMPLETED — Grade 1 2 3 4 5 6 7 8 9 10 11 12   College 1 2 3 4

Name(s) of School(s) other than high school:	Location	Major	Dates	Degree (if any)
_____	_____	_____	_____	_____
_____	_____	_____	_____	_____
_____	_____	_____	_____	_____

Is there anything else you would like us to know about you? _____

US MILITARY

BRANCH	LAST RANK	DATE OF SEPARATION
_____	_____	_____

Your most important duties and training during service: (include schools attended) _____

6-170175 (6/78)

All Information Treated Confidentially

125

LIST PREVIOUS JOBS STARTING WITH YOUR PRESENT OR MOST RECENT ONE. PLEASE DESCRIBE DUTIES AS COMPLETELY AS SPACE ALLOWS.

WORK EXPERIENCE

Present or Last Employer: _____

Address: _____
Number   Street

_____
City   State   Zip

Telephone No.: _____
(Area Code)   Number

Your Duties: _____

Reason for Leaving: _____
_____
Supervisor: _____

Dates Start	Salary Start
/ /	$
Left	Left
/ /	$

Employer: _____

Address: _____
Number   Street

_____
City   State   Zip

Telephone No.: _____
(Area Code)   Number

Your Duties: _____

Reason for Leaving: _____
_____
Supervisor: _____

Dates Start	Salary Start
/ /	$
Left	Left
/ /	$

Employer: _____

Address: _____
Number   Street

_____
City   State   Zip

Telephone No.: _____
(Area Code)   Number

Your Duties: _____

Reason for Leaving: _____
_____
Supervisor: _____

Dates Start	Salary Start
/ /	$
Left	Left
/ /	$

Employer: _____

Address: _____
Number   Street

_____
City   State   Zip

Telephone No.: _____
(Area Code)   Number

Your Duties: _____

Reason for Leaving: _____
_____
Supervisor: _____

Dates Start	Salary Start
/ /	$
Left	Left
/ /	$

REFERENCES

One of HP's pre-employment steps is to contact your previous employers.
May we contact your present employer?   ☐ Yes   ☐ No

IN THE SPACE BELOW PLEASE LIST PERSONAL REFERENCES WHO CAN COMMENT ON YOUR EDUCATIONAL OR JOB RELATED EXPERIENCE: (DO NOT GIVE RELATIVES OR YOUR EMPLOYERS LISTED ABOVE)

NAME _____   PHONE NO. — 8AM–5 PM

NAME _____   PHONE NO. — 8AM· 5 PM

NAME _____   PHONE NO. — 8 AM· 5 PM

LOCA-TION

PLEASE CHECK LOCATIONS WHERE YOU ARE WILLING TO WORK:

☐ Palo Alto   ☐ Cupertino   ☐ Mountain View   ☐ Santa Rosa
☐ Santa Clara   ☐ San Jose   ☐ Sunnyvale

SIGNATURE

THIS APPLICATION IS NOT COMPLETE UNTIL THE FOLLOWING STATEMENT HAS BEEN READ AND SIGNED:

I certify that all of the information furnished on this form is true, complete, and correct to the best of my knowledge. I understand that such information is subject to verification by Hewlett-Packard.

....
SIGNATURE   DATE

EMPLOYMENT OFFICE COMMENTS

_____
_____
_____

DISPOSITION OF APPLICATION: Post Card _____   _____   RLC
                                        Date   Date

126

Courtesy of Hewlett-Packard Company

INTERVIEW RATING

UNIVERSITY OF SANTA CLARA
CAREER PLANNING AND PLACEMENT OFFICE

FIRM: _____

RECRUITER: _____   DATE: _____

I.   CHARACTERISTICS OF CANDIDATE:
     A = Interview preparation
     B = Clarity of career objectives
     C = Realistic career objectives
     D = Appropriate academic preparation
     E = Personal appearance
     F = Communicative ability
     G = Emotional maturity
     H = Self-confidence
     I = Motivation
     J = Overall rating

II. EMPLOYER INTEREST:
     1 = Particularly high interest
     2 = Interest with further consideration necessary
     3 = Prefer not to make offer
     4 = Need placement counseling

III. ADDITIONAL COMMENTS:

RATING SCALE: 1) Outstanding   2) Above average   3) Average   4) Below average   5) Poor

NAME	I. CHARACTERISTICS OF CANDIDATE										II.	III. COMMENTS
	A	B	C	D	E	F	G	H	I	J		

SAMPLE
This is an interview rating form used by campus recruiters. Note the characteristics that some interviewers may find important. You may wish to use it to rate members of a group role playing the interview.

Figure 7-8 Interview Rating Scale

3. The Job Hunt Checklist

If you are job hunting now, establish a goal: You will contact 100 people by information interviewing, networking, applying for jobs, writing letters, making telephone calls, and sending résumés upon request. To check your progress, answer the following questions yes or no.

_____ Have you interviewed 25 people to obtain information about jobs and companies?

_____ Have you applied for work directly to 50 companies?

_____ Have you written an effective résumé for each job title?

_____ Have you contacted a network of at least 25 people who could help you to get hired?

_____ After each interview, do you critique yourself honestly?

_____ Have you written letters to thank the people who interviewed you?

Eight

Decisions, Decisions: What's Your Next Move?

The last step in the career search process is making a good decision. Will you go back to school, start a new job, keep the same job but with a new approach, or keep the status quo by deciding not to decide? The decision will be easier to make if your values are clear. It also helps to be aware of the behavior pattern that is characteristic of your own personality type.

Each personality type has its own decision-making style. The social person acts out of caring for others but is not always "practical." Both the realistic and the conventional types tend to stay within societal norms. The conventional type follows the lead of others. Realistic types tend to make their own decisions, but they sometimes disregard the feelings of others. The creative/artistic person, on the other hand, will see so many possibilities—including some that follow no known guidelines—that it's hard to choose. While the enterprising person leaps first and gets the facts later, the investigative types seem to research in the library forever.

We can fantasize a perfectly self-actualized person bringing all of these factors into balance: caring for others, with just enough "hard-headed" realism; creating new systems while following guidelines when appropriate; searching out just enough facts before risking the decision. Since most of us aren't troubled with such perfection, we often need help with decision-making. In this chapter we will consider four attitudes and four options and, finally, a four-phase decision-making process.

The first rule is *keep calm*. If possible, make the career decision when you are not under pressure because of a crisis in your life. In times of crisis, a million fantasies arise: Quit work altogether and drop out; start my own company; join the navy; end my marriage; run off with my secretary; sell everything, hitch up the wagon, and head West! The uncertainties are as numerous as the fantasies: Am I OK? Is this all there is? Will my health hold up? Will my kids ever get settled? Will I? Will I look like a fool if I go back to school? Can I keep on succeeding? Do I even want to?

215

216/Eight

**Decisions,
Decisions:**

Where are you on
the Career Choice
Continuum?

Are you just drifting?
Start gathering information
about careers.

Are you swamped with
information?
It's time to start narrowing
the choices.

Stay calm, stay on course,
and you'll reach your
destination.

Second, *take small steps* with courage. Remember that you don't have to put a decision into action immediately and in one leap! You can set a reasonable time limit and proceed by taking tiny steps. Just as you analyzed past activities, you can analyze a decision down into its minicomponents. If a decision to get a four-year degree seems overwhelming, looking at college catalogs in the library is a manageable first step.

Third, *keep perspective.* Review all the relevant facts you've been collecting, and record them in the space provided at the end of this book. You can use Maslow's hierarchy from Chapter 1, for example, to identify the weak spots in your life. Some people feel they want material success after long periods of "doing without!" Others wish to move away from materialism so that they can develop nurturing relationships, grow intellectually, and search for more meaning to their lives.

Fourth, *be confident.* Know that you *can* take the necessary steps to make your decision happen. Since we cannot know the future, every decision involves risking, then trusting that it will work out. In order to improve our lives, we change what can be changed, accept what can't be changed, and hope we have the wisdom to know the difference. We have to take the first step, however small.

Let's approach the first step by examining the options.

Back to School

For the first time in the history of the United States, more than half of all U.S. workers have white-collar jobs. As the need for unskilled labor decreases, more adults choose to go back to school. Today 69 percent of all Americans 25 years and older have graduated from high school, and 17 percent have completed four years of college.[1] The concept of life-long learning encourages adults to change and grow on many different levels. In today's fast-moving, technological world, workers need to "keep up." Learning to learn, to be a generalist, to have a broad view of the world are essential skills for the future.

You may be wondering if you should return to school. Or you may be in college and wondering what courses to take if you continue. You could take courses to improve your basic skills, to explore various majors, to prepare for possible careers, or just to foster personal enrichment and growth. Do not let your age or your previous school record discourage you. The average age of all adults returning to school is rising to the 30-year-old level, and there is no maximum in sight. A recent newspaper article described a man of 92 receiving his associate of arts degree.

Twenty years after publication of *The Feminine Mystique,* women who have worked little or not at all for pay outside their homes are still returning to college in record numbers. Studies show that the great majority of such women are fearful: "Am I too old to learn, too old to compete with young college students?" The surprise comes when, with few exceptions, the re-entry woman reports a great growth in confidence and the discovery of new-found goals. Many returning students have previous school records that qualify as disasters, but now, because they are mature and motivated, they can reach their goals. So can you.

If your high school education was incomplete or deficient, consider basic skill courses in language and math at community colleges or adult education centers. Usually counselors are available to help you decide which courses to take. Search for someone who understands exactly where you are now, and how you feel about it.

A two-year community college (junior college) is a good place to explore various majors and prepare for a career. Obtain a catalog at the college bookstore and look for introductory courses. The titles of these courses frequently include terms such as "beginning," "orientation to," "introduction to," or "principles of." The catalog will tell you the required courses and general degree requirements for each major. Usually advisors or counselors will be available to help you through the maze of choices.

If you want a college degree at the four-year level, you can go directly to a four-year institution, or you can attend a community college for two years and then transfer to a four-year college or university to complete your junior-and senior-level courses. The four-year "package" can be outlined as follows:

First year: general education (GE), introduction to a major and electives
Second year: major requirements, GE, and electives
Third year: major requirements, electives, and remaining GE
Fourth year: major requirements and electives

ALTERNATIVE ROUTES TO EDUCATIONAL CREDIT

High School Credit

Adults can earn high school equivalency certificates through the General Educational Development (GED) program:

> GED Testing Service
> One Dupont Circle N.W.
> Suite 20
> Washington, DC 20036-1163

College Credit

At various colleges, look for flexible alternatives such as TV courses, weekend programs, credit by examination, and credit for work experience.

Credit by Examination

You can take examinations to earn college credit. Contact the College-Level Examination Program (CLEP) for information:

> CLEP College Board
> Department C
> 888 Seventh Avenue
> New York, NY 10019

Or contact the Proficiency Examination Program (PEP):

> ACT-PEP
> P.O. Box 168
> Iowa City, IA 52243

Credit for Noncollege Learning

The Office on Educational Credit (OEC) at the American Council on Education evaluates courses given by private employers, community organizations, labor unions, government agencies, and military education programs. Contact:

> American Council on Education
> Office of Educational Credit
> One Dupont Circle N.W.
> Washington, DC 20036

Credit for Experience

You can apply for college credit for your work experience. Contact:

> Council for Advancement of Experiential Learning (CAEL)
> American City Building
> Suite 212
> Columbia, MD 21044
> 800-638-7813 (toll free)

The Task Force on Volunteer Accreditation of the Council of National Organizations for Adult Education has developed a series of "I Can" lists to help volunteers identify skills for which college credit might be given. The Council's book *I Can: A Tool for Assessing Skills Acquired Through Volunteer Experience* may be purchased for $4.75. Contact:

> Ramco Associates
> 228 East 45th Street
> New York, NY 10017

You will probably need more math if you are interested in science, four-year business or technical fields, architecture, or engineering. The usual sequence is as follows:

High school: Arithmetic, introductory algebra, plane geometry, intermediate algebra, trigonometry, college (pre-calculus) algebra or "senior math"
College: College algebra, calculus (two to three semesters or five quarters), other advanced courses as needed and required

Educational Testing Service publishes *How to Get Credit for What You Have Learned as a Homemaker or Volunteer*. It may be purchased for $3. Contact:

Educational Testing Service
Princeton NJ 08540

Credit for Correspondence and Independent Study

The Division of Independent Study of the National University Extension Association (NUEA) sponsors a wide variety of correspondence and independent study courses and programs, which are available through its membership institutions. The Association publishes *NUEA Guide to Independent Study Through Correspondence Instruction, 1980 Edition* ($2), and *On-Campus Degree Programs for Part-Time Students* ($4). For information, contact:

NUEA
Suite 360
One Dupont Circle N.W.
Washington, DC 20036

To order the publications, contact

Peterson's Guides
P.O. Box 978
Book Order Department
Edison, NJ 00817

Home Study Schools

A book entitled *Bear's Guide to Nontradi-* *tional College Degrees* (1981) is available from:

John Bear
P.O. Box 646
Mendocino, CA 95460

Another relevant publication is *There Is a School in Your Mail Box: A Book on Home Study* by Dr. G. Howard Poteet, available from:

National Home Study Council
1601 18th Street N.W.
Washington, D.C. 20009

For additional information, contact the following organizations:

National Home Study Council
1601 18th Street N.W.
Washington, DC 20009

Regents External Degree Program
State Education Department
Cultural Education Center
Room 5C85
Albany, NY 12230

Thomas A. Edison College
New Jersey College for External Degrees
101 West State Street
Trenton, NJ 08625

National University Consortium for
    Telecommunications in Teaching
University College
University of Maryland
College Park, MD 20742

First, check to see how much math you need for various programs. (You may not need any at all.) Then try to start where you left off or where you feel most comfortable. Before you try to enroll in a course, however, find out whether you must complete any prerequisites; a *prerequisite* is an elementary course that you need in order to understand a more advanced course.

Adult education programs offer math courses at the high school level and possibly beyond. Community colleges offer not only high school level courses but also most of the college courses at the freshman and sophomore level. Both offer remedial arithmetic.

You can find courses for personal growth and enrichment in colleges, adult education programs, and community centers. Many are noncredit courses, which provide an easy way to start back to school.

If returning to school seems impossible—because of distance, for example—investigate tutoring services, correspondence courses, and courses by TV. Some colleges and universities administer tests like the College Level Examination Program (CLEP), which enable you to earn credit by examination. Some give credit for work experience. You may be required to attend the school in order to complete courses, but such credits decrease the time that you need to spend on campus.

If finances are a problem, apply for financial aid. Sometimes students of all ages can get grants and low-interest loans for education. Some people change their lifestyles, mortgage or sell their houses, sell their cars and ride a bike.

Remember, too, that much learning takes place off campus. You can teach yourself many things, and you can find others who will help you learn. Much depends on having a goal and working toward it—or being flexible enough to see alternatives.

Remember that most jobs require only average to somewhat above average skills. Talking to people "in the field" can help you to assess your motivation to go on with it, especially if it looks as though you'll need years of training. Remember, however, when you meet a competent professional all trained, experienced, and "'way up there," it wasn't done in one step. Most valuable in acquiring high-level ability is the patience to stay with it until you learn it. But hard work is fun if you are doing what you enjoy.

As you go along, new horizons will open up. You can also float to your level. Before the end of your training, you may choose to stop out at a point where you feel comfortable. Instead of going straight on to become a certified public accountant, for example, you might try work experience as an accounting clerk, which might lead you in a direction that you hadn't seen before.

You may find along the way that you'd like to float sideways to a different area with similar satisfiers. The more homework you've done regarding your interests, the more quickly you'll be able to make such changes.

If you simply must get more detailed information about your skills, your aptitudes to develop skills, or where you skills need sharpening, you can contact a counselor at a local college, state employment office, or in private practice. You can arrange to take such tests as the DAT (Differential Aptitude Test) or the GATB (the General Aptitude Test Battery).

Back to Work

You may decide to by-pass further training and go directly out into the job market. Perhaps your decision-making and job-hunting skills will need to be reviewed and

If she doesn't make it as a dancer, she wants to be a dentist.

THE PICK OF PUNCH

sharpened. For some, going back to work is a "natural." For others, it's a scary prospect. One woman's experience is worth sharing:

> Last fall, quaking and shaking, I had made up my mind I must not put off any longer the job-hunting ordeal. During a bridge game on a Wednesday, I announced I was going to find secretarial work. My partner announced her husband needed a secretary; she phoned him, he said, "Sure." On Thursday I made an appointment for Friday, and two weeks later I was sitting at a desk, secretary to a very fine man who has been very understanding of my initial lack of self-assurance (starting to work again at 56 after 27 years). My 60-day performance report was a very satisfactory one (was delighted to have "initiative" get the best grading); and at six-months received a 12 percent raise; but, best of all, the following remarks: "in recognition of outstanding contribution to the department." I love the work, and most of all, I love the self-assurance it's given me. Tell other women as quaking and shaking as I that it's not all that hard. Take that first plunge, and you've got it made.
>
> I should add that my husband and family are delighted with the New Me. I hear no more complaints about what doesn't get done at home, they do the work instead. They are all being most supportive.*

*Courtesy of Carol Shawhan.

221

Same Job/New Approach

If you are already employed, a brief exploration of the job market may convince you that your present job isn't so bad after all. "Then why," you will wonder, "do I feel dissatisfied?" A most common explanation is, "I'm not comfortable with my co-workers." Often communications problems are at the root of this discomfort. Would some fine tuning in human relations improve your work life?

You may wish to check these items: Are you pleasant and easy to get along with? Do you overlook other people's minor shortcomings? Do your appearance and manner fit in with the style of your workplace? Do you give others credit and praise?

If your job is beginning to call for new duties, such as public presentations or writing, some of your basic skills may need improving. Try to put energy into your job, and to learn as much as you can in order to grow and develop. Your self-confidence will improve along with your skills.

Some people create a job within a job by assessing the tasks they like or dislike. Sometimes it's possible to trade tasks with others, ask for a reorganization, or even hire someone to work with you if your work load warrants it. Taking on a new project, changing departments, doing the same function in a new locale—each of these can be a creative way to get a fresh start.

Amazingly, some people are so successful they are promoted beyond the level of their own self-confidence. Suddenly they discover that everyone believes in them except themselves, and they need to grow in confidence to meet those expectations. Sometimes a step down can be a welcome change if the pressures of the job are really unbearable. An executive, laid off and then rehired into a lower position says, "The money doesn't add up. But for the first time in my life I don't give a damn. I haven't felt this good in years!"[2] "Stepping down" is a career direction we rarely consider, but it may be a good move toward actualizing our values. If you are dissatisfied with yourself, consider enrolling in some growth classes—or at least do some reading in the area of personal growth. If a problem is weighing on you, discuss it with a trusted friend or a counselor. Many problems have obvious solutions that we miss when searching alone.

Deciding Not to Decide

When you keep the status quo, you are deciding not to decide—which can be a good decision. You might stay in the same job, take more classes, or continue to be at home with your children. You may need to do more exploring and evaluating, but try to set a time limit for your next move, say six months to a year.

Decision-Making: A Four-Phase Process

Decision-making is a four-phase process that involves gathering information, weighing alternatives and outcomes, checking values, and designing strategies.

Gather information. Every decision calls for accurate information. In this book you have been gathering all the information that you need to make a career decision. You have learned how to pull information from a variety of sources and resources.

Weigh the alternatives and outcomes. There are alternatives to every decision, and each alternative will have several outcomes, both positive and negative. Every decision involves some risk.

Some people envision only one type of outcome. Some, burdened by fears, see only disasters—major and minor. Other overly optimistic folks see grandiose positive events occurring. Most major decisions, however, result in a mixture of outcomes. You take a job with a good salary, for example, but have to get extra training or work overtime. Hardly any decision has perfect results. Without a crystal ball, it's hard to predict exactly how a decision is going to work out. Even the most carefully reasoned decision can bring disappointing results. In such cases, try to avoid blaming yourself, but give yourself credit for having taken the risk.

Some decisions that won't work do result in lost time and money, or even physical injury. But many risks involve merely the approval of others: What will people think? Indeed, you may find yourself preserving the status quo solely out of fear of others' opinions. If so, you're giving others a great deal of power over your life. There is no way to change and grow without some risk.

Every change, even if it's only re-arranging the garage, has an impact on others. Caring for those around you involves bringing them along with your decision-making, that is, communicating your own needs honestly while listening to theirs, keeping them informed as you make changes. Hardly any change is perfect. There will be advantages and disadvantages to most moves. The idea is to *maximize the advantages.*

One way to assess the risks is to imagine all the possible results, ranging from worst to best, if you decide to act. Rate each result on the degree of risk it represents for you. Look at the results most likely to occur to see if you are willing to accept those outcomes. Look at the results least likely to occur to see if it's acceptable that they *not* happen. Do you tend to imagine just the worst or the best outcomes? Either tendency can lead you to make a poor decision.

Check values. As you make choices, you express your value system—because values are revealed in what you *do,* not in what you *say.* As a final check, consider your decision in terms of values. If you want to live very simply, why seek a high-powered, energy-consuming job whose only reward is money? On the other hand, if money is important to you, aim for it. If you want both a family and a career, plan for it. Your decision should reflect your personal priorities.

Design strategies. This book outlines a great many strategies that you can use in launching your career. How will you carry out your decision? Develop a good set of strategies, a step-by-step procedure for putting your decision into practice. Think of each step as a goal, and set a time limit for reaching each successive step. The time limit helps to discourage procrastination.

If time is a problem for you, learn to manage it. Some people pack their lives with so many activities that the end result is failure, frustration, or frenzy instead of accomplishment. Others take on too little and end up feeling bored and uninvolved. There are various techniques for managing time:

- List all the tasks on your agenda and rank them in the order of importance.
- Keep a "very important" list, a "so-so" list, and a "nice if I can get around to it" list of tasks that need doing.
- For one week, keep track of all your activities to find out where you are spending your time.

For further help with time management, read Alan Lakein's *How to Get Control of Your Time and Your Life.*[3]

Some people complete the entire career search process without making the big decision. If you are still unable to choose a career, you may need more time to gain confidence. To find out what is holding you back, ask yourself if you are

- Locked into your stereotypes
- Too complacent to change the status quo
- Caught in health or emotional problems
- Bogged down in transitions like divorce, widowhood, immigration adjustment
- Burdened by family responsibilities
- Longing for improved personal relationships
- Afraid to make a commitment
- In need of money, education, other resources
- Blocked by office politics
- Caught in a shrinking job market
- In the habit of procrastinating
- Overresearching—losing yourself in the library
- Experiencing conflicts about values

Perhaps you need to take a "dynamic rest" along the road to success. Read some books about the problem that's holding you back. Talk to a trusted friend or counselor. Paradoxically, sometimes we need to accept the status quo before we can change it, even just a little.

If you have assessed your needs, wants, values, interests, and skills, made decisions, set goals, and determined strategies—then your next step is effective action.

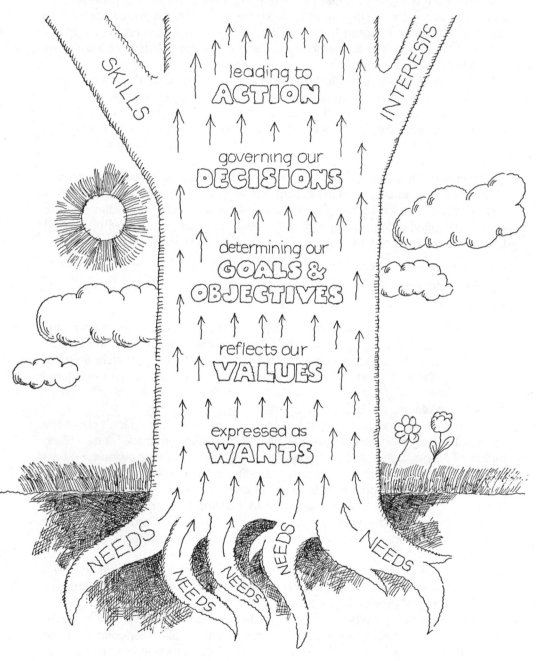

leading to
ACTION

governing our
DECISIONS

determining our
GOALS &
OBJECTIVES

reflects our
VALUES

expressed as
WANTS

SKILLS

INTERESTS

NEEDS
NEEDS
NEEDS
NEEDS
NEEDS

How to Define Success

As you move toward a career decision, you need to have an image of the successful you. But what is success? Some people equate it with money and prestige. The fact is that success is "all in your head"—everyone's definition is different. Failure also is whatever you choose to call it. Both success and failure are only steps in the experiment of living: Some steps work and some don't. What we learn from all this is called *experience.*

Success most often comes to those who set realistic goals and work hard persistently without giving up when things go wrong. Most successful people admit they have had some good luck that helped them along the way. Chances are, they have had bad luck too, and have made some mistakes, but were not defeated. They were able to maintain their enthusiasm and commitment, which are the keys to success for everyone, especially those with little experience or education.

A common hazard on the road to success is the "I don't deserve it" syndrome. Since the desire for success is the strongest of all motivators, this feeling can block a good decision. If you tune in to your mental conversations, you will recognize yourself as friend or foe. As Ken Keyes, Jr., says, "Beware what you tell yourself!"[4] Consider how each of these messages might affect an individual's career:

"I don't deserve success. My goal is only to work hard."

"No matter how much money I've got, it's never enough."

"Everyone—including me—deserves self-actualization."

As surprising as it may seem, some people are afraid to succeed. Success brings more responsibility and higher visibility. It leads others to expect you to keep on performing well. Success requires a great deal of continued effort, both to get there and to stay there. The one who accepts failure no longer has to keep on trying. In some cases, failing is a way to exert independence against the real or imagined demands of others.

Some days our bad feelings send us in search of a problem. "Don't cheer me up or tell me anything good because it will ruin my misery program." Jerry Gillies, author of *Money Love,* says some people have a "poverty consciousness," others a "prosperity consciousness."[5] Margaret Anstin, in her career guide to *Voyages,* says that we can use a potential salary loss as an excuse to avoid changing careers. We tend to let money indicate our value as persons and measure our success. Anstin points out, "Prosperity is much more likely to flow to and through you if you are doing work you enjoy."[6] Enjoyment of work is another way to define success.

Affirmations, both positive and negative, are so powerful that the authors of the children's book *Make It So!* have children speculate, "So—I've been wondering—could most of my problems be caused by me?"[7]

In this book, you have been learning good things about yourself: your interests, values, and skills. You've learned how to find or make a place for yourself in the job market. You've learned to assess jobs and workplaces and how to network

And what if the stress of success turns out to be as bad as the stress of failure?

THE NOW SOCIETY by William Hamilton

effectively. Now it's time to "own" all the good things about yourself by positive affirmations. Affirmation can change outcomes because they change attitudes and feelings. When you believe in yourself as a capable person, you are on your way to further growth and fulfillment. Fulfillment is another word for success.

Both success and failure are only temporary. The excited, enthusiastic, newly hired graduate, the 40-year company man, and the secure civil servant may have a hard time recognizing themselves as people in transition. But the fact is that *all* people are in transition. No one stands still on the same job forever. Growth, promotion, transfers, new technology, layoffs, cutbacks, mergers, reorganizations, changes of management, company bankruptcy, life transitions, illness, disability, and retirement are just a few of the changes that affect careers.

Perhaps you have made a good career decision but now find that things are changing. You may have put a great deal of energy into your job. You may have earned a degree and learned new skills in preparation for your career. Still your job doesn't seem to be working out well, so you (or your employer) decide to call it quits. Suddenly you are jobless and worried about where to go next. But you are also sleeping-in some mornings, catching up on errands, enjoying an occasional walk on the beach. That's good: the more you can enjoy your new leisure, the better you'll be able to plan your next step. Be open to new ideas at times like this.

Some questions you need to answer are: Do I want to do almost exactly the same job in a similar setting? Do I want to get out of the old line of work or into another type of workplace? Do I want to make a career change, create my own career, start a new business, go back to school? Most important, what changes can I make in myself to put me in harmony with my choices? What skills did I learn and develop on my last job? Did that job put me in touch with new interests? What did I dislike about that job?

If you were fired or laid off, evaluate the causes to see how they can be avoided in the future. Ask for help from friends, relatives, and neighbors without hiding your job loss. As everyone knows, it can happen to anyone. Despite the very real trauma involved in being jobless, you can use the experience to advantage by preparing for your next job: Learn to pick up cues that will help you to make changes or seize opportunities *before* you are laid off or fired. Keep up contacts and keep other options open, instead of sinking into mindless security on your job. You can't always plan your career step by step, but you can adopt a game plan that provides alternatives.

Even if you plan to stay at the same place in the same job for a lo-o-o-o-ong time, chances are that some day job burnout or boredom will prompt you to wonder, "Is this all there is?" You may have assessed yourself and found out exactly who you are. You have found that dream job that embodies your most important values and interests and is encouraging you to develop your skills. You have a growing family and a hefty mortgage. You seem to "have it all," but still you experience a nagging discontent. You feel "stuck," as if there is nowhere else to go. Now it's reassessment time—time to renew the career search and look for new directions.

You will find a workplace where your skills are needed and appreciated. Knowing that your skills are needed, you will have the confidence to take action. Having proved yourself as a capable person, you will be on your way to further growth and self-fulfillment.

The steps you take create your life. May your career choice make you a "true person." May your dreams be actualized.

Self-Assessment Exercises

The following exercises illustrate some aspects of the decision-making process.

1. Decision-Making Style

Remember that you, and only you, have the ability to make your decisions and take responsibility for them. You make many decisions every day. It's helpful to reflect on how you do it. Check (√) the appropriate columns. Then double-check (√√) answers that indicate areas you'd like to improve.

	Usually	Sometimes	Rarely

1. I make decisions after considering many alternatives. _____ _____ _____

2. I make decisions easily, without undue agonizing, and on time. _____ _____ _____

3. I base my decisions on "reasoned judgment" of the information available. _____ _____ _____

4. I base my decisions on feelings and intuition. _____ _____ _____

5. I make my own decisions, not shifting responsibility to others. _____ _____ _____

6. I consult with others, but my decisions are my own. _____ _____ _____

7. I compromise when the needs of others are involved. _____ _____ _____

8. I make some decisions to fulfill my own needs. _____ _____ _____

9. I "test out" major decisions ahead of time where possible. _____ _____ _____

10. I take responsibility for the consequences of my decisions. _____ _____ _____

11. If a decision doesn't work, I try another plan. _____ _____ _____

2. Making Changes: Risk Assessment

a. List four changes you'd like to make. Consider changes in your career, skills, education, family, friends, lifestyle, and all phases of your intellectual and altruistic/spiritual development.

Change 1 _____

Change 2 _____

Change 3 _____

Change 4 _____

b. Select one change and on the next page list as many possible results as you can, both positive and negative. Rate the risk for each result high, medium, or low as it applies to you.

Change: I would like to _____

Possible Results and Degree of Risk

Positive	High	Medium	Low		Negative	High	Medium	Low

Cross out any results that are *unlikely to happen.*

If any high-risk results are both unacceptable and likely to happen, you may want to make an alternate decision.

3. Decision Target

a. Write your possible decision from Exercise 2, "Making Changes: Risk Assessment," in the center circle of the target.

b. Review your values rating from Chapter 1. Think about which of your values would be affected if you carried out that decision.

c. Arrange those values in the outer circles according to their importance to you and whether they support or oppose the decision. Since outcomes represent values, include results from Exercise 2

d. Do the positive values outweigh the negative values?

Yes _____ No _____

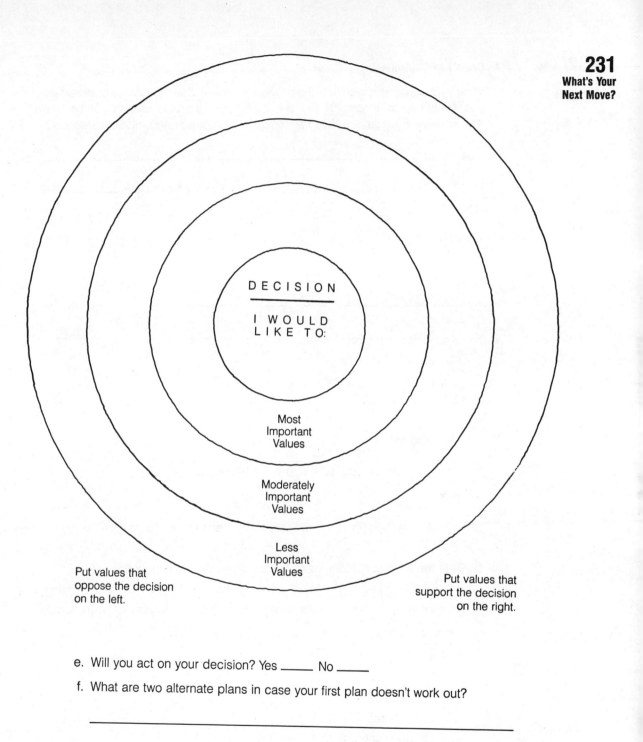

DECISION
I WOULD
LIKE TO:

Most
Important
Values

Moderately
Important
Values

Less
Important
Values

Put values that
oppose the decision
on the left.

Put values that
support the decision
on the right.

e. Will you act on your decision? Yes _____ No _____

f. What are two alternate plans in case your first plan doesn't work out?

_____

_____

4. Goals and Strategies

Write your goal or decision from the previous exercise. State four steps or strategies you would take to accomplish this change. In the right-hand column, set the time line. How soon would you like to accomplish this change and related strategies?

Goal or decision: _____

Is the goal realistic? _____ Does it agree with your values? _____

	Date to accomplish
Steps I must take	
a. _____	_____
b. _____	_____
c. _____	_____
d. _____	_____
e. _____	_____

5. Time Management

How will you manage your time in order to reach your goals?

a. State the number of college credits you plan to carry.   a. _____

b. Allow at least two hours of study for each credit or unit (units ×
   2).   b. _____

c. State the number of hours you will work per week. (Include family
   care.)   c. _____

d. Total the number of hours each week you have committed so far.   d. [____]

e. Estimate the number of hours per week you devote to:

   Sleeping   _____

   Eating   _____

   Commuting   _____

   Household chores   _____

   Business (bank, dentist, shopping, etc.)   _____

   Recreation   _____

   Communicating with family and friends   _____

Exercise   _____

Miscellaneous/unexpected   _____

Add the total.   e. ☐

f. Add the totals in boxes *d* and *e* to see how many hours per week you spend in all activities—the big total!   f. ☐

Remember, there are only 168 hours in a week! How do you stand? Are you overcommitted or undercommitted?

_____

6. Your Weekly Schedule

Once you have chosen some goals and strategies, it's important to fit them into your time schedule. Are you trying to do too much? Do you let too much time slip away? To find out, fill in the schedule chart on the next page for a week. At the end of the week, cross out the unnecessary activities that are overcrowding your schedule, and fill empty spaces with things you would like to do. Don't crowd every minute of every day. Try to schedule only the activities that have value for you.

7. Back to School

If going to college is on your list of possibilities, check (✓) the answers that explain why. If college isn't for you, check any other training alternatives that appeal to you.

Why college?

_____ Not sure, but wish to explore and find out about it

_____ Personal enrichment

_____ Hope to improve basic skills

_____ Wish to earn a career program certificate

_____ Would like to finish high school work and earn a diploma

_____ Plan to earn a two-year degree at a community college

_____ Want to earn a B.A. or B.S. degree from a four-year college or university

_____ Pressure from mother, father, boss

Weekly Schedule

Time	Monday	Tuesday	Wednesday	Thursday	Friday	Saturday	Sunday
6:30							
7:00							
7:30							
8:00							
8:30							
9:00							
9:30							
10:00							
10:30							
11:00							
11:30							
12:00							
12:30							
1:00							
1:30							
2:00							
2:30							
3:00							
3:30							
4:00							
4:30							
5:00							
5:30							
6:00							
6:30							
7:00							
7:30							
8:00							
8:30							
9:00							
9:30							
10:00							
10:30							
11:00							
11:30							
12:00							

Other training alternatives?

_____ Apprenticeship programs with unions in various crafts

_____ Adult education through my local school district

_____ Proprietary schools (private schools that teach a special job skill)

_____ On-the-job training programs or management training programs

_____ Off-campus or extension college work by TV, job experience, weekend college, and other options for the working person

8. School Subjects

a. Check (√) the columns that describe your feelings about school subjects.

	Like	Dislike	Did well	Did not do well	Avoided
Reading	_____	_____	_____	_____	_____
Writing	_____	_____	_____	_____	_____
Speech/drama	_____	_____	_____	_____	_____
Math	_____	_____	_____	_____	_____
Science	_____	_____	_____	_____	_____
Social studies	_____	_____	_____	_____	_____
Art/crafts	_____	_____	_____	_____	_____
Music	_____	_____	_____	_____	_____
Industrial/technical	_____	_____	_____	_____	_____
Business	_____	_____	_____	_____	_____
Health	_____	_____	_____	_____	_____
Agriculture	_____	_____	_____	_____	_____
Physical education	_____	_____	_____	_____	_____
_____	_____	_____	_____	_____	_____
_____	_____	_____	_____	_____	_____
_____	_____	_____	_____	_____	_____

b. Circle the subjects you'd like to study further.

c. Now look at your "worst" subjects. Are there any that you'd like to try again? Few people have the time and energy to become good at everything. But often our work is poor only because we don't want to make the effort to improve. Getting rid of this "excess baggage" can be a liberating experience.

9. College Majors

The listing of major subjects on the next page is arranged by predominant personality type and the twelve interest areas from the Job Group Chart; a few subjects have been listed in two places. Check all of the subjects that interest you at this time.

10. Transition Tune-up

Check (√) the items you need to work on to smooth the way for a possible transition.

_____ a. Keep on assessing your needs, wants, interests, skills, and prospects.

_____ b. Keep your contacts up to date, stay in the network, watch the job action in your field.

_____ c. Stay one step ahead by retraining for tomorrow's job market.

_____ d. Shoulder to the wheel, nose to the grindstone! Make an energetic, enthusiastic, prideful commitment to the job.

_____ e. Keep one ear to the ground. Anticipate changes that are likely to affect you.

_____ f. Be aware of the political games in your workplace, but keep your sense of humor.

_____ g. Make friends, not enemies. Avoid hostile strategies to get ahead.

_____ h. Be aware of a promotion leading you into a job that doesn't match your skills and interests. It may end in a dead end or a detour you dislike.

_____ i. Check values to avoid conflicts over unethical, unacceptable practices.

_____ j. Develop a satisfying personal life to prevent you from drowning in work and losing perspective.

_____ k. Consider a job change, rather than a career change, if you are dissatisfied.

_____ l. Save enough to carry you through a month or two of unemployment.

_____ m. Avoid debt. Live below your income until your next step is clear.

College Majors Arranged by Personality Type and Job Group

R REALISTIC

Mechanical
- ___ Aero maintenance/Operations
- ___ Air conditioning/Refrigeration/ Solar technology
- ___ Anaplastology
- ___ Automotive technology
- ___ Biomedical technology
- ___ Construction technology
- ___ Electronics technology
- ___ *See* Engineering under Investigative
- ___ Fabrication technology
- ___ Food service
- ___ Industrial administration/ Engineering
- ___ Industrial engineering and technology
- ___ Laser technology
- ___ Machine/Tool technology
- ___ Manufacturing technology
- ___ Quality control
- ___ Radiologic technology
- ___ Semiconductor management
- ___ Technological drafting/ Modelbuilding
- ___ Transportation
- ___ Welding technology

Industrial
- ___ No majors

Nature
- ___ Agriculture
- ___ Animal health technology
- ___ Nursery management
- ___ Park management technology
- ___ Wildlife management technology

Protective
- ___ Administration of justice
- ___ Fire science
- ___ Safety engineering

Physical performance
- ___ Physical education/ Kinesiology

I INVESTIGATIVE

Scientific/Analytic
- ___ Biological/Life science
  - ___ Agricultural science
  - ___ Animal/Avian science
  - ___ Bacteriology
  - ___ Biology
  - ___ Botany
  - ___ Conservation
  - ___ Enology

I INVESTIGATIVE *continued*

- ___ Entomology/Pest science
- ___ Environmental science
- ___ Food science
- ___ Forest science
- ___ Genetics
- ___ Kinesiology
- ___ Marine biology
- ___ Microbiology
- ___ Nutrition
- ___ Soil/Water/Wood science
- ___ Toxicology
- ___ Zoology
- ___ Consumer economics/ Science
- ___ Cybernetics
- ___ Engineering
  - ___ Aeronautical/Aerospace
  - ___ Agricultural
  - ___ Bio engineering
  - ___ Civil
  - ___ Computer science
  - ___ Electrical/Electronic
  - ___ Environmental
  - ___ Material science
  - ___ Naval architecture
  - ___ Nuclear
  - ___ Science
  - ___ Systems
  - ___ Transportation
- ___ Linguistics
- ___ Mathematics/Statistics/ Applied
- ___ Medical
  - ___ Dentistry
  - ___ Optometry
  - ___ Pharmacy
  - ___ Medicine/Surgery
  - ___ Veterinary medicine
- ___ Physical sciences
  - ___ Chemistry
  - ___ Geology/Earth science
  - ___ Meteorology
  - ___ Oceanography
  - ___ Physics/Astronomy
- ___ Social sciences
  - ___ Anthropology
  - ___ Consumer economics
  - ___ Economics
  - ___ Ethnic studies
  - ___ Geography
  - ___ History
  - ___ Psychology
  - ___ Sociology
  - ___ Urban/Rural studies
  - ___ Women's studies

A ARTISTIC

Applied Arts
- ___ Architecture
- ___ Commercial art
- ___ Film/Photography
- ___ Home economics
  - ___ Fashion design
  - ___ Interior design
- ___ Industrial design
- ___ Graphics
- ___ Journalism
- ___ Landscape design/ Ornamental horticulture
- ___ Media specialty
- ___ Modelbuilding
- ___ Radio/TV
- ___ Technical illustrating

Fine Arts
- ___ Art/Art history
- ___ Dance
- ___ Drama
- ___ English
- ___ Foreign language
- ___ Humanities
- ___ Literature
- ___ Music
- ___ Philosophy
- ___ Speech

S SOCIAL

Human Services
- ___ Community health worker
- ___ Counseling
- ___ Dental assistant/hygiene
- ___ Dietician
- ___ Health science
- ___ Inhalation therapy
- ___ Nursing RN, LVN, assistant
- ___ Occupational therapy
- ___ Pediatric assistant
- ___ Physical therapy/also assistant
- ___ Primary care associate
- ___ Psychiatric technician
- ___ Psychology—clinical
- ___ Public health
- ___ Social service
- ___ Speech pathology and audiology

Accommodating
- ___ Cosmetology
- ___ Food service
- ___ Travel careers

S/E SOCIAL / ENTERPRISING

Leading/Influencing
- ___ Advertising
- ___ Business administration
- ___ Convalescent hospital administration
- ___ Education
- ___ Health care management
- ___ Insurance
- ___ Labor studies
- ___ Law
- ___ Library science
- ___ Management/Supervision
- ___ Manpower administration
- ___ Office administration
- ___ Public relations
- ___ Recreation
- ___ *See* Social sciences under Investigative
- ___ Volunteer administration

E ENTERPRISING

Persuading
- ___ Business administration
- ___ Fashion/Retail merchandising
- ___ International trade
- ___ Law
- ___ Marketing/Sales
- ___ Political science
- ___ Purchasing
- ___ Real estate
- ___ Speech

C CONVENTIONAL

Business Detail
- ___ Accounting
- ___ Attorney assistant
- ___ Banking
- ___ Court reporting
- ___ Data processing
- ___ Insurance
- ___ Secretarial
  - ___ Administrative
  - ___ Clerical
  - ___ Medical assistant/Records
  - ___ Legal
  - ___ Unit clerk
  - ___ Word processing

11. Positive Affirmations

Fveryone is a mixture of faults, foibles, and failings along with skills, successes, and strengths. Check (√) the statements that match your thought patterns. Select one positive statement and say it many times a day over a week's time. Know that attitudes and feelings can be changed.

Negatives	Positives
_____ I don't think I'll ever figure out what I want to do.	_____ I can take steps to figure out what to do.
_____ I'm not interested in anything.	_____ I'm interested in many things
_____ Nothing is much fun.	_____ I enjoy many of my activities.
_____ I'm dumb.	_____ I can learn.
_____ If my first choice doesn't work out, I'm stuck.	_____ I can plan alternatives.
_____ I'm tired of trying because nothing works.	_____ I have the energy to make things happen.
_____ I'm afraid.	_____ I'm brave.
_____ I never have fun.	_____ I can create a good time.

_____ I can make a good decision!

 Group Discussion Questions

1. Share your educational plans.
2. Discuss the concept of life-long learning and what form it can take in your own life.
3. If you are working (or going to school), what are some new approaches you could take to improve your situation?
4. What factors might cause someone to "decide not to decide"?
5. Describe the steps you take in making decisions.
6. How do values relate to decisions?
7. Define success.
8. Define failure.
9. What values might prompt a manager to "step down" to a lower job status?
10. What values might take the place of work in your life?

Nine

Work Affects the Soul:

The Final Analysis

The Self-Assessment Exercises in this book were designed to help you focus on the personal qualities you will bring to the workplace and the rewards you hope to receive from it. The "Final Analysis" gives you a place to summarize all this information. It will give you an overview of most of the areas of your life affected by work. It will help you assess your career search process and how effectively it has helped you choose the career that will lead to your personal growth and self-fulfillment on all levels. It will help you make those final decisions and provide a handy future reference.

To complete the "Final Analysis," review the Self-Assessment Exercises and summarize the data below. Feel free to add additional information about yourself and the career you are considering.

Chapter 1   Needs, Wants, and Values: Spotlighting YOU

1. Review "Tapping into Feelings" (p. 22) and "Life Problems Checklist" (p. 23). Then list areas you would like to develop or improve and those you would like to change or eliminate.

I want to develop:

_____

_____

_____

_____

I want to change:

_____

_____

_____

_____

2. Review "Needs and Wants and Shoulds," section g (p. 27). Check the balance in your life. Do you have enough? What do you need or want on these four levels?

	I have enough of:	I want:
Physical level	_____	_____
	_____	_____
	_____	_____
	_____	_____
Emotional level	_____	_____
	_____	_____
	_____	_____
	_____	_____
Intellectual level	_____	_____
	_____	_____
	_____	_____
	_____	_____
Altruistic level	_____	_____
	_____	_____
	_____	_____
	_____	_____

Is your life in balance on these four levels? Yes _____ No _____

If not, how can you improve the balance? _____

_____

_____

_____

3. Review "Rating Values," section a (p. 27). List your three most important career values.

   a. _____

   b. _____

   c. _____

4. Review your autobiographical data. In reviewing "Free Spirit Years" (p. 29), "Your Life Line" (p. 30), and "Create an Autobiography" (p. 35), what did you learn about yourself?

   _____

   _____

   _____

5. Review "Candid Camera—3-D" (p. 32). List the five activities that you enjoy the most.

   a. _____

   b. _____

   c. _____

   d. _____

   e. _____

Chapter 2   Roles and Realities: Sinking the Stereotypes

Review the roles you play and the roles of others (p. 60). Then finish the following statements:

1. I enjoy being a _____

2. I would like to improve in my role as a _____

3. I'd like to be more accepting of people who are _____

_____

Chapters 3 and 4   Job Satisfiers

1. Review the Personality Mosaic (pp. 67–78); then list your types and scores for each type in order from highest to lowest.

First _____   Fourth _____

Second _____   Fifth _____

Third _____   Sixth _____

2. Check your Data, People, Things Indicator (p. 94). Explain your high, medium, or low ratings here:

Data _____

_____

_____

_____

People _____

_____

_____

_____

Things _____

_____

_____

_____

3. From your Work Qualities Inventory (p. 96), list your "must have" work qualities by key word:

a. _____   c. _____

b. _____   d. _____

List your "must avoid" work qualities:

a. _____   c. _____

b. _____   d. _____

4. Are you a "mind person," a "body person," or both? _____
Of the basic eight skills (pp. 97–98), which skills are most important to you?

_____

_____

_____

From the Personal Skills Checklist (p. 88), list your best skills and the ones you could improve.

Best skills	Could improve
_____	_____
_____	_____
_____	_____
_____	_____
_____	_____

5. Which work-specific skills do you have?

_____

_____

What work-specific skills do you wish to acquire?

_____

_____

6. List three job groups by decimal code and title from the Job Groups Chart (p. 101) in the order of your own interests.

    a. _____

    b. _____

    c. _____

7. Why did you choose your top job group? How does it match your personality, skills, interests, and work qualities?

_____

_____

_____

8. Do you want a career or just a job? Explain your answer.

_____

_____

_____

9. List the job title you'd like the most: _____

10. How does your career choice match your values?

_____

_____

_____

1. Of the five major trends (pp. 128–29), which would you like to change? How would you change it?

_____

_____

_____

2. Consider your altruistic feelings. What contribution would you like to make to the world?

_____

_____

_____

3. What does the *Occupational Outlook Handbook* or similar references say about the employment outlook for the career of your choice?

_____

_____

_____

4. What is the salary range for the career of your choice? _____
Would this career support your lifestyle? Yes _____ No _____

5. List five alternate careers that you would consider. List one positive and one negative feature of each.

Career	Positive feature	Negative feature
a. _____	_____	_____
b. _____	_____	_____
c. _____	_____	_____
d. _____	_____	_____
e. _____	_____	_____

Chapter 6   Workplaces and Styles: Scanning the Subtleties

1. Use findings from your research to describe the ideal workplace. Consider size and complexity, type of environment, and emotional rewards you would like to receive.

_____

_____

_____

_____

_____

_____

2. Review Figure 6-1, the Career Ladder (p. 156). How far up the ladder do you want to go?. Explain your answer.

_____

_____

_____

3. Would you like to help plan your own work routine? If so, explain how.

_____

_____

_____

4. Review "Researching Workplaces" and "Workplace Checklist" (pp. 174–78). Then list the five corporate values that are most important to you (see "Workplace Values," p. 178). Would you take a job if any of those values were missing? Check (✓) any "must have" values on your list.

a. _____

b. _____

c. _____

d. _____

e. _____

5. Describe your ideal job.

_____

_____

_____

_____

_____

6. Describe your ideal boss.

_____

_____

_____

_____

_____

7. Do you prefer working alone or with a team? Explain your answer.

_____

_____

_____

8. Describe your ideal work day.

_____

_____   _____

_____

9. Describe your ideal balance of work and leisure.

_____

_____

_____

10. What motivates you to work? Describe your personal work ethic. What does work mean to you?

_____

_____

_____

Chapter 7   The Job Hunt: Tools for Breaking and Entering

1. To prepare for the job hunt:

   Name the title of a job you might apply for _____

   List ten of your characteristics that relate to that job:

   _____

   _____

   _____

   _____

   _____

   _____

   _____

   _____

   _____

2. Write your résumé on a separate sheet of paper. Use your notes from pages 207–208.

3. What is the most important thing you've learned from this book?

_____

_____

_____

Chapter 8   Decisions, Decisions: What's Your Next Move?

1. What is your next move in the career search?

_____

_____

_____

2. Educational planning sheet:

   a. Do you now have the skills and training you need to obtain a job in the field of your choice? Yes _____ No _____
   If you need more preparation, which of the following do you need (see p. 235)?

   _____ Apprenticeship

   _____ On-the-job training

   _____ Workships or seminars

   _____ Other: _____

   b. If you need more education, which of these are you considering (see p. 233)?

   _____ A few courses   _____ A B.A. or B.S. degree

   _____ A certificate   _____ Graduate school

   _____ An A.A. or A.S. degree   _____ Other: _____

   c. List an appropriate major (or majors) for your career choice (see p. 237).

   _____

d. What kind of school do you plan to attend?

_____ Two year

_____ Four year

_____ Local college

_____ College in your state

_____ Out-of-state college

_____ Public

_____ Private

e. List colleges or universities that offer the major you have chosen. (Use the educational reference section of your library, and ask for assistance from a college counseling center.)

_____

_____

_____

f. Obtain catalogs for colleges of interest. To gather as much information as possible, visit the campuses, talk to people who are familiar with each school. For example, will you need:

_____ Financial aid

_____ Housing

_____ Special entrance tests

_____ A specific grade point average

_____ Other: _____

g. Begin course planning in the space below:

Major requirements	General or graduation requirements	Electives
_____	_____	_____
_____	_____	_____
_____	_____	_____
_____	_____	_____

3. Complete the bottom line: I plan to be employed in the job of my choice by

   (date): _____

4. Review all of the inventories you have taken. Read your autobiography again. Check each item in "The Final Analysis" to make sure there are no contradictions.

5. Does it hang together?   Yes _____   No _____

Hang Loose

MICHELE F. BAKARICH

I'm
just
going
to
hang
loose
,
that's
the
best
way
to
go

© 1978 Reprinted with permission

Appendix

Sample Résumés and Letters

The sample résumés and letters in this Appendix are those of real job seekers ranging from college student to senior citizen, from engineer to housewife returning to work. Each résumé is unique to one person, as your résumé will be unique to you. But you can use these sample résumés in a number of ways. Notice the variety of forms and styles. Select the ones that seem to fit your situation best, and use them as models to create your own unique résumé.

The sample résumés can be used for role playing also. As you read them, pay attention to the person behind the résumé as an interviewer would. Think of questions you might ask the owner of each résumé, and use these questions in mock interviews.

The letters that accompany résumés are called "cover letters." In addition to "covering" your résumé, letters may be used to thank people who have interviewed you and to keep in touch with them until you are actually employed.

5096 W. Monroe Street
Kokomo, Indiana 46901

May 22, 1983

Mr. William A. Cline
115 E. Birch Bark Lane
Sault Ste Marie, Michigan 49783

Dear Mr. Cline:

This is to let you know that I am still interested in working with the Forest Service in the Michigan area. I expect to be in touch with you around November regarding the jobs of recreation assistant and resource assistant that you mentioned to me for next year.

By the way, I applied for the spotted owl project job at Gifford Pinchot National Forest last summer. Thanks for notifying me about that job. (It was never listed with Civil Service.)

If you know of any promising late-opening summer jobs in your area this year, I would appreciate it if you would let me know.

Thanks again.

Yours truly,

Daniel P. Magee

Daniel P. Magee
(906) 555-1212

September 17, 1984

Mr. Archibald Manx
The Arrogant Cat
1000 Main Street
Los Gatos, CA 95030

Dear Sir:

Recently it has come to my attention that you have an opening for a managerial position.

I have had four years supervisory experience working in various phases of the restaurant business. My intention is to continue in this field. The excellent quality of The Arrogant Cat is well known. I feel that I could be of assistance in maintaining this fine level of service.

Enclosed is a copy of my resume. I will call you next week for an appointment to discuss this with you further.

Sincerely yours,

Kathleen M. Neville

Kathleen M. Neville
791 Peony Lane
Aptos, CA 95003
(415) 555-1730

KATHLEEN M. NEVILLE
791 Peony Lane
Aptos, CA 95003
(408) 555-1730

POSITION OBJECTIVE:

Restaurant Management Trainee

QUALIFICATIONS IN BRIEF:

AA in Restaurant Management
BA candidate in Business Management
Supervisory experience
Good human relations skills
Reliable, responsible, creative worker

EDUCATION:

SAN JOSE STATE UNIVERSITY, San Jose, CA   Present
Major: Business Management

FOOTHILL COMMUNITY COLLEGE, Los Altos Hills, CA   1984
AA Degree in Restaurant Management (Core Courses at West Valley College)

WORK EXPERIENCE:

LINDA'S DRIVE-IN, Santa Cruz, CA   August 1981 to Present
Supervisor/Cook

Inventory, order, prepare, and stock food supplies. Settle employee and customer problems and complaints. Orient/train new employees; evaluate employee performance. Do minor repairs/maintenance. As occasional acting manager, open and close shop, handle cash/cash register.

                                                              Previous
Babysitting and housekeeping throughout junior high and high school.

ACTIVITIES:

GIRL SCOUTS   1972-82
Supervised day camp; planned activities, taught games, arts and crafts, sports, camping skills, and first aid. Solved conflicts. Received art award.

MUSIC   1976-83
Foothill Youth Symphony, Jazz, Symphony, Marching/Pep Bands at various times from elementary school through community college. Toured Expo 1980, Spokane, Washington.

DRAMA—AWALT HIGH SCHOOL   1981-82
As Assistant Director supervised making costumes, sets, props. Performed in Summer Theatre Workshop.

REFERENCES: Provided upon request.

Figure A-2 Chronological Résumé and Cover Letter of a College Student

Kathleen Neville is the college student whose work skills provided the example in the "Candid Camera—3-D" exercise in Chapter 1. Her limited work experience is amplified by high school activities. Her brief statement of qualifications emphasizes education and transferable and personal responsibility skills. Her cover letter mentions her commitment to use her skills in the desired position.

RUBY F. GARCIA
404 Lark Drive
Honolulu, Hawaii 96815
(808) 555-1212

POSITION OBJECTIVE: Office Manager, preferably in a small setting

EXPERIENCE:

RUBY'S TYPING SERVICE   Present
Professional typist   11 years
Manuscripts, resumes, term papers, theses, letters typed and edited.

ST. PATRICK'S CATHOLIC CHURCH, Honolulu, Hawaii
Addressograph Operator
Typed names and addresses on plate machine. Operated addressograph. Kept files up to date with changes of address and registered new parishioners. Mailed out monthly bulk mail. Substituted for the parish secretary when needed.

McKINLEY HIGH SCHOOL, Honolulu, Hawaii   1 year
Secretary to Vice-Principal and Textbook and Supply Clerk
Took dictation, typed, filed. Delivered and picked up textbooks for teachers. Filled out supply orders and ordered new supplies as needed.

BUREAU OF RECLAMATION, Honolulu, Hawaii   1 year
Secretary Pool
Took dictation from engineers and typed their reports.

HICKAM AIR FORCE FIELD, Honolulu, Hawaii   1 year
Secretary
Took dictation from job analysts and typed their reports.

DIVISION OF DISBURSEMENTS, Honolulu, Hawaii   1 year
Typist
Typed names and addresses on U.S. Savings Bonds.

BALDWIN HIGH SCHOOL, Wailuku, Maui   1 year
Secretary to Night School Principal
Registered students. General office work for night school.

LAWRENCE CHRYSLER, PLYMOUTH DEALER, Wailuku, Maui   2 years
Secretary
Took dictation, typed, bookkeeping, made out payroll, worked with parts manager in checking supplies ordered and received.

HALEAKALA REALTORS, Wailuku, Maui   3 years
Secretary
General office work, took dictation, and typed for three realtors.

EDUCATION:
HEALD'S BUSINESS COLLEGE, Honolulu, Hawaii
BALDWIN HIGH SCHOOL, Wailuku, Maui

COMMUNITY SERVICE ACTIVITIES:
Leader in Brownies, Girl Scouts. Den Mother for Cub Scouts. Helped in fund-raising affairs for PTA, Patron's Guild, Little League. Volunteer in special education classes

---

RUBY F. GARCIA
404 Lark Drive
Honolulu, Hawaii 96815
(808) 555-1212

POSITION OBJECTIVE:
Office Manager, preferably in small setting

QUALIFICATIONS IN BRIEF:
Twenty-two years of secretarial experience. Responsible, efficient, careful of detail, tactful, and supportive of co-workers.

EXPERIENCE:

SECRETARIAL/CLERICAL: Both general and technical, took dictation, typed, kept books. Operated addressograph, did monthly mailing. Typed church bulletins, letters, resumes, theses, and manuscripts.

INVENTORY: Took inventory of stockroom. Ordered, checked, and delivered supplies.

HUMAN RELATIONS: Interacted with engineers and job analysts doing technical reports, registered students, supervised/taught children in a variety of settings. Cooperated with groups in fund raising.

EDUCATION:
Heald's Business College, Honolulu, Hawaii
Baldwin High School, Wailuku, Maui

Figure A-3 Chronological and Functional Résumés for the Same Person
The functional résumé shows just two work-specific areas. In this case the chronological résumé highlights the broader experience more impressively. It's good practice to prepare both types of résumés to see which works best for you.

BARBARA A. CLINE
409 Long Island Drive
College Point, NY 11356
(212) 555-3600

POSITION OBJECTIVE: Administrator of Ambulatory Health Care Facility

EXPERIENCE SUMMARY:

FASHION MERCHANDISE WORKERS HEALTH CENTER, New York, N.Y. 1977 to present
Assistant Administrative Director

Administer ambulatory care health center serving 900 patients daily. Personnel administration: recruit, administer salary, negotiate contracts
for two unions, counsel 165 lay staff. Coordinate 20 administrative
department supervisors and their activities. Key role in development of
computerized appointment and pharmacy system for HP 3000 on-line; all
related MIS activities. Plan, evaluate, and administer $5 million budget.
Purchase supplies. Prepare annual report text. Direct physical plant
maintenance, repair, and renovation. Do publicity and patient relations
including articles, personal appearances, and health fair.

Executive Secretary to Administrative Director   1972-1977

Supervised and trained clerical personnel. Secretarial responsibilities.

NATIONAL CAMPING AND HIKING ASSOCIATION, New York, N.Y.   1971
Convention Coordinator/Administrative Assistant

Maintained membership; planned convention and publicity and employment
referral service for members. Coordinated and implemented NCHA 1971 convention in Waterville Valley, New Hampshire.

JUICE & BEVERAGE MAGAZINE, New York, N.Y.   1970
Administrative Assistant to Managing Editor

Supervised department secretaries in editorial unit; researched articles;
wrote NEW PRODUCTS section of magazine (60 items/month).

BIOKEM INSTITUTE, Pittsburgh, Pa.   1968-1969
Administrative Secretary for Research Scientists and Professors

Prepared grant proposals to NIH, NSF, USAF. Coordinated convention, American Chemical Society.

EDUCATION:

FORDHAM UNIVERSITY: MBA   1982

EMPIRE STATE COLLEGE, SUNY New York   1980
B.S. in Business Management, 3.6 avg.

OTHER EXPERIENCE:

Free-lance writing. Community activities: teen counseling, volunteer
ambulance corps, church groups. Member APHA, GHAA, NYPHA, and N.Y. Pers.
Mgt. Assoc. Invited Paper, GHAA 1980 on computerized patient appointment
system. Member, Hewlett-Packard Users' Group.

REFERENCES: Available upon request.

---

409 Long Island Drive
College Point, NY 11356
June 10, 1984

Ms. Margaret Moss
Personnel Director
Deerpark Medical Center
Boulder, CO 80301

Dear Ms. Moss:

It was enjoyable meeting your representative, Jack Fosse, at the Health
Care Management Association Conference on June 6. I was interested to learn
that you are looking for an administrator with computer capability.

I feel that my background would prove valuable in the reorganization and
expansion that you are planning for your Center. My expertise lies in two
areas. The first is in the way health care is actually planned for, scheduled,
and delivered in an outpatient ambulatory care or HMO setting. The second area,
and my most recent experience, has been in setting up a complete computer system
to handle doctor and patient appointment scheduling, patient needs and flow,
and statistics.

Since I am planning a visit to Boulder this summer, I look forward to
getting together with you to review my qualifications for the administrative
position. I will call you in about ten days for an appointment.

Sincerely yours,

Barbara A. Cline

Barbara A. Cline
(212) 555-3600

Resume enclosed

Figure A-4 Chronological Résumé and Cover Letter of Career Woman Moving Up

Barbara Cline's résumé shows the career path of a clerical person moving into professional management. She carefully selects "other experience" that shows her involvement
in her profession and community. Her cover letter indicates her awareness of the center's planned reorganization. She indicates how her skills and experience fit in.

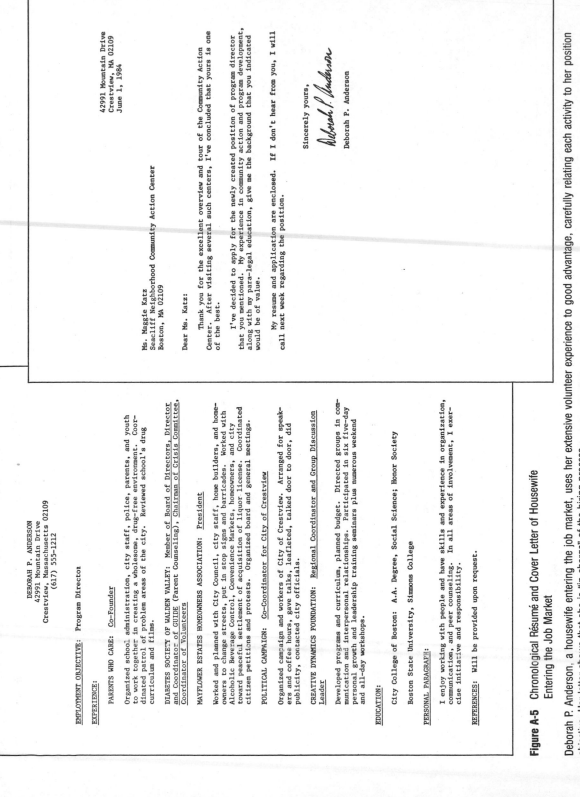

Figure A-5 Chronological Résumé and Cover Letter of Housewife Entering the Job Market

Deborah P. Anderson, a housewife entering the job market, uses her extensive volunteer experience to good advantage, carefully relating each activity to her position objective. Her letter shows that she is "in charge" of the hiring process.

LARRY ANDERSON
32881 Amazon Drive
Silicon Valley, CA 94040   (415) 555-7218

POSITION OBJECTIVE:

    Management facilitator of advanced semiconductor products from design to
    production.

QUALIFICATIONS IN BRIEF:

    BSEE and graduate work. Fourteen years of management/engineering experi-
    ence. Excellent human relations skills.

WORK EXPERIENCE:

    ELECTRONIC SYSTEMS, Mountain View, CA   April 1968 to Present
    Manager of Manufacturing Engineering

    Manage product engineering, instrumentation, and test data processing.

    Product Line Manager

    Managed transfer of new products from design to production. Directed yield
    improvement programs on RAMS and EPROMS.

    Instrumentation Manager

    Directed personnel, budget, and interdepartmental policies.

    Section Head—Instrumentation

    Computerized in-house test equipment, both hard and software design.
    Supervised assembly groups and electronic stores.

    Senior Engineer

    Designed and checked all high-speed sections of the in-house MOS test sys-
    tem. Supervised documentation of the complete system.

    NATIONAL MICROELECTRONIC DIVISION   May 1965 to April 1968
    Supervisor of Instrumentation

    Proposed designs for, modified, ordered, and maintained test equipment.
    Began as junior engineer in device evaluation and became designer of test
    equipment of complex MOS IC's.

EDUCATION:

    SAN JOSE STATE UNIVERSITY, San Jose, CA
    Major: Electrical Engineering, BSEE Degree   1965
            Sixteen units of graduate work   1965-67

REFERENCES: Provided upon request.

```
                        BOBBIE CLARK
                      510 S. 39th Street
                    Escanaba, Michigan 49829
                      H - (906) 555-1212
                      W - (906) 555-1313


JOB OBJECTIVE:  Personnel Interviewer

QUALIFICATIONS

     Ability to:  Organize and promote programs and activities
                  Perform effectively under pressure
                  Use tact and diplomacy with people
                  Speak extemporaneously with originality and inventiveness
                  Implement suggestions and findings.


PERSONNEL EXPERIENCE

     BAY DE NOC COMMUNITY COLLEGE, Escanaba, Michigan              Present
     Placement Interviewer

     Interview applicants to determine their suitability for employment; advise
     applicants in interview preparation techniques and assist students in
     completing job applications.  Contact employers concerning job openings
     and refer properly qualified applicants.  Develop new job listings.

     JOB SERVICE, MICHIGAN EMPLOYMENT SECURITY COMMISSION, Escanaba, Michigan
     Employment Interviewer

     Interviewed job applicants to select persons meeting employer's qualifica-
     tions.  File-searched job orders, and matched applicant's qualifications
     with job requirements and employer's specifications.  Performed reference
     and background checks and often referred applicants to vocational counsel-
     ing and testing services.  Followed up with employer on interviewers for
     hiring results and future recommendations.  Developed jobs through contacts
     with employers.


PUBLIC RELATIONS EXPERIENCE

     8TH ASSEMBLY DISTRICT OFFICE, Green Bay, Wisconsin

     WINNEBAGO FOUNDATION, Green Bay, Wisconsin
     Public Relations Representative

     Liaison between State Capitol and Assembly District Office reviewing con-
     stituent problems applicable to state jurisdiction.  Representative for the
     Assemblyman.  Wrote press releases.  Effective in establishing rapport with
     media personnel to obtain coverage.  Promoted community and civic programs
     by speaking to groups.  Coordinated scheduling of activities.  Made pre-
     sentations on philosophy of foundation.  Recruited for workshops and taught
     related classes.  Managed funds for budget.  Counseled clients.


REFERENCES

     References are available and provided upon request.
```

HUONG-MAI VAN
369 Rose Lane
Monte Sereno, California 95030
(408) 555-1212

POSITION OBJECTIVE: Employee Trainer in Pharmaceutical Industry

QUALIFICATIONS IN BRIEF:

    Excellent in human relations, communications, organizational leadership.
Extensive pharmaceutical experience. Speak Vietnamese, French, and
English. Chemistry-English education equivalent to AA degree. Dedicated
worker.

EDUCATION:

    UNIVERSITY OF CALIFORNIA, SAN FRANCISCO. Pharmacy Degree Candidate   1985
WEST VALLEY COLLEGE, Saratoga, California. AS: Chemistry   1982
SAIGON UNIVERSITY, Saigon, Vietnam. Two years English Education Major

EXPERIENCE SUMMARY:

    WEST VALLEY COLLEGE, Saratoga, California.   Present
Educational Opportunity Program Student Advisor

    Recruit, support, orient, motivate students. Developed and implemented
system of tutoring; coordinate tutoring schedule. Founder and President:
Vietnamese Student Association. Planned/organized cultural events.

    Chemistry Student Lab Assistant   February 1979-1980

    Prepared materials for laboratory classes.

    EQUAL OPPORTUNITY COMMISSION, San Mateo County. October 1977-January 1979
Health Training Coordinator

    Organized training for low-income parents as child care provider. Inter-
viewed, evaluated, trained, supervised 52 participants.

    PARKE-DAVIS CORPORATION, Washington, D.C.   February 1977-October 1977
Pharmaceutical Representative

    Visited medical offices, pharmacies, hospitals to present new products and
take orders.

    INDOCHINA CENTER (U.S. CATHOLIC CONFERENCE)   April 1976-January 1977
Case Aide

    JOHNS HOPKINS UNIVERSITY, Baltimore, Maryland.   February 1976-April 1976
Medical Transcriber

    RED CROSS, Baltimore, Maryland.   February 1976-April 1976
Receptionist Volunteer

    PHAM HONG THAI PHARMACY, Saigon, Vietnam.   February 1968-April 1975
Sales and inventory clerk, cashier

REFERENCES: Available upon request.

AMALIA LENA
1643 W. Peachwood Drive
Fort Lauderdale, FL 33325
(305) 555-3669

JOB OBJECTIVE:

Manager: Savings and Loan

QUALIFICATIONS IN BRIEF:

Three and one half years' experience as bank teller, preceded by four years
of clerical work in a variety of settings. Extensive community service
activities. Special skills: especially good at business contact with
people; fluency in Italian; limited fluency in Spanish; excellent memory
for names.

WORK EXPERIENCE:

CIVIC FEDERAL SAVINGS, Fort Lauderdale, FL   Present
Head Teller, occasional Acting Manager

Type, cashier, deal with public at teller window, pay bank bills. Work
on-line with computer. Handle transactions and answer banking questions
by phone. As acting manager, do general supervision of personnel and
procedures, including management of vault cash.

DADE COUNTY SANITATION DISTRICT, Miami, FL   Previous
Office Clerk

Filed, typed, radio communication with personnel in the field, general
telephone work, paid department bills, occasional payroll management.

MIAMI MEDICAL CLINIC, Miami, FL
Medical Records Clerk

Checked for medical records, delivered same to doctors' offices.

ATLANTIC TELEPHONE AND TELEGRAPH, Ft. Lauderdale, FL
Yellow Pages Clerk

WOOLWORTH AND COMPANY, Ft. Lauderdale, FL
Sales Clerk

EDUCATION:

ST. VINCENT'S HIGH SCHOOL, Ft. Lauderdale, FL
Concentration in business education courses.
Subsequent workshops dealing with human relations and crisis counseling.

COMMUNITY SERVICE ACTIVITIES:

Girl Scout/Cub Scout Leader, seven years
Elementary School Teacher Aide
Hospital Chairperson for PTA Group
Crisis counseling, individually and in small groups

GEORGE R. URCIUOLI   (817) 555-6060 (Home)
462 Great Plains Drive
Waco, Texas 76701   (817) 555-2211 (Work)

CAREER OBJECTIVE:

   Management position in the area of materials planning and control for
   manufacturing firm.

CURRENT STATUS:

   U.S. Army Officer completing 20 years of active duty with rank of Lt.
   Colonel. Leaving military service to start second career in business.

EXPERIENCE:

   MATERIALS CONTROL: Stored and allocated $4.5 million inventory of food,
   fuel, ammunition, repair parts, construction material. Coordinated resup-
   ply operation for 22,000 combat troops. Commanded 127 men providing supplies and services to 2,000 combat troops. Directed 90-person team furnish-
   ing materials and electronic instrumentation for R & D project.   Implemented
   supply and service program for 800 logistics personnel. Scheduled and
   coordinated use of ranges, classrooms, training areas, drill fields, test
   facilities.

   OFFICE ADMINISTRATION: Managed administrative services for command group.
   Coordinated projects between senior executive, section chiefs, subordinate
   commanders. Participated in forming organizational directorate and organization training center.

   HUMAN RELATIONS: As Inspector General, conducted inspections, inquiries,
   surveys. Reported allegations, complaints, requests of military personnel
   and families. Recommended corrective actions. Advised Commanding General
   on activities, attitudes, status of the organization. Performed internal
   audits/reviews. Personnel officer for 2,500-person task force.

   BUDGETING/ACCOUNTING: As Central Accounting Officer, prepared $1 million
   annual budget for Command Sport and Recreation Fund. Administered $600,000
   budget for R & D support group. Raised and distributed $20,000 for relief
   program. Raised $14,000 for Red Cross drive. Formulated policies and
   accounting procedures for various post clubs.

   INSTRUCTION: Wrote lesson plans for and conducted weapons training for
   18,000 recruits. Directed committee of 104 instructors. Initiated two
   training innovations now accepted as standard throughout entire U.S. Army.
   Taught management and economics part-time at community college level.

EDUCATION:

   BBA, University of the City of New York   1959
   MMAS, U.S. Army Command and General Staff College   1974
   MBA, Golden Gate University, San Francisco, CA   1978

Notes

Introduction

1. Studs Terkel, *Working* (New York: Avon, 1972), p. 233.

Chapter 1   Needs, Wants, and Values: Spotlighting YOU

1. Victor Frankl, *Man's Search for Meaning* (New York: Washington Square Press, 1963).
2. Nena O'Neill and George O'Neill, *Shifting Gears* (New York: Avon, 1974), p. 140.
3. Ken Keyes, Jr., *Handbook to Higher Consciousness* (St. Mary's, Ky.: Cornucopia Institute, 1975), p. 52.
4. See Gary Carnum, "Everybody Talks About Values," *Learning* (December 1972); and S. B. Simon, S. W. Howe, and H. Kirschenbaum, *Values Clarification* (New York: Hart, 1972).
5. Edward Goss, "Patterns of Organizational and Occupational Socialization," *The Vocational Guidance Quarterly* (December 1975), p. 140.
6. Abraham Maslow, *Motivation and Personality* (New York: Harper and Row, 1954) p. 91; see also Marilyn M. Bates and Clarence Johnson, *A Manual for Group Leaders* (Denver: Love Publishing, 1972); and Keyes, *Handbook to Higher Consciousness.*
7. Lance Morrow, *Time,* May 11, 1981, p. 94.
8. "Special Report," *Oxfam America News* (Winter 1983), p. 3.
9. Garrett DeBell, "A Future That Makes Ecological Sense," *The Environmental Handbook* (New York: Ballantine Books, 1970), pp. 153–58.
10. Terrence E. Carroll, "The Ideology of Work," *Vocational Guidance Quarterly* (December 1975), p. 154.
11. Morrow, *Time.*
12. U.S. Department of Health, Education, and Welfare, *Work in America* (Cambridge, Mass.: M.I.T. Press, 1973), pp. 186–87.
13. Hans Selye, *Stress Without Distress* (Philadelphia: J. B. Lippincott, 1974).

1. Daniel J. Levinson, *The Seasons of a Man's Life* (New York: Ballantine Books, 1978), p. 229.
2. *Federally Employed Women, October 1980* (Sacramento: California Commission on the Status of Women, January–February 1982); *Earnings Gap Between Men and Women* (Washington, D.C.: U.S. Department of Labor, Women's Bureau, 1979); *Job Options for Women in the 80's* (Washington, D.C.: U.S. Department of Labor, Women's Bureau, 1980); *20 Facts on Women Workers* (Washington, D.C.: U.S. Department of Labor, Women's Bureau, 1980). See also *Statistical Abstract of the United States* (Washington, D.C.: Bureau of the Census, 1981), pp. 380, 407; *Time*, August 4, 1980, p. 52; and Carolyn Jacobson, "New Challenges for Women Workers," *The AFL-CIO American Federationist* (April 1980), p. 3.
3. Virginia Y. Trotter, "Women in Leadership and Decision Making: A Shift in Balance," *Vital Speeches*, April 1, 1975, pp. 373–75.
4. Betty Friedan, *The Feminine Mystique* (New York: Dell Books, 1963).
5. Levinson, *The Seasons of a Man's Life*, pp. 20, 43–6, 158.
6. Ruth B. Kundsin, ed., *Women and Success: The Anatomy of Achievement* (New York: William Morrow, 1974), p. 176.
7. Bess Myerson, "Someday I'd Like to Walk Slowly," *Redbook* (September 1975), p. 76.
8. Alice Cook, "The Working Mother," address to Center for Research on Women, Stanford University, January 1976.
9. Caryl Rivers, *San Francisco Chronicle*, January 1, 1975.
10. Aletha Huston Stein and Margaret M. Bailey, "The Socialization of Achievement Orientation in Females," *Psychological Bulletin* 80, no. 5 (November 1973), p. 353.
11. *Time*, January 21, 1980.
12. Lillian Hellman, *An Unfinished Woman: A Memoir* (Boston: Atlantic Monthly Press, 1969).
13. *Working Women Speak*, National Advisory Council on Women's Educational Programs, p. 5, 24.
14. Tish Sommers, "Where Sexism Meets Ageism," *Modern Maturity* (October–November 1975), p. 60.
15. Terence Wright, "Liberation, My Nation, Migration," *Diaspora* (Fall 1980).
16. National Advisory Council on Economic Opportunity, "Report to the President," *San Francisco Chronicle-Examiner*, October 19, 1980, Section A, p. 19.
17. Marilyn Power Goldberg, "The Economic Exploitation of Women," *Review of Radical Political Economics* 2, no. 1 (Spring 1970).
18. John Kenneth Galbraith, "The Economics of the American Housewife," *Harper's* (June 1973), p. 78.
19. Betty Friedan, *The Second Stage* (New York: Summit Books), 1981.
20. Marilyn Ferguson, *Aquarian Conspiracy: Personal and Social Transformation in the 1980's* (Los Angeles: J. P. Tarcher, 1980).
21. Jean Houston, "The Church in Future Society," taped address to the Lutheran Brotherhood Colloquium, University of Texas, Austin, January 1979. See also Jean Houston, *The Possible Human* (Los Angeles: J. P. Tarcher, 1982).

Chapter 3   Personality and Peformance: Pieces of the Puzzle

1. John L. Holland, *Making Vocational Choices: A Theory of Careers* (Englewood Cliffs, N.J.: Prentice-Hall, 1973).
2. Jean Houston, "The Church in Future Society."
3. See Sydney A. Fine, "Counseling Skills: Target for Tomorrow," *Vocational Guidance Quarterly* (June 1974); and "Nature of Skills: Implications for Education and Training," *Proceedings*, 75th Annual Convention of the American Personnel Association, 1967.

4. Ray A. Killian, "The Working Woman . . . A Male Manager's View," American Management Association Paper, 1971.
5. Genita Kovacevich Costello, "How Women are Recasting the Managerial Mold," *San Jose Mercury News*, April 25, 1982.

Chapter 4   The Career Connection: Finding Your Job Satisfiers

1. U.S. Department of Labor, *Dictionary of Occupational Titles*, 1978.
2. U.S. Department of Labor, *Guide for Occupational Exploration*, 1979.
3. Compiled from the following sources: U.S. Department of Labor, *Dictionary of Occupational Titles*, vol. 2, 1965; U.S. Department of Labor, *Guide for Occupational Exploration*, 1979; U.S. Army, *Career and Education Guide*, Counselor Edition, 1978; U.S. Department of Labor, *Handbook for Analyzing Jobs*, 1972.
4. *Worker Trait Group Guide* (Bloomington, Ill.: McKnight Publishing Co., 1978).

Chapter 5   The Job Market: Facts, Trends, and Predictions

1. Norris McWhirter, ed., *Guiness Book of World Records* (New York: Bantam Books, 1982).
2. See Joseph Luft, *Group Processes: An Introduction to Group Dynamics*, 3rd ed. (Palo Alto, Calif.: Mayfield Publishing Co., 1984).
3. François Dusquesne, "The Making of a Sacred Planet," *One Earth* 1, no. 2, p. 6.
4. Marvin Cetram and Thomas O'Toole, "Careers with a Future," *Futurist* (June 1982).
5. John Peers, lecture at Mission College, Santa Clara, Calif., November 11, 1982.
6. David R. Francis, "The Demographic Touch: Will the 80's Be Golden?" *Christian Science Monitor*, December 29, 1981, p. 11.
7. "The Job Outlook for College Graduates During the 1980's," *Occupational Outlook Quarterly* (Washington, D.C.: U.S. Department of Labor, Bureau of Labor Statistics, Summer 1982); *Statistical Abstract of the United States* (Washington, D.C.; Bureau of the Census, 1981), p. 145.
8. Peter J. Michelozzi, "Jobs, Wages and Reading Ability," Fall 1981.
9. John P. Beck, "Unions, the Economy and the 'Right to Useful Work'" (Ann Arbor: University of Michigan, Summer School on Extending Workplace Democracy, Institute of Labor and Industrial Relations, 1980).
10. Alvin Toffler, *The Third Wave* (New York: Bantam Books, 1980).
11. Thomas W. Foster, "The Amish Society, a Relic of the Past, Could Become a Model for the Future," *Futurist* (December 1981), p. 33.
12. Frances, Moore Lappé and Joseph Collins, *Food First: Beyond the Myth of Scarcity* (New York: Ballantine Books, 1977).
13. *Futurist* (April 1942), p. 3.
14. Marvin Feldman, "Work, Employment and the New Economics," Occasional Paper no. 70, National Center for Research in Vocational Education (Columbus: Ohio State University, 1981).
15. Colin Norman, "The Staggering Challenge of Global Unemployment," *Futurist* (August 1978), p. 224.
16. Alvin Toffler, *The Third Wave*, p. 350.
17. "The Job Outlook in Brief," *Occupational Outlook Quarterly* (Washington, D.C.: U.S. Department of Labor, Bureau of Labor Statistics, Spring 1982), pp. 7–33.
18. Cetram and O'Toole, "Careers with a Future."
19. *Futurist* (December 1980), p. 4.

20. "Where Future Jobs Will Be, " *World Press Review* (March 1981), p. 21.
21. Walter Chandoha, *Book of Kittens and Cats* (New York: Bramhall House, 1973), p. 8.

Chapter 6   Workplaces and Work Styles: Scanning the Subtleties

1. Erving Goffman, *Asylums* (New York: Doubleday, 1961).
2. Barbara Garson, "Women's Work," *Working Papers* (Fall 1973), p. 5.
3. *Time*, March 10, 1975, p. 42.
4. Part-Time Professionals, P.O. Box 3419, Alexandria, VA 22304
5. *Christian Science Monitor*, March 18, 1982.
6. Ritchie P. Lowry, "Social Investing," *Futurist* (April 1982); "Socially Sensitive Investing' (Boston: U.S. Trust Co.); Theodore V. Purcell, "Institutionalizing Ethics on Corporate Boards," *Review of Social Economy 36*, no. 1 (April 1978).
7. Meyer Friedman and Ray H. Rosenman, *Type A Behavior and Your Heart* (New York: Fawcett, 1974).
8. John Kenneth Galbraith, "The Economics of an American Housewife," *Atlantic Monthly* (August 1973), pp. 78-83.
9. Terkel, *Working*, p. 4.
10. Robert Schrank, "How to Relieve Worker Boredom," *Psychology Today* (July 1978), pp. 79-80.
11. Charles McCabe, *San Francisco Chronicle*, September 1974.
12. James Michener, *The Fires of Spring* (New York: Bantam Books, 1949).
13. Jeremy Joan Hewes, *Worksteads* (Garden City, NY: Doubleday, 1981), pp. 7, 5. See also Bernard Lefkowitz, *Breaktime: Living Without Work in a Nine-to-Five World* (New York, Penguin Books, 1979).
14. "The Freedom to Succeed," *Christian Science Monitor*, April 26, 1982.
15. Ferguson, *Aquarian Conspiracy*.
16. Toffler, *Third Wave*, p. 387.
17. Richard H. Pitcairn and Susan Hubble Pitcairn, *Dr. Pitcairn's Complete Guide to Natural Health for Dogs and Cats* (Emmaus, Pa.: Rodale Press, 1982).
18. Bill Cane, *Through Crisis to Freedom* (Chicago: Acta Books, 1980), p. 8.

Chapter 7   The Job Hunt: Tools for Breaking and Entering

1. Toni St. James, Interview Workshop, California Employment Development Department, 1977.
2. Ibid.

Chapter 8   Decisions, Decisions: What's Your Next Move?

1. *Statistical Abstract of the United States*, (Washington, D.C.: U.S. Department of Commerce, Bureau of the Census, 1981), pp. 130, 142.
2. *San Jose Mercury News*, October 25, 1981.
3. Alan Lakein, *How to Get Control of Your Time and Your Life* (New York: Wyden, 1973).
4. Ken Keyes, Jr., "Oneness Space," Living Love Recording (St. Mary's, Ky.: Cornucopia Center).
5. Jerry Gillies, *Money Love* (New York: Warner Books, 1978).
6. Margaret Anstin, *Voyages: A Chartbook for Career Life Planning* (Dubuque, Ia.: Kendall/Hunt Publishing, 1980), p. 115.
7. Betts Richter and Alice Jacobsen, *Make It So! From That Special Something Within* (Sonoma, Calif.: Be All Books, 1979).

Index

271